Young People Using Family V

Kate Fitz-Gibbon · Heather Douglas ·
JaneMaree Maher
Editors

Young People Using Family Violence

International Perspectives on Research, Responses and Reforms

Springer

Editors
Kate Fitz-Gibbon
Monash University
Clayton, VIC, Australia

Heather Douglas
University of Melbourne
Melbourne, VIC, Australia

JaneMaree Maher
Monash University
Clayton, VIC, Australia

ISBN 978-981-16-1333-3 ISBN 978-981-16-1331-9 (eBook)
https://doi.org/10.1007/978-981-16-1331-9

This Springer imprint is published by the registered company Springer Nature Singapore Pte Ltd.
The registered company address is: 152 Beach Road, #21-01/04 Gateway East, Singapore 189721, Singapore

Acknowledgements

This collection emerged from conversations between the editors about the need to build and connect the evidence based on young people's experiences and use of family violence. We are grateful to all the contributors who have generously shared their research and insights in this area with us through the chapters contained in this collection.

We are extremely grateful to Ellen Reeves for working with us to prepare this manuscript for submission. Ellen's careful editing work, organisation and attention to detail were an invaluable assistance in bringing this collection together.

As always, we extend our appreciation to our colleagues at Monash University and the University of Queensland. Our writing is always enriched by the discussions, meetings and other research activities that we are involved in with colleagues across both universities and particularly our Monash Gender and Family Violence Prevention Centre colleagues, including Prof. Sandra Walklate, Prof. Jude McCulloch, Assoc. Prof. Silke Meyer, Assoc. Prof. Marie Segrave, Dr. Naomi Pfitzner and Dr. Jasmine McGowan.

Thank you also to Springer for supporting this project.

We are also very grateful to all of those with lived experience of adolescent family violence who have been willing to participate in the studies that underpin the chapters in this collection.

Introduction

Young People Using Family Violence: International Perspectives on Research, Responses and Reforms

Family violence is an increasingly recognised problem globally, and the adequacy of service and justice system responses for young people who use violence in the family home is heavily debated and recognised as an under-researched area. This collection offers an original contribution to this important topic. The collection is particularly timely given that governments worldwide and the United Nations (UN) are presently engaging in reviews of responses to intimate partner violence and gender-based killings. There has to date, however, been a paucity of research which has held children who use different forms of family violence in its focus. *Young people using family violence* directly addresses the gap by bringing together a range of international contributions that consider the use of violence in the home by children and how best to respond from diverse perspectives.

Extending the Story: Examining Young People Using Family Violence

There have been extensive policy developments and active national reform agendas surrounding domestic and family violence (DFV) in many countries over the last decade. In Australia, at the state level, most notably, this process included the 2016 Victorian Royal Commission into Family Violence (RCFV, 2016) and the Queensland *Not Now, Not Ever* Report (Special Taskforce on Domestic and Family Violence in Queensland, 2015). The RCFV (2016) identified adolescent family violence as a form of family violence for which there was increasing evidence of prevalence but few targeted responses or prevention efforts. The RCFV estimated that one in ten family violence incidents reported to police in Victoria involved a child under 19 years of age using violence (see also O'Brien and Fitz-Gibbon, 2016). Recognising that there are currently 'no systemic responses to the needs of these young people and their families', the RCFV (2016) recommended a number of reforms targeted at the development of specialist trials, programmes and responses. The Queensland Special Taskforce Report (2015) on the other hand did not look at the use of violence by young people, and none of its 140 recommendations directly sought to address response or prevention efforts for this form of family violence.

Nationally, in Australia, the Council of Attorney Generals (COAG), *Advisory Panel on Reducing Violence against Women and their Children* (COAG report, 2016) and work undertaken through *Australia's National Plan on violence against women and girls* has sought to establish a broad national reform agenda for improving responses to and prevention of family violence, among other forms of violence against women. While the COAG report (2016) recognises the need to develop better responses to children as victims of DFV, it is largely silent on the reforms required to improve responses to children using violence in the home and support for affected family members.

Beyond Australia, recent international law reform and relevant review activity have been limited. The UK Parliament Domestic Abuse Bill (2019) includes a number of sections relating to children as victims of domestic abuse but does not propose any legislative reform for children who use violence in a domestic setting. Despite the early development of intervention programmes specifically designed to address adolescent family violence in America (the Step Up programme, for example, see Buel, 2002) in more recent times, many American scholars have turned their attention to the study of teen dating and college intimate partner violence (see, inter alia, Lehrner & Allen, 2018; Thomas & Weston, 2019). There is currently little research or policy attention directed at the use of violence by adolescents within the family home. Similarly, in New Zealand, when it comes to adolescents, the focus of recent attention has been on teen dating violence (Beres, 2017).

In this broader political context, the international momentum for effective responses to domestic and family violence, combined with continued attention to responses to youth offending, offers a critical opportunity for criminologists, sociologists and legal scholars and practitioners to contribute new evidence and analysis to inform policy, practice and reform. This is the aim of this collection. In *Young people using family violence*, we locate the family unit, in all its manifestations, as central in understanding the circumstances in which children use violence in the home and as central in effective responses and prevention strategies. The focus of this collection and all its the contributions builds on the previous work that has examined the complexities of the family as a social unit as well as research which maps the inequalities in which families operate (see, inter alia, Brown et al., 2015; Forby et al., 2020; Meyer & Carlson, 2014).

A Note on Language

There are numerous terms used to refer to a young person's use of violence in the home. In the Australian context, the term adolescent family violence (AFV) has been favoured in recent years (see, for example, Douglas and Walsh, 2018; Fitz-Gibbon et al., 2018), while, in the UK, the term child to parent violence (CPV) is more routinely utilised. Other terms used include adolescent violence in the home (AVITH), youth violence, youth violence in the home (Broadhead & Francis, 2015), teen violence, teen abuse and adolescent violence towards parents (Howard, 2010) as well as sibling violence (on this, see Elliott et al., 2020). Throughout this collection, contributors have used their own preferred term and we, as editors, have not imposed uniformity across chapters. Knowledge of this type of family violence is still emerging, and the variation in terms reflects this.

Likewise, there are numerous definitions and changing uses of the term child, young person and adolescent across research in this area. The proposed UK Domestic Abuse Bill (2019) defines a child as any person under the age of 18 years (section (3)), and recent Australian research has included definitions of adolescent in both legislation and research as anywhere between children 'as young as 10 years and (young people) as old as 21 years' (Douglas & Walsh, 2018). While one chapter in this collection considers the response to sibling abuse, the remaining chapters focus on adolescent to parent abuse. The roles of parent and/or carer may be understood in a variety of ways. The contributors to this collection have focused their attention on those contexts where biological, adopted and 'step' parents are subjected to abuse. However, we recognise there is a growing literature that explores the use of violence by adolescents towards their carers in state residential care (see, inter alia, Baidawi & Sheehan, 2020; Gerard et al., 2019). We are also cognisant that the experiences of young First Nations people using violence in family contexts have not yet been mapped and cannot be understood using either existing paradigms of intimate partner violence or family violence.

The Need for a New Paradigm for Understanding and Developing Specialist Responses to Young People Who use Violence in the Home

The research that does exist on the topic of adolescent family violence has considered the degree to which the phenomena is gendered in similar ways to intimate partner violence and the extent to which young people are likewise motivated by desires to control, intimidate and threaten (see, inter alia, Daly & Nancarrow, 2010; Daly & Wade, 2016; Howard, 2015). The small body of the literature available almost universally agrees that there is a need for a specialist response that departs from the assumptions used in developing responses to intimate partner violence and/or the resort to youth justice system responses (on the latter, see Douglas & Walsh, 2018; Miles & Condry, 2016; Thomas et al., 2019), namely the goal of maintaining familial relationships and parental connections where safe to do so (Haw, 2010).

The legal system is increasingly recognised as a blunt tool that has all too often failed to deliver justice and safety outcomes for women victim-survivors of intimate partner violence (see Goodmark, 2018). While calls to reduce the reliance on the criminal justice system in responses to violence against women have been largely focused on adult-perpetrated intimate partner violence (see, inter alia, Goodmark, 2020; Walklate and Fitz-Gibbon, 2019), there is an emerging body of work which documents the limits of the criminal law in responding to children who use family violence (see, inter alia, Campbell et al., 2020; Douglas & Walsh, 2018). This research has begun to highlight the complexity faced by families who experience adolescent family violence, including the high rates of disability, mental health and substance abuse issues, and pre-existing exposure to family violence. While we appreciate this form of violence cannot be disentangled from the broader problems that some of these families are facing, this collection seeks to bring this form of violence into view and to mount a call for specialised, whole of system responses and tailored interventions. Such a complex problem requires a more developed and specific suite of tools.

Standardised approaches that do not allow for discretion and are inherently punitive in nature are arguably ill-suited to provide meaningful responses to this form of family violence. To progress the efficacy of responses, there is a need to build the evidence base on the complex needs of families experiencing adolescent family violence, and the roles and capacities of the existing service structures in responding to them. A number of the chapters in this collection interrogate why both criminal justice and the support service systems have failed to date to deliver meaningful responses to parents experiencing this form of family violence. Understanding the limits of the existing responses provides an important opportunity to ensure that any future reforms do not repeat the mistakes of the past, developing responses that are neither trusted by parents (contributing to underreporting) nor effective in providing meaningful support to the children directly involved and the family members impacted. This analysis of limits also requires a reconsideration of the point at which a response can be offered; as several chapters within this collection demonstrate, there is a need to move to earlier models of intervention and more proactive responses (e.g. education systems) rather than reactive ones (e.g. police and child protection intervention).

In seeking to set a new agenda, we argue that the current punitive climate for youth justice policy and practice in Australia and elsewhere should not be used as a template to inform the design and delivery of responses to children using family violence. This is a particular concern for First Nations peoples: the disproportionate criminalisation of young Indigenous Australians is a critical concern (Australian Institute of Health and Welfare 2018, see also Australian Human Rights Commission, 2020). This issue presents significant challenges in the context of domestic and family violence. Government responses to family violence in recent years have emphasised the importance of perpetrator responsibility and accountability (RCFV, 2016). However, children who use family violence may not have the developmental capacity to understand their behaviour and they are likely to continue to rely on their victim for nurturing and support. Research suggests that many young people who use family violence in the home may also have experienced family violence and/or witnessed intimate partner violence themselves (Howard, 2015; Simmons et al., 2018), and that criminal justice system responses may not be the most effective way forward (Douglas & Walsh, 2018; Fitz-Gibbon et al., 2018; Miles & Condry, 2016). Several of the contributions in *Young people using family violence* argue for the need to develop specialised and age appropriate justice and service system responses to children who use violence in family settings.

Contributing New Insights to a Hidden Problem

This collection brings together a range of international scholars leading innovative research agendas in this field. While each of the contributions provides a country-specific focus, emerging from either Australia, the UK, USA or Canada, the themes and findings can be situated within a global context and provide insights into lessons beyond their jurisdiction's legal and specialist service system responses to children using family violence. *Young people using family violence* brings together international experts to examine the following questions:

- How can we best understand and respond to the problem of adolescent to parent violence?
- To what extent do traditional family violence responses address the experiences of adolescents who use family violence?
- What barriers to help seeking exist for parent victims of adolescent family violence?
- To what degree do the existing support and justice services provide adequate responses to victims of adolescent family violence?
- In what circumstances do children kill their biological and adopted parents?

The chapters explore the nature of adolescent family violence as well as the adequacy and effectiveness of the current service and justice system responses.

The collection begins with two chapters which further enhance the current understandings of different forms of adolescent family violence, or adolescent to parent violence (Chap. 1, Condry and Miles) and sibling violence (Chap. 2, Desir and Karatekin). Building on their extensive research into child to parent violence (see, inter alia, Condry & Miles, 2014; Miles & Condry, 2015), Condry and Miles tease out the inherent difficulty of recognising the seriousness of the harm inflicted by adolescents in some families alongside the need to steer away from criminal justice intervention. They argue that this form of family violence brings two paradigms into conflict—the youth justice approach and a family violence perspective. In Chap. 2, Desir and Karatekin address sibling violence—a form of adolescent family violence that has been subjected to minimal scrutiny worldwide. Their chapter reviews what is known in the current literature about sibling violence and how this can inform policy directions and service responses.

Chapters 3 and 4 are focused on service system responses to adolescent family violence. In Chap. 3, Fitz-Gibbon, Maher and Elliott draw from the findings of an Australian study involving victim-survivors to explore the barriers to help seeking experienced by women victims of adolescent family violence. Finishing with a focus on the possibilities of intervention in the education system, this chapter argues that there is a need for targeted service responses and stronger referral pathways. Continuing the focus on responses to mothers' experiences of adolescent family violence, in Chap. 4, Burck examines the merits of a specific group therapy intervention programme trialled in the Australian state of Queensland. Grounded in attachment theory, the programme under examination is one of only a few non-punitive interventions currently tailored to families experiencing AFV in Australia.

Extending the collection's analysis of service responses, Chaps. 5 and 6 encourage a rethink of how policy-makers should respond to children who use family violence by examining the degree to which traditional legal system responses and programmes may be ill-suited for this cohort of young offender. In Chap. 5, Douglas draws on interviews conducted in Australia with mothers and stepmothers who have experienced adolescent family violence to critically analyse the merits of legal interventions and responses. Highlighting the need for greater recognition of the overlap between experiences of adolescent family violence and intimate partner violence, Douglas calls for improved understanding and awareness of adolescent family violence among those working within the justice system. Building on this, in Chap. 6, Campbell questions the degree to which the 'blunt instrument' of the criminal justice system can offer any effective responses to this form of family violence. In the second half of her chapter, Campbell considers what more effective responses may look like and how the harm experienced and used by adolescents who use family violence in the home may be better recognised.

The final two chapters in our collection turn the focus to lethal violence and provide detailed examinations of what is known about child to parent homicide in Canada and the USA. In Chap. 7, Dawson and Hill examine child to parent homicide in Canada. Drawing from a dataset including 135 cases of parricide committed over a 30-year period, Dawson and Hill identify the characteristics of and precursors to this form of lethal violence before moving into an analysis of responses and how this research can inform improved prevention and intervention agendas in this area. Building on Heide's significant body of work examining parricide in the US context (see, inter alia, Heide, 1993, 1995, on the UK context see Holt, 2017), the final chapter in this collection (Chap. 8) by Hubbell, Heide and Khachatryan draws on media articles to examine the characteristics and variables present in homicide cases where a child kills their adoptive parent(s). Acknowledging the challenges of collecting data on this specific subset of homicide cases, the authors extend the current research by providing one of the first detailed illustrations of this form of parricide.

Setting an Agenda for Change

This edited volume is one of the first international collections to subject children's use of family violence and responses to adolescent family violence to deep critical scrutiny. By adopting a focus on children who use family violence, this collection seeks to contribute valuable new knowledge to the current policy debates surrounding the merits and viability of responses to family violence and how they may need to be adapted, changed and reformed to better respond to children using family violence and their families. Several of the contributions recognise the family violence reform activity that is underway in many Australian states and territories at the moment, as well as political debates and unprecedented levels of advocacy in Australia and other countries worldwide. However, to date, the majority of this activity has been focused upon understanding, responding to and preventing intimate partner violence in adult heterosexual relationships. Children as users of family violence have been largely absent from these discussions. We acknowledge with regret that the specific issues of First Nations families and communities are not addressed in this collection and urge the commitment of policy and research resources to build knowledge critical for these communities (see also Australian Human Rights Commission, 2020). It is our hope that this collection acts to intensify focus on the impacts and effects of children using violence in the home and supports the push for more research, better support and new programmes. We hope that the analyses here will contribute to the work of informing new responses to and programmes for children using family violence. We also hope that better support for families and new approaches to prevention can emerge.

Kate Fitz-Gibbon
Heather Douglas
JaneMaree Maher

References

Australian Human Rights Commission. (2020). *Wiyi Yani U Thangani (Women's Voices): Securing our rights, securing our future report.* Australian Human Rights Commission. https://humanrights.gov.au/our-work/aboriginal-and-torres-strait-islander-social-justice/publications/wiyi-yani-u-thangani

Australian Institute of Health and Welfare. (2018). *Youth detention population in Australia 2018.* https://www.aihw.gov.au/reports/juv/128/youth-detention-population-in-australia-2018/contents/table-of-contents

Baidawi, S., & Sheehan, R. (2020). Maltreatment and delinquency: Examining the contexts of offending amongst child protection-involved children. *The British Journal of Social Work, 50*(7), 2191–2211.

Beres, M. (2017). *Preventing adolescent relationship abuse and promoting healthy relationships. Issues Paper.* New Zealand Family Violence Clearinghouse, Auckland.

Broadhead, S., & Francis, R. (2015). *Responding to youth violence in the home and its harmful impacts on families and communities in Western Australia: Summary Report.* Women's Health and Family Services, Perth.

Brown, S., Manning, W., & Stykes, B. (2015). Family structure and child well-being: Integrating family complexity. *Journal of Marriage and Family,77*(1), 177–190.

Buel, S. (2002). Why juvenile courts should address family violence: Promising practices to improve intervention outcomes. *Juvenile and Family Court Journal* (Spring).

Campbell, E., Richter, J., Howard, J., & Cockburn, H. (2020). *The PIPA project: Positive interventions for perpetrators of adolescent violence in the home (AVITH)* (Research report, 04/2020). Sydney, NSW: ANROWS.

Condry, R., & Miles, C. (2014). Adolescent to parent violence: Framing and mapping a hidden problem. *Criminology & Criminal Justice, 14*(3), 257–275.

Council of Australian Governments (COAG). (2016). *Advisory panel on reducing violence against women and their children.* Department of the Prime Minister and Cabinet, Australian Government, Canberra.

Daly, K., & Nancarrow, H. (2010). Restorative justice and youth violence towards parents. In J. Ptacek (Ed.), *Feminism,restorative justice and violence against women* (pp. 150–176). Oxford: Oxford University Press.

Daly, K., & Wade, D. (2016). Gender and adolescent-to-parent violence: A systematic analysis of typical and atypical cases. In A. Holt (Ed.), *Working with adolescent violence and abuse towards parents: Approaches and contexts for intervention* (pp. 148–168). Abingdon, NY: Routledge.

Douglas, H., & Walsh, T. (2018). Adolescent family violence: What is the role for legal responses? *Sydney Law Review, 40*(4), 499–526.

Elliott, K., Fitz-Gibbon, K., & Maher, J. M. M. (2020). Sibling violence: Understanding experiences, impacts and the need for nuanced responses. *British Journal of Sociology, 71*(1), 168–182.

Fitz-Gibbon, K., Elliott, K., & Maher, J. (2018). *Investigating adolescent family violence in Victoria: Understanding experiences and practitioner perspectives.* Monash Gender and Family Violence Research Program: Faculty of Arts, Monash University.

Fomby, P., Ophir, A., & Carlson, M. (2020). Family complexity and children's behaviour problems over two US cohorts. *Journal of Marriage and Family.* https://doi.org/10.1111/jomf.12706

Gerard, A., McGrath, A., & Colvin, E. (2019). 'I'm not getting out of bed!' The criminalisation of young people in residential care. *Australian & New Zealand Journal of Criminology, 52*(1), 76–93.

Goodmark, L. (2018). *Decriminalizing domestic violence: A balanced policy approach to intimate partner violence.* University of California Press.

Goodmark, L. (2020). Reimagining VAWA: Why criminalization Is a failed policy and what a non-carceral VAWA could look like. *Violence Against Women.* https://doi.org/10.1177/1077801220949686

Haw, A. (2010). *Parenting over violence: Understanding and empowering mothers affected by adolescent violence in the home—Report.* The Patricia Giles Centre, Perth.

Heide, K. M. (1993). Parents who get killed and the children who kill them. *Journal of Interpersonal Violence, 8*(4), 531–544.

Heide, K. M. (1995). The phenomenon of parricide. In *Why kids kill parents: Child abuse and adolescent homicide* (pp. 3–18). Thousand Oaks: SAGE.

Holt, A. (2017). Parricide in England and Wales (1977–2012): An exploration of offenders, victims, incidents and outcomes. *Criminology and Criminal Justice, 17*(5), 568–587.

Howard, J. (2010, November 9). A coordinated response to adolescent violence in the home. *Domestic Violence Resource Centre blog.*

Howard, J. (2015, December 8). Adolescent violence in the home: How is it different to adult family violence? *Australian Institute of Family Studies.*

Lehrner, A., & Allen, N. E. (2018). A qualitative investigation of the role of gender in young women's dating violence in the United States. *Violence Against Women, 24*(14), 1697–1717.

Meyer, D., & Carlson, M. (2014). Family complexity: Implications for research. *The ANNALS of the American Academy of Political and Social Science, 654*, 259–276.

Miles, C., & Condry, R. (2015). Responding to adolescent to parent violence: Challenges for policy and practice. *British Journal of Criminology, 55*(6), 1076–1095.

Miles, C., & Condry, R. (2016). Adolescent to parent violence: The police response to parents reporting violence from their children. *Policing and Society, 26*(7), 804–823.

O'Brien, W., & Fitz-Gibbon, K. (2016, April 1). 'Silent victims': Royal commission recommends better protections for child victims of family violence. *The Conversation.*

Royal Commission into Family Violence (RCFV). (2016). *Report and recommendations.* Royal Commission into Family Violence: Victoria, Australia.

Simmons, M., McEwan, T. E., Purcell, R., & Ogloff, J. R. P. (2018). Sixty years of child-to-parent abuse research: What we know and where to go. *Aggression and Violent Behavior, 38*, 31–52.

Special Taskforce on Domestic and Family Violence in Queensland. (2015). *Not now, not ever: Putting an end to domestic and family violence in Queensland*. Queensland Government, Brisbane.

Thomas, K., Fitz-Gibbon, K., & Maher, J. M. M. (2019). The use of protection orders in response to adolescent family violence: mapping divergent Australian approaches and the merits of this criminal justice intervention. *Current Issues in Criminal Justice, 31*(4), 461–475.

Thomas, R. A., & Weston, R. (2019). Gender differences in the association of intimate partner violence and relationship values among college students. *Journal of Aggression, Maltreatment & Trauma, 28*(9), 1110–1129.

Walklate, S., & Fitz-Gibbon, K. (2019). The criminalisation of coercive control: The power of law? *International Journal for Crime, Justice and Social Democracy, 8*(4), 94.

Contents

Editors and Contributors

About the Editors

Kate Fitz-Gibbon is Director of the Monash Gender and Family Violence Prevention Centre and an Associate Professor in Criminology in the Faculty of Arts at Monash University (Victoria, Australia). She is also an Honorary Research Fellow in the School of Law and Social Justice at University of Liverpool (UK) and a Research Associate of the Research Centre of Violence at West Virginia University (US). Her research examines family violence, femicide, the law of homicide and the impact of criminal law reform across Australian and international jurisdictions. Kate has advised on homicide law reform reviews and family violence inquiries in several Australian and international jurisdictions. Her recent publications include *Towards a Global Femicide Index: Counting the costs* (2020, Routledge) and *The Emerald Handbook on Femicide, Criminology and Social Change* (2020, Emerald), both with Sandra Walklate, Jude McCulloch and JaneMaree.

Heather Douglas is a Professor of Law in the Melbourne Law School at the University of Melbourne. Recent research focuses on women's experience of legal engagement as part of their response to domestic and family violence. Currently, she is exploring the legal response to non-fatal strangulation. She is the project lead on Australia's National Domestic and Family Violence Bench Book and the author of many books and articles on domestic and family violence. Her most recent book is *Women, Intimate Partner Violence and the Law* (2021, Oxford University Press). Heather was appointed a Fellow of the Australian Academy of Law in 2013 and a Fellow of the Academy of Social Sciences in Australia in 2017.

JaneMaree Maher is Professor in the Centre for Women's Studies and Gender Research, Sociology, in the School of Social Sciences at Monash University. Her research two key areas of gendered social science: women's work, mothering and family, and gendered violences. Current research projects are focused on the impacts of family violence on mothering and intimate partner homicide. She is the author of over 60 peer-reviewed journal articles and five books: most recently *Towards a Global Femicide Index: Counting the costs* (2020, Routledge) with Sandra Walklate, Kate Fitz-Gibbon and Jude McCulloch and *Policing Hate Crime: Understanding Communities and Prejudice* (Routledge 2017) with Gail Mason, Jude McCulloch, Sharon Pickering, Rebecca Wickes and Carolyn McKay.

Contributors

David Burck Youth and Family Services (YFS) Queensland, Logan/Jimboomba, Australia;
School of Nursing, Midwifery and Social Work, University of Queensland, Brisbane, Australia

Elena Campbell Centre for Innovative Justice, RMIT University, Melbourne, Australia

Rachel Condry University of Oxford, Oxford, UK

Myrna Dawson Centre for the Study of Social and Legal Responses to Violence, University of Guelph, Guelph, Canada

Michelle Patrice Desir Institute of Child Development, University of Minnesota, Minneapolis, MN, USA;
Child Abuse Pediatrics, Penn State Hershey Medical Center, Hershey, PA, USA

Heather Douglas Law School, University of Melbourne, Melbourne, Australia

Karla Elliott Faculty of Arts, School of Social Sciences, Monash Gender and Family Violence Prevention Centre, Monash University, Melbourne, Australia

Kate Fitz-Gibbon Faculty of Arts, School of Social Sciences, Monash Gender and Family Violence Prevention Centre, Monash University, Melbourne, Australia

Kathleen M. Heide Department of Criminology, University of South Florida, Tampa, FL, USA

Emily Hill Centre for the Study of Social and Legal Responses to Violence, University of Guelph, Guelph, Canada

James T. Hubbell School of Criminal Justice, University at Albany, State University of New York, Albany, NY, USA

Canan Karatekin Institute of Child Development, University of Minnesota, Minneapolis, MN, USA

Norair Khachatryan Department of Criminology, University of South Florida, Tampa, FL, USA

JaneMaree Maher Faculty of Arts, School of Social Sciences, Monash Gender and Family Violence Prevention Centre, Monash University, Melbourne, Australia

Caroline Miles University of Manchester, Manchester, UK

Chapter 1
Children Who Perpetrate Family Violence Are Still Children: Understanding and Responding to Adolescent to Parent Violence

Rachel Condry and Caroline Miles

Abstract This chapter explores ways of understanding and responding to the problem of adolescent to parent violence, drawing upon data from a UK study. We focus on the tension between recognizing the harm caused by violence and the suffering of a parent victim, without over-criminalising children who perpetrate this violence. Family violence perpetrated by children is a problem that must be taken seriously and one which requires a rigorous response, but this response needs to hold the age of the child in the foreground. This can be understood as a collision of two paradigms: a youth justice approach which emphasises diversion wherever possible and the rights of children on the one hand; and a family violence perspective which emphasises gendered patterns of power and control and the rights of victims on the other. We argue that responses to this form of violence need to hold different imperatives in balance, which include the complexities of family histories, dimensions of blame and culpability, shame and guilt, and an understanding of how violence is enacted through particular adolescent-specific dynamics of power and control.

1.1 Introduction

Adolescent to parent violence (defined here as physical assaults, threats of violence and criminal damage from an adolescent aged 13 to 19 years towards a parent/step-parent) has gained some recognition in the UK over the past decade amongst academics, practitioners and policy makers (for example, Bonnick, 2019; Condry & Miles, 2014; Holt, 2012; Home Office, 2015; Miles & Condry, 2015; SafeLives, 2017). This form of family violence falls under the cross-governmental definition of domestic violence, the criminal offence of coercive control, and is included in the

R. Condry (✉)
University of Oxford, Oxford, UK
e-mail: Rachel.condry@crim.ox.ac.uk

C. Miles
University of Manchester, Manchester, UK

K. Fitz-Gibbon et al. (eds.), *Young People Using Family Violence*,
https://doi.org/10.1007/978-981-16-1331-9_1

definition of domestic violence in the 2019 draft Domestic Abuse Bill.[1] In 2015, following the completion of our research study on adolescent to parent violence (APV), the Home Office published an information guide for third sector agencies on responding to Adolescent to Parent Violence and Abuse.[2] Notwithstanding the increased awareness of APV and the serious impact it can have on families, responses to the problem remain under-developed and piecemeal. Outside of the criminal justice system, families seeking help are at the mercy of ad hoc support agencies or individuals, and the police justice response lacks consistency due to a lack of understanding, training, and specific policy (Miles & Condry, 2014).

At the heart of the problem is a tension between the recognition of parents as victims of sometimes severe levels of abuse, who need their experiences to be taken seriously and safeguarding to be put in place, and the simultaneous recognition of the potential vulnerabilities of children who engage in violence towards their parents. In justice terms, this reflects the long-standing bifurcation of youth justice, wherein there exists tension between punishing and diverting children away from the criminal justice system (Muncie & Hughes, 2002). Added to this is the dominant victim-focused approach to responding to family violence, wherein criminal justice responses are centred around the rights of victims and based upon assumptions of power dynamics typical of (abusive) intimate partner relationships, rather than parent–child relationships. In the discussion below, we argue that although there is a need to give parent victims a voice and recognise their experiences, there is equally a need to give voice to the children who are violent towards their parents. It is essential to understand children's perceptions, perspectives and reflections, so that we can develop appropriate responses that serve the needs of both parents and children, with the age of the child paramount in determining how the violence is responded to.

1.2 Literature on Adolescent to Parent Violence (APV)

Academic literature on APV (also frequently referred to as adolescent family violence, adolescent violence in the home, child to parent violence/abuse, parent abuse) has been steadily growing over the past four decades, with particular pockets of research emerging in the UK, US, Canada, Spain and Australia (for example, see Condry & Miles, 2014; Cottrell & Monk, 2004; Gallagher, 2004; Calvete et al., 2013a, 2013b, 2015; Fitz-Gibbon et al., 2018; Holt, 2013; Howard & Rottem, 2008; Miles & Condry, 2015, Thomas et al., 2019). Much of this literature has been concerned with establishing the extent and prevalence of APV (for example, Agnew & Huguley, 1989; Brezina, 1999; Calvete et al., 2013a, 2013b; Edenborough et al.,

[1] https://assets.publishing.service.gov.uk/government/uploads/system/uploads/attachment_data/file/772202/CCS1218158068-Web_Accessible.pdf.

[2] https://assets.publishing.service.gov.uk/government/uploads/system/uploads/attachment_data/file/732573/APVA.pdf.

2008; Elliott et al., 2011; Ibabe et al., 2013; Kratcoski, 1985; Pagani et al., 2004; Paulson et al., 1990; Peek et al., 1985; Snyder & McCurley, 2008; Strom et al., 2010; Ulman & Straus, 2003; Walsh & Kreinert, 2007, 2009), the characteristics of families who experience APV (Boxer et al., 2009; Evans & Warren-Sohlberg, 1988; Howard, 2011; Ibabe et al., 2013; Kethineni, 2004; McKenna et al., 2010; Nock & Kazdin, 2002; Routt & Anderson, 2011; Sheehan, 1997; Stewart et al., 2007; Strom et al., 2010; Walsh & Kreinert, 2007, 2009), the nature/characteristics of APV (for example, Agnew & Huguley, 1989; Elliott et al., 2011; Evans & Warren-Sohlberg, 1988; Walsh & Kreinert, 2007), potential causal factors/explanations of APV (Biehal, 2012; Calvete et al., 2013a, 2013b, 2014; Contreros & Cano, 2016a, 2016b; Cottrell, 2004; Howard & Rottem, 2008; Ibabe & Bentler, 2015; Ibabe & Jaureguizar, 2010; Ibabe et al., 2014; Kethineni, 2004; Kennedy et al., 2010; Lyons et al., 2015; Margolin & Raucom, 2014; McCloskey & Lichter, 2003; Paulson et al., 1990; Routt & Anderson, 2011) and how the violence and abuse is experienced by parents (for example, Eckstein, 2004; Edleson, 1999; Edenborough et al., 2008; Jackson, 2003; Paterson et al., 2002; Stewart et al., 2007).

There is also a small body of literature focusing on responses to APV (for example, Daly & Nancarrow, 2010; Holt, 2009; Holt & Retford, 2012; Hunter et al., 2010; Routt & Anderson, 2011; Sheehan, 1997; Condry & Miles, 2014; Miles & Condry, 2014, 2015), highlighting the complexity of this form of family violence and the quandaries it presents to social and criminal justice services. In our own writing on responses to APV, we have identified the challenges faced by police and youth justice services, drawing upon practitioners' experiences of responding to APV (Condry & Miles, 2014; Miles & Condry, 2014, 2015), and argued for tailor-made, holistic responses that meet the complex needs of parent victims.

In this chapter, we develop this work by focusing on the perspectives of young people, whose voices are for the most part lacking in existing literature. We argue that in addition to working closely with parents to ensure a victim-led approach (which may well incur a non-prosecutorial response) and recognising their needs, it is essential that young people are treated as such, and recognised as (potentially vulnerable) children. We seek to document some of the contexts of APV through the eyes of young people and highlight their safeguarding needs, which require addressing alongside those of their parents.

1.3 Our Study

The narratives of young people, expert practitioners, and parents presented below derive from the first large study of adolescent to parent violence (APV) in the UK, which was conducted between 2010 and 2013. Given the previous lack of knowledge surrounding APV, the study aimed to document the broad extent and characteristics of APV (as reported to the police), generate accounts of APV from parent-victims and young people who had engaged in APV, and also examine the conceptualisation of and responses to APV from a police, youth justice and practitioner perspective.

As such, the study incorporated a mixed-methods methodology consisting of police statistical data (from two police forces in England), quantitative and qualitative data from 100 police case files, and over 100 in-depth interviews with police, expert practitioners working with families experiencing APV, parents of children engaged in APV, and the adolescents themselves.

The focus here is on children's accounts, which are largely missing in the literature on APV. As detailed above, much of the research in the field is concerned with measuring the extent of the problem, articulating parents' experiences of abuse at the hands of their child(ren), and identifying potential explanations for the behaviour. When trying to understand what leads to APV, parents' accounts or case file analyses are frequently used to identify correlations between the perpetration of APV and a variety of factors such as problematic family histories, offending outside of the home, problematic peers, etc. Similarly to the broader arena of domestic abuse, the voices of people who engage in violence and other forms of abuse towards their parents are curiously lacking, and there tends to be a victim-focused approach to understanding and responding to the problem of APV. One of the crucial aims of our research was to enable the voices of young people to be heard, in order to try and understand their behaviour and hear their perspectives of the context surrounding APV. In so doing, a complex picture emerged of children who are often simultaneous victims and perpetrators, with sometimes severe vulnerabilities and safeguarding needs that require recognition and incorporation into the response to APV.

The discussion below incorporates direct quotes from interviews we conducted with 18 young people aged 13–19, all of whom were accessing support services for families experiencing adolescent to parent violence. Seven of these interviews were individual, semi-structured interviews, including three females and four males who were violent towards their parents. The remaining eleven participants derived from two focus groups conducted with young people attending a group support session (6 males, 5 females). We also draw upon semi-structured interviews we conducted with twenty expert practitioners working with families experiencing adolescent to parent violence. This group of participants included individuals from local and national domestic abuse support organisations, Independent Domestic Violence Advocates (IDVAs), specialist child to parent violence support organisations, and clinical psychologists.

1.4 Young People's Understanding of the Problem

> When people, like, hear of teenagers being aggressive towards parents, they don't look towards the emotional side of it. They just think, oh, well, they're either spoilt and they're not getting their own way, so they're doing that; or, or it's, they're just a bad child. Where, I don't know, I just think there's always something behind everyone. And there's always some, a reason why someone acts a certain way. But everyone doesn't see that. You just need to look behind the aggression, and look towards the emotions. (Daughter, aged 16)

The quote above is from a 16 year old girl who had been violent towards her mother for some time. As she articulately explains, APV does not take place in a vacuum and is often contextualised by a complex set of circumstances or, as she says, 'a reason why someone acts in a certain way'. Although it is important to recognise the agency and responsibility of young people who are violent towards their parents, it is also incumbent to understand the pathways leading to the behaviour and how the context of the violence is conceptualised by the young person using violence.

The young people we spoke to were all involved in support groups relating to their behaviour, and were able to articulate examples of incidents in which they had acted violently towards their parents quite clearly and openly:

> I'll tell you about the time that I got locked up for hitting. I'd just, I'd been out all night, and I didn't tell my Mum I was staying out. And I came back, and she, and she were asking me where I'd been and all this. And I just got shower, got changed, and went to go out. And she, like, stopped me from going out. And, and then we started arguing. Just, like, she was saying, 'no, you're not allowed out.' And I were going, 'yeah, I am. I'm going out.' She locked the front door, so I couldn't go out front door. And then I tried going out back gate, but she grabbed me. And I don't like people grabbing me, so I pushed her away. And then she pushed me back, so I punched her. (Daughter, aged 16)

> I just started hitting things and stuff like that. And then when we moved into new house, when I were angry I used to punch my door and put, like, holes in my door, to take my anger out on something. And then my bedroom door got took off, so I started hitting bathroom door. That been took off. And then I hit kitchen door. I went like that, elbow kitchen door. And I put a little dint in that. And then that's about it. (Son, aged 15)

These quotes illustrate the frankness of the young people we interviewed, and also provide an insight into the nature of many incidents narrated by young people, characterised by child–parent conflict, expressions of anger, and manifestations via physical assaults to parents and damage to property in the home. Many parents we spoke to who were experiencing violence from their child emphasised the substantial effects of damage to their home, which was often described as more harmful than personal assaults. Those parents in social housing could not keep calling out repair teams repeatedly; those in private housing could often not afford to keep repairing damage and even if they could, they reported shame at having to explain to contractors (and visitors) how the damage had happened. As a result, families often lived with visible damage in the home, a daily reminder of their predicament. Reflecting this sentiment, the leading UK website collating research and practice developments on child to parent violence and abuse is called 'Holes in the Wall', because of the importance of this aspect of the problem of APV to families' experiences.[3]

The young people who we interviewed referred to a range of precursory factors or pathways to APV that did not necessarily excuse or justify their behaviour, but provided some rationale from their perspective. Across the interviews, talking both about their own experiences and more generally about how they understood the problem of APV, they described factors such as learning difficulties; ADHD; Autistic Spectrum Disorder; mental health problems and self harm; substance use by both

---

[3]https://holesinthewall.co.uk/.

themselves and their parents; previous experience of domestic violence and abuse; and parental conflict, separation/divorce and step parents.

Sometimes parental conflict was characterised by strained relationships with parents, which might have a long history, as illustrated in these two quotes:

> My relationship with my Mum's like strained and … I don't know. It's really strange. It's strained. We don't really talk about us feelings about stuff, or we don't, like, talk about, I don't know, like the normal thing that a daughter and a mum talks about. (Daughter, aged 16)

> I think I've never got along with my Mum … It started off basically just maybe, like, like vocally aggressive, like swearing at her and calling her names and stuff. And then it just gradually got to being aggressive, like physically aggressive towards her. (Daughter, aged 16)

And for others, they admitted that they had difficulties accepting boundaries:

> My Mum and Dad do try to be strict, but [I] don't really listen … Like if they'd completely banned me like they had before, and locked all doors in the house, I'll just jammy window open with paper clips and jump straight out, jumping over fence. (Daughter, aged 13)

> I used to just like kick off and stuff … [about] like anything. Just like, don't know, like petty things … Like if my Mum told me to do like one of me chores or owt, I'd just like, if I didn't want to do it, I wouldn't do it and stuff. (Son, aged 13)

And some children contextualised their problematic relationship with their parents within the conflict they experienced and lived with between their parents:

> Since I were maybe seven, I can remember them arguing. And then they split up for like good they said. And then after a couple of months they started like seeing each other to try and make it work. And I used to hate it because I used to just like think about my Mum and Dad arguing, and like when he used to hide vodka. And he used to get, not aggressive, but my Mum used to get aggressive towards my Dad. (Daughter, aged 13)

Some of the young people also described experiencing problems at school and getting into trouble outside of the home:

> Well my behaviour's quite bad at school like. It's improving a bit now. But I used to, I got detentions at least every day. And they found out I were cutting myself. So they like, they referred me to here cos they knew that I used to come and that I enjoyed coming and it helped. So they referred me to here. (Daughter, aged 13).

In addition to disharmony at home and sometimes outside of the home, some of the factors referred to in the interviews clearly reflected the vulnerability of young people, for example, experiencing mental health problems and self-harm, adverse home-lives (including for example, parental alcoholism or being in care), and direct or indirect experiences of domestic and sexual abuse.

Some young people had witnessed parental domestic abuse in their childhoods while others had direct experience of physical and sexual abuse. The data collected in our study does not allow us to estimate the number of adolescents who are violent in the family that have previous experience of domestic violence (this is not recorded in police data, and estimates cannot accurately be drawn from smaller samples in qualitative research). However, a number of services reported to us anecdotally that over 50% of their case load reported such histories (in some services, it was more). This may be one pathway to young people being violent in the home, but it is by no means the only explanation.

In the interviews, some young people also described indirect victimisation, in terms of witnessing or living in a home in which there was domestic abuse between their parents. This led to resentment and a lack of faith in their parents, and a shift in the child–parent dynamic:

> Like they'll never just split up like I guess normal people would. There's some sort of massive argument, lots of blood on the floor. And then someone will storm off. Not just like a normal person will walk off with a suitcase. Got to be an argument or some drama… (Daughter, aged 13)

> Because she used to keep giving him chances and like she'd see how much it were upsetting me and my Sister and like she'd kick him out for like a couple of days and then he'd come back and he'd do the exact same. And she just like, she used to put me down about him. Like make it out as if it were my fault, because he were my Dad. (Daughter, aged 13)

Other young people experienced direct physical violence and/or sexual abuse. In the quotes below, the interviewees refer to being abused in the home by their parents, or in the first quote, by extended family who were caring for him at the time:

> [B]ecause of my molestation and what people did in my past, I've kept it inside me and bottled it up. And then, 'cause that's why I have my kick-offs and stuff like that. 'Cause with my, my Dad's step-auntie, I used to get whatever I wanted whenever I wanted. Now I've come to live with my Mam, it's like I'm not getting my own way. (Son, aged 15)

> I think it's 'cause I resent her for something in past. It's basically, when I was younger, my Brother raped me daily for about a year. And I told her. It happened between, between the ages of seven and eight. And I told her, when I were, like, seven, it was happening. … I think, in my head, if she can't look after me, what's point? (Daughter, aged 16)

> Because they've both been aggressive to me before … like sometimes it's just been like a hit or a slap. And then it's been to when my Dad's been like full on beat me up. Went all black and blue with steel toecaps on so… (Daughter, aged 13)

For these children, their relationships with their parents were severely damaged for various reasons, and they talked about having a lack of faith in their parents/carers' ability to look after them and protect them, often levelling blame at the non-abusive parent, usually their mother. As one young person stated, 'emotionally it's her fault that I'm the way I am' (Daughter, aged 16). In addition to the detrimental effects of their direct victimisation, their child–parent relationship could not be conceived of in traditional terms and, although they had all perpetrated (sometimes severe) violence towards their parents, their self-accounts clearly portray them as simultaneous victims.

In our study we also interviewed practitioner experts who worked directly with families in a range of settings. They too pointed to histories of violence in many families experiencing violence from an adolescent:

> A typical family would be a family who have experienced domestic violence over many years. Maybe at this point, the perpetrator has left the family, the child is reaching adolescence, they're going through all the changes associated with being a teenager at that point.

> There is also a power vacuum that's missing. The child usually has had some sort of traumatic experience, around witnessing or directly experiencing violence and are full of rage and sort of anger towards everything and anything, perpetuated by hormonal, physiological and psychological changes going on during that time; and somehow, you know, this becomes expressed towards the mum. Now mums have in a, I mean this a very kind of broad generalisation, you know, but the mum has had years of experience of domestic violence and that's, you know, affected her self-esteem, affected her confidence as a mother … So you often get this kind of typical dialogue between sort of child saying to their parent, "You're too weak," and you know, being abusive towards mum. (Expert interview 2)

As this expert suggests, APV may be rooted in a perceived lack of parental power and control, resentment and anger towards a parent, a lack of faith in that parent, and learning to use abuse and violence in conflictual situations:

> And actually, these young people who are committing the acts of violence, they stepped into a vacancy. So they didn't create the violence in the family, in a lot of the cases. The majority of cases that we see the violence is a sort of an organising principle. They step into a vacancy of the person who delivers the violence. And sometimes that's better than being the person who receives the violence, you know. (Expert interview 12)

1.5 Why Is It Difficult to Make Sense of APV Through Currently Available 'Frames'?

The problem of adolescent to parent violence is constructed in very particular ways through the different paradigms of family violence, youth justice, and children's services. In this section, we critically discuss the construction and response to APV as a form of domestic abuse, and also outline some of the key problems with existing criminal justice responses, within the context of current approaches to youth justice and the associated responsibilisation of parents. We highlight the complex challenge of responding to young people who are violent towards their parents, but also vulnerable, with particular safeguarding needs. We argue for the foregrounding of these safeguarding needs in responding to APV, which require careful balancing with the needs of parents.

1.5.1 The Family Violence Paradigm

In England and Wales, APV currently falls within the policy framework surrounding domestic violence and abuse, given that it involves abusive behaviour between relatives. Women's Aid defines domestic abuse as an incident or pattern of incidents of controlling, coercive, threatening, degrading and violent behaviour, including sexual violence, in the majority of cases by a partner or ex-partner, but also by a family member or carer. On their website, Women's Aid explains clearly how this is gendered[4]:

[4]https://www.womensaid.org.uk/information-support/what-is-domestic-abuse/.

> Domestic abuse is a gendered crime which is deeply rooted in the societal inequality between men and women. It is a form of gender-based violence, violence "directed against a woman because she is a women or that affects disproportionately."
>
> Women are more likely than men to experience multiple incidents of abuse, different types of domestic abuse (intimate partner violence, sexual assault and stalking) and in particular sexual violence. Any woman can experience domestic abuse regardless of race, ethnic or religious group, sexuality, class, or disability, but some women who experience other forms of oppression and discrimination may face further barriers to disclosing abuse and finding help.
>
> Domestic abuse exists as part of violence against women and girls; which also includes different forms of family violence such as forced marriage, female genital mutilation and so called "honour crimes" that are perpetrated primarily by family members, often with multiple perpetrators.

This framework is reminiscent of our analysis of police recorded APV, which revealed that 78% of parent victims who reported APV to the police were female (mothers); indeed, 67% of all recorded APV across the London Metropolitan Police Service over a one year period (2009–2010) involved a son–mother relationship (Condry & Miles, 2014). APV is, therefore, a gendered problem—yet 22% of victims in the cases reported to the Metropolitan Police were male and 13% of perpetrators were female (Condry & Miles, 2014), so it is not exclusively a male to female phenomenon.

The current cross-government definition of domestic violence and abuse in England and Wales, as amended in March 2013 (Home Office, 2013), defines DVA as follows:

> Any incident or pattern of incidents of controlling, coercive or threatening behaviour, violence or abuse between those aged 16 or over who are or have been intimate partners or family members regardless of gender or sexuality. This can encompass but is not limited to the following types of abuse:

- psychological
- physical
- sexual
- financial
- emotional.

Although the intention of lowering the age parameters of DVA from 18 to 16 was to include young perpetrators and victims of intimate partner violence (IPV), a concurrent outcome was to capture more incidents of APV, which would previously not have been flagged as domestic abuse due to the young age of perpetrators. Indeed, over the past decade, numbers of APV incidents recorded by the police have reportedly doubled (BBC, 2019; Clough, 2018), which is potentially a direct result of the revised definition informing police recording decisions and more precise identification.

In some ways, it seems logical to conceptualise APV within the DVA framework, given that the abusive behaviours experienced by parent victims of APV are very similar in nature to those experienced by victims of IPV, consisting of threats of violence, verbal and physical assaults, and coercive control (for a more detailed discussion, see Miles & Condry, 2015). This was also identified by practitioners working to support families, many of whom also had experience of working with victims of IPV:

> [I]t was very hard to make the distinction usefully between violence to partners and violence particularly against mothers, but violence to parents. (Expert 10)

> Well you're looking at the same as a perpetrator of domestic abuse, apart from it's from a child. Cos they've, you know, it's manipulation, verbal, physical intimidation, psychological … the behaviour's exactly the same. (Expert 5)

There were also similarities in the impact of the abuse, in terms of parents feeling fearful, worn down, and constantly 'walking on eggshells' or changing their behaviour in order to avoid potential conflicts:

> [S]he was really scared of what he was able to do physically to her. She, she was really frightened by that and that's why she gave him all the money, and ran around after him and did all sorts of things cos she, she was scared about the violence. (Expert 16)

> I wouldn't identify the ones I've spoken to as being kind of parenting, teenage and parenting issues. I would look at the, the woman's really unhappy and, and scared cos that, that is the thing with Domestic Abuse, it's about that kind of fear and about changing your behaviour as well, so women will change their behaviour … (Expert 16)

In this sense, it is understandable that APV has been constructed as and is responded to under the broad umbrella of other types of family violence, particularly IPV. However, as we have documented elsewhere (Miles & Condry, 2015), there are important distinctions to be drawn between the context surrounding APV and other types of family violence, which render dominant responses (characterised by separation, termination of relationship and where possible, prosecution) inappropriate. Many of the differences stem from the distinctive nature of the child–parent relationship, which brings with it both a legal and moral responsibility for the (albeit abusive) child's welfare and a strong emotional drive for parents to maintain a relationship with their child. As such, parents are understandably reluctant to disclose to and work with agencies who they fear will prioritise prosecuting their child over providing support. Relatedly, as documented above, many young people who are abusive towards their parents are also vulnerable in a number of ways (including mental health difficulties, disharmonious home lives, direct and/or indirect experiences of abuse). As such, there is a blurred line between 'victim' and 'perpetrator', and many young people are simultaneous victims and perpetrators, with clear safeguarding needs.

1.5.2 The Criminal Justice/Youth Justice Paradigm

> [The] vast majority of [young people] have had quite difficult and complex problems in their lives, on an on-going basis for a number of them. And at which point do you, are you able to challenge them around responsibility and accountability for their own behaviour? And that's a real tension in this work really, is that you're working with them, a lot more than

> you are in adult work, you're working with them both as victims and as abusers, in a sense. And, and finding that balance can be tricky. (Expert interview 4)

The vulnerability of many young people who are abusive towards their parents was also highlighted by youth justice case workers we interviewed, who were often working with young people due to their offending outside of the home, but were also aware of their violent behaviour within the home. As the quotes above and below convey, there was a strong recognition that criminalising these young people was antithetical to their needs and almost certainly counter-productive.

> [P]articularly the young people that we work with, for them to be engaged with the criminal justice system, to be criminalised and treated as offenders, is almost compounding what they've already been through. So rather than label them as bad, what we do is try to help them to understand how they're feeling, their emotions and how to change their behaviour, and that abusive relationships versus healthy relationships. So it's a more supportive, rather than a judgemental, I suppose on the face of it. (Expert interview 6)

There was a strong sense from all practitioners that rather than in need of criminalising, young people who are abusive towards their parents are vulnerable and in need of support and safeguarding, as opposed to a criminal justice response pre-occupied with punitive measures, and that such measures should anyway be a last resort. Other studies have similarly highlighted concerns about criminal justice responses in this context (Fitz-Gibbon et al., 2018; Douglas & Walsh, 2018; Thomas et al., 2019).

Furthermore, there is a long history within youth justice of parents being held accountable for their children's behaviour, which stands in stark contrast to understanding a parent as a victim of their child's actions. This has strengthened in England and Wales in recent decades with a focus on 'problem families' and a 'parenting deficit' as a cause of youth offending under the New Labour administration of 1997–2010 and in the years since (Burney & Gelsthorpe, 2008; Muncie, 1999). What has remained constant throughout this period is the construction of young people as offenders outside the home, rather than within the home, and as young people lacking in parental control and guidance. A new body of knowledge, and ways of talking and thinking about parenting developed which constructed parents of young offenders and parent–child relationships in very particular ways (for a more detailed discussion, see Condry & Miles, 2012). Specifically, parents who were thought to be shirking their responsibilities could be made to control their children through measures such as Parenting Orders. As Muncie has argued, this ultimately resulted in criminalizing 'inadequate parenting' (Muncie, 1999) and in an individualized analysis which failed to take account of structural inequalities. These assumptions are particularly problematic in the case of parents being victimized by their adolescent children and this construction of parent and child relationships in the youth justice system leaves little room for understanding parents as victims (see Condry & Miles, 2016; Condry, 2016 for further discussion).

1.5.3 The Safeguarding/Social Work Paradigm

Young people who perpetrate violence in the home are vulnerable children, and it is important that any responses to that violence do not lose sight of this. Parents in our study often described a lack of response or understanding from children's services, as in the case of this mother:

> And then in end I tried phoning social services – they didn't want to know, they wouldn't touch me. Said "[your son] is not at harm from you or you're not at harm from him". I says "Not yet. Not yet." I says "I'll tell you now" I says "this is how it's going to play out" I says "he's going to carry on. Do this, do that, do the other. And in the end" I says "I won't be able to cope and he'll end up in care and then that's it" I says "and then you'll all be all over us then won't you?" "No… this, that, and the other" and I thought "Oh, whatever." And I used to phone them up sometimes and I used to say "If you don't come and get him, I'm going to kill him" …I mean I was trying to get social services involved for twelve months. When they actually were involved, it were worst thing I ever did. I should never have tried to get 'em involved because they made it worse. (Mother aged 32, son aged 16)

Some of these parents described how social services did not see the child using violence in the home as at risk and would only see the problem of APV as within their remit if there were younger siblings in the family who could be said to have child protection needs because of the violence. The response to APV from social services is a topic that is an under researched area and there is little systematic evidence to draw upon. However, recent discussions with those in the profession suggest that this may have improved in recent years with more nuanced understandings of children's wellbeing (see also Bonnick, 2019).

The policy and academic literature on safeguarding is instructive here and draws attention to a broader understanding of the needs of children and how this should be viewed holistically and contextually. This definition of safeguarding from the NSPCC's website describes the different elements of safeguarding, three of which go beyond protecting children from abuse or maltreatment [emphasis added]:

> Safeguarding is the action that is taken to promote the welfare of children and protect them from harm. Safeguarding means:
>
> protecting children from abuse and maltreatment
>
> *preventing harm to children's health or development*
>
> *ensuring children grow up with the provision of safe and effective care*
>
> *taking action to enable all children and young people to have the best outcomes.*
>
> Child protection is part of the safeguarding process. It focuses on protecting individual children identified as suffering or likely to suffer significant harm. This includes child protection procedures which detail how to respond to concerns about a child.[5]

A key point is that a child using violence in the home, even if not abused or maltreated, will not be achieving a satisfactory level of health and development, receiving safe and effective care, or having the best outcomes. Our research suggests that young people who are using violence might have a range of safeguarding needs,

[5] https://learning.nspcc.org.uk/safeguarding-child-protection/.

including previous or current victimisation; being witnesses to violence in the family; mental health problems; self harm; learning difficulties; substance misuse; vulnerabilities to peer violence or sexual exploitation, not being safe; not thriving and developing; and potential poor outcomes across a range of domains, including mental health and education. If they are using violence in the home they will not be growing up with safe and effective care, and their health and development will clearly be affected.

It is worth noting the parallels between the safeguarding needs of young people who are violent in the home and the antecedents to adolescent suicide. An analysis in 2014 of serious case reviews for children who had taken their lives found that pathways to harm for these young people were complex and difficulties were often enduring (Sidebotham et al., 2016). Pathways included parental conflict and acrimonious separation; parental and/or child substance misuse; mental health problems, including self-harm, and involvement with children and adolescent health services; involvement with a youth offending team; bullying; domestic abuse, time spent in local authority care or secure units; going missing and homelessness; and experiences of being a young carer. The authors highlight a cumulative risk of harm and particularly the impact of domestic abuse on young people:

> There is cumulative risk of harm to a child when different parental and environmental risk factors are present in combination or over periods of time. We previously noted this particularly in relation to domestic abuse, parental mental ill-health, and alcohol or substance misuse, but it also includes other risks such as adverse experiences in the parents' own childhoods, a history of violent crime, a pattern of multiple consecutive partners, acrimonious separation, and social isolation. When presented with any of these risk factors, practitioners should explore whether there may be other cumulative risks of harm to the child, as well as any protective factors. The impact of all domestic abuse is harmful to children and a step-change is required in how we understand and respond to domestic abuse. There is a need to move away from incident-based models of intervention with domestic abuse to a deeper understanding of the ongoing nature of coercive control and its impact on women and children, and also on men. (Sidebotham et al., 2016, p. 13)

Young people who are using violence in the home need to be understood as at risk and at point of crisis. Recent work on contextual safeguarding (Firmin, 2017) emphasises the need to look holistically at children's lives and think about all the influences and potential sites of risk, not just focusing on the parent–child relationship. In developing the contextual safeguarding approach, Firmin (2017) argues the importance of considering children's lives holistically and including risks to them outside of the home, for example amongst peer groups or in the community. Such an approach is important when considering children who use violence who may be more likely to be detached from the protective influence of parents and potentially subject to other risks.

1.6 Conclusion

This chapter has argued that children and young people who perpetrate family violence are still children with safeguarding and wellbeing needs, and need to be defined as such, rather than being defined as troubled young adults and seen through the lens of responses designed for adults. Young people using violence in the home are the concern of all services that work with children and families, and there remains a need for a greater recognition and understanding of the problem and more consistency in how young people are understood across these services A guiding principle in a consistent approach should be a contextual and holistic approach to children's lives which allows a broad capture of pathways or antecedents to the problem of APV. It is important to hold a child-centred approach in balance with an understanding of the harm caused to parent victims: responses to this form of violence need to hold different imperatives in balance, which include the complexities of family histories, dimensions of blame and culpability, shame and guilt, and an understanding of how violence is enacted through particular adolescent-specific dynamics of power and control.

References

Agnew, R., & Huguley, S. (1989). Adolescent violence toward parents. *Journal of Marriage and the Family, 51*(3), 699–711.

BBC. (2019). Domestic violence: Child-parent violence doubles in three years. https://www.bbc.co.uk/news/uk-england-49207887

Biehal, N. (2012). Parent abuse by young people on the edge of care: A child welfare perspective. *Social Policy and Society, 11*(2), 251–263.

Bonnick, H. (2019). *Child to parent violence and abuse: A practitioner's guide to working with families*. Pavilion Publishing and Media Limited.

Boxer, P., Gullen, R., & Mahoney, A. (2009). Adolescents' physical aggression toward parents in a clinic-referred sample. *Journal of Clinical Child and Adolescent Psychology, 38*(1), 106–116.

Brezina, T. (1999). Teenage violence toward parents as an adaption to family strain: Evidence from a national survey of adolescent males. *Youth and Society, 30*(4), 416–444.

Burney, E., & Gelsthorpe, L. (2008). Do we need a "naughty step"? Rethinking the parenting order after ten years. *The Howard Journal, 47*(5), 470–485.

Calvete, E., Orue, I., & Gamez-Gaudix, M. (2013a). Child-to-parent violence: Emotional and behavioural predictors. *Journal of Interpersonal Violence, 28*(4), 755–772.

Calvete, E., Gamez-Gaudiz, M., Orue, I., Gonzalez-Diez, Z., Lopez de Arroyabe, E., Sampedro, R., Pereria, R., Zubizarreta, A., & Borrajo, E. (2013b). Brief report: The adolescent child-to-parent aggression questionnaire: An examination of aggression against parents in Spanish adolescents. *Journal of Adolescence, 36*(6), 1077–1081.

Calvete, E., Orue, I., Bertino, L., Gonzalez, Z., Montes, Y., Padilla, P., & Pereira, R. (2014). Child-to-parent violence in adolescents: The perspectives of the parents, children, and professionals in a sample of Spanish focus group participants. *Journal of Family Violence, 29*(3), 343–352.

Calvete, E., Gamez-Gaudiz, M., & Orue, I. (2015). Reciprocal longitudinal associations between substance use and child-to-parent violence in adolescents. *Journal of Adolescence, 44,* 124–133.

Clough, L. (2018). What happens when your child becomes violent… with you. https://www.theguardian.com/society/2018/dec/09/what-happens-when-your-child-becomes-violent-with-you

Condry, R. (2016). The parent as paradoxical victim: Adolescent to parent violence and contested victimization. In D. Spencer & S. Walklate (Eds.), *Reconceptualizing critical victimology: Interventions and possibilities* (pp. 45–62). Lexington Books.
Condry, R., & Miles, C. (2012). Adolescent to parent violence and youth justice in England and Wales. *Social Policy and Society, 11*(2), 241–250.
Condry, R., & Miles, C. (2014). Adolescent to parent violence: Framing and mapping a hidden problem. *Criminology and Criminal Justice, 14*(3), 257–275.
Condry, R., & Miles, C. (2016). Adolescent to parent violence and the challenge for youth justice. In M. Bosworth, C. Hoyle, & L. Zedner (Eds.), *The changing contours of criminal justice* (pp. 257–269). Oxford University Press.
Cottrell, B. (2004). *When Teens Abuse Their Parents.* Nova Scotia: Fernwood Publishing
Contreras, L., & Cano, M. (2016a). Child-to-parent violence: The role of exposure to violence and its relationship to social-cognitive processing. *The European Journal of Psychology Applied to Legal Context, 8*(2), 43–50.
Contreras, L., & Cano, M. (2016b). Social competence and child-to-parent violence: Analyzing the role of the emotional intelligence, social attitudes, and personal values. *Deviant Behavior, 37*(2), 115–125.
Cottrell, B., & Monk, P. (2004). Adolescent to parent abuse: A qualitative overview of common themes. *Journal of Family Issues, 25*(8), 1072–1095.
Daly, K., & Nancarrow, H. (2010). Restorative justice and youth violence toward parents. In J. Ptacek (Ed.), *Feminism, restorative justice, and violence against women* (pp. 150–176). Oxford University Press.
Douglas, H., & Walsh, T. (2018). Adolescent family violence: What is the role for legal responses? *Sydney Law Review, 40*(4), 499–526.
Eckstein, N. (2004). Emergent issues in families experiencing adolescent-to-parent abuse. *Western Journal of Communication, 68*(4), 365–388.
Edenborough, M., Jackson, D., Mannix, J., & Wilkes, L. M. (2008). Living in the red zone: The experience of child-to-mother violence. *Child and Family Social Work, 13*(4), 464–473.
Edleson, J. L. (1999). The overlap between child maltreatment and woman battering. *Violence Against Women, 5*(2), 134–154.
Elliott, G., Cunningham, S., Colangelo, M., & Gelles, R. (2011). Perceived mattering to the family and physical violence within the family by adolescents. *Journal of Family Issues, 32*(8), 1007–1029.
Evans, E. D., & Warren-Sohlberg, L. (1988). A pattern analysis of adolescent abusive behaviour towards parents. *Journal of Adolescent Research, 3*(2), 201–216.
Firmin, C. (2017). *Contextual safeguarding: An overview of the operational, strategic and conceptual framework.* Institute of Applied Social Research. https://contextualsafeguarding.org.uk/assets/documents/Contextual-Safeguarding-Briefing.pdf
Fitz-Gibbon, K., Elliott, K., & Maher, J. M. (2018). *Investigating adolescent family violence in Victoria: Understanding experiences and practitioner perspectives.* Monash Gender and Family Violence Research Program, Faculty of Arts, Monash University.
Gallagher, E. (2004). Parents victimised by their children. *Australian and New Zealand Journal of Family Therapy, 25*(1), 1–12.
Holt, A. (2009). Parent abuse: Some reflections on the adequacy of a youth justice response. *Internet Journal of Criminology,* 1–11.
Holt, A. (2012). *Adolescent-to-parent abuse: Current understandings in research, policy and practice.* Policy Press.
Holt, A. (2013). *Adolescent-to-parent abuse: Current understandings in research, policy and practice.* Policy Press.
Holt, A., & Retford, S. (2012). Practitioner accounts of responding to parent abuse—A case study in ad hoc delivery, perverse outcomes and a policy silence. *Child and Family Social Work, 18*(3), 1–10.

Home Office. (2013). *New government domestic violence and abuse definition* (Home Office Circular 003/2013). Home Office. Retrieved May 22, 2014 from https://www.gov.uk/government/publications/new-government-domestic-violence-and-abuse-definition

Home Office. (2015). *Information guide on adolescent to parent violence and abuse*. Home Office. Retrieved May 15, 2020 from https://assets.publishing.service.gov.uk/government/uploads/system/uploads/attachment_data/file/732573/APVA.pdf

Howard, J. (2011). *Adolescent violence in the home: The missing link in family violence prevention and response* (Stakeholder paper 11). Australian Domestic & Family Violence Clearinghouse.

Howard, J., & Rottem, H. (2008). *It all starts at home: Male adolescent violence to mothers*. Inner South Community Health Service.

Hunter, C., Nixon, J., & Parr, S. (2010). Mother abuse: A matter of youth justice, child welfare or domestic violence? *Journal of Law and Society, 37*(2), 264–284.

Ibabe, I., & Bentler, P. M. (2015). The contribution of family relationships to child-to-parent violence. *Journal of Family Violence, 31*(2), 259–269.

Ibabe, I., & Jaureguizar, J. (2010). Child-to-parent violence: Profile of abusive adolescents and their families. *Journal of Criminal Justice, 38*(4), 616–624.

Ibabe, I., Jaureguizar, J., & Bentler, P. M. (2013). Risk factors for child-to-parent violence. *International Research on Aggression and Violence, 28*(5), 523–534.

Ibabe, I., Ainara, A., & Elgorriaga, E. (2014). Behavioral problems and depressive symptomatology as predictors of child-to-parent violence. *The European Journal of Psychology Applied to Legal Context, 6*(2), 53–61.

Jackson, D. (2003). Broadening constructions of family violence: Mothers' perspectives of aggression from their children. *Child and Family Social Work, 8*(4), 321–329.

Kennedy, T. D., Edmonds, W. A., Dann, K. T. J., & Burnett, K. F. (2010). The clinical and adaptive features of young offenders with histories of child-parent violence. *Journal of Family Violence, 25*(5), 509–520.

Kethineni, S. (2004). Youth-on-parent violence in a central Illinois County. *Youth Violence and Juvenile Justice, 2*(4), 374–394.

Kratcoski, P. (1985). Youth violence directed toward significant others. *Journal of Adolescence, 8*(2), 145–157.

Lyons, J., Bell, T., Frechette, S., & Romano, E. (2015). Child-to-parent violence: Frequency and family correlates. *Journal of Family Violence, 30*(6), 729–742.

Margolin, G., & Raucom, B. (2014). Adolescents' aggression to parents: Longitudinal links with parents' physical aggression. *Journal of Adolescent Health, 55*(5), 645–651.

McCloskey, L. A., & Lichter, E. L. (2003). The contribution of marital violence to adolescent aggression across different relationships. *Journal of Interpersonal Violence, 18*(4), 390–411.

McKenna, M., O'Connor, R., & Verco, J. (2010). *Exposing the dark side of parenting: A report of parents' experiences of child and adolescent family violence*. The Regional Alliance Addressing Child and Adolescent Violence in the Home, South Australia, Regional Alliance.

Miles, C., & Condry, R. (2014). Adolescent to parent violence: The police response to parents reporting violence from their children. *Policing and Society, 26*(7), 804–823.

Miles, C., & Condry, R. (2015). Responding to adolescent to parent violence: Challenges for policy and practice. *British Journal of Criminology, 55*(6), 1076–1095.

Muncie, J. (1999). Institutionalised intolerance: Youth justice and the 1998 Crime and Disorder Act. *Critical Social Policy, 19*(2), 147–175.

Muncie, J., & Hughes, G. (2002). Modes of youth governance: Political rationalities, criminalization, and resistance. In J. Muncie, G. Hughes, & E. McLaughlin (Eds.), *Youth justice: Critical readings* (pp. 1–18). Sage.

Nock, M. K., & Kazdin, A. E. (2002). Parent-directed physical aggression by clinic-referred youths. *Journal of Clinical Child and Adolescent Psychology, 31*(2), 193–205.

Pagani, L., Tremblay, R., Nagin, D., Zoccolillo, M., Vitaro, F., & McDuff, P. (2004). Risk factor models for adolescent verbal and physical aggression toward mothers. *International Journal of Behavioural Development, 28*(6), 528–537.

Paterson, R., Luntz, H., Perlesz, A., & Cotton, S. (2002). Adolescent violence towards parents: Maintaining family connections when the going gets tough. *Australian and New Zealand Journal of Family Therapy, 23*(2), 90–100.
Paulson, M. J., Coombs, R. H., & Landsverk, J. (1990). Youth who physically assault their parents. *Journal of Family Violence, 5*(1), 121–133.
Peek, C. W., Fischer, J. L., & Kidwell, J. A. (1985). Teenage violence toward parents: A neglected dimension of family violence. *Journal of Marriage and the Family, 47*(4), 1051–1058.
Routt, G., & Anderson, L. (2011). Adolescent violence towards parents. *Journal of Aggression, Maltreatment & Trauma, 20*(1), 1–18.
SafeLives. (2017). *Safe young lives: Young people and domestic abuse.* https://safelives.org.uk/sites/default/files/resources/Safe%20Young%20Lives%20web.pdf
Sheehan, M. (1997). Adolescent violence—Strategies, outcomes and dilemmas in working with young people and their families. *Australian and New Zealand Journal of Family Therapy, 18*(2), 80–91.
Sidebotham, P., Brandon, M., Bailey, S., Belderson, P., Dodsworth, J., Garstang, J., Harrison, E., Retzer, A., & Sorensen, P. (2016). *Pathways to harm, pathways to protection: A triennial analysis of serious case reviews 2011 to 2014: Final report*. Department for Education. https://assets.publishing.service.gov.uk/government/uploads/system/uploads/attachment_data/file/533826/Triennial_Analysis_of_SCRs_2011-2014_-__Pathways_to_harm_and_protection.pdf
Snyder, H. N., & McCurley, C. (2008). *Domestic assaults by juvenile offenders.* Juvenile Justice Bulletin, U.S. Department of Justice: Office of Justice Programs.
Stewart, M., Burns, A., & Leonard, R. (2007). Dark side of the mothering role: Abuse of mothers by adolescent and adult children. *Sex Roles, 56*(3), 183–191.
Strom, K. J., Warner, T. D., Tichhavsky, L., & Kahn, M. A. (2010). Policing juveniles: Domestic violence arrest policies, gender, and police response to child-parent violence. *Crime and Delinquency, 60*(3), 427–450.
Thomas, K., Fitz-Gibbon, K., & Maher, J. M. (2019). The use of protection orders in response to adolescent family violence: Mapping divergent Australian approaches and the merits of this criminal justice intervention. *Current Issues in Criminal Justice, 31*(4), 461–475.
Ulman, A., & Straus, M. (2003). Violence by children against mothers in relation to violence between parents and corporal punishment by parents. *Journal of Comparative Family Studies, 34*(1), 41–60.
Walsh, J. A., & Krienert, J. L. (2007). Child-to-parent violence: An empirical analysis of offender, victim, and event characteristics in a national sample of reported incidents. *Journal of Family Violence, 22*(7), 563–574.
Walsh, J. A., & Krienert, J. L. (2009). A decade of child-initiated family violence: Comparative analysis of child-parent violence and parricide examining offender, victim and event characteristics in a national sample of reported incidents, 1995–2005. *Journal of Interpersonal Violence, 24*(9), 1450–1477.

Rachel Condry is Professor of Criminology and Fellow of St Hilda's College at the University of Oxford. Her work focuses broadly on the intersections between crime and the family, which has included research projects on the families of serious offenders, prisoners' families, parenting expertise in youth justice, adolescent to parent violence, adult filial violence, and parricide. She is currently researching the relationship between school exclusion and youth offending as a co-investigator on the the multi-disciplinary Excluded Lives project at the University of Oxford, and collaborating with Caroline Miles (University of Manchester) researching fatal and non-fatal filial violence across the lifecourse. Rachel is a co-editor of the Howard Journal of Crime and Justice, Associate Editor of The Journal of Criminology, and Editor of the book series Routledge Studies in Crime, Justice and the Family.

Caroline Miles is a Senior Lecturer in Criminology and Director for Postgraduate Research in the Department of Criminology at the University of Manchester. Caroline's research interests incorporate violence and homicide, with specific interests in child to parent violence and abuse, honour-based violence and abuse, domestic homicide, parricide, and homicide trends. Most recently, Caroline has worked on an ESRC-funded project 'Understanding and improving risk assessment in domestic violence' (with Juanjo Medina-Ariza, University of Manchester) and an N8-funded project, 'Early identification of honour-based abuse' (with Claire Fox, University of Manchester and West Yorkshire Police). She is also collaborating with Rachel Condry (University of Oxford) to research fatal and non-fatal filial violence across the lifecourse, building on their previous ESRC-funded project 'Investigating adolescent violence towards parents'.

Chapter 2
Prevalent but Overlooked: Current Literature, Policy, and Service Responses to Sibling Abuse

Michelle Patrice Desir and Canan Karatekin

Abstract When people think of family violence, they often think of domestic violence between adults or child maltreatment. However, sibling abuse is often overlooked and normalized despite being the most common form of family violence and despite evidence of its associations with various detrimental emotional and behavioral outcomes. This chapter describes the current state of the literature on sibling abuse with an emphasis on definitions, prevalence estimates, the association of sibling abuse with adverse outcomes, and current interventions available to address this pervasive phenomenon. We discuss suggestions for future research to highlight the gaps and limitations in the current literature including the need to address definitional and methodological issues, understand the various dynamics of abusive sibling relationships, and build on current intervention research. Finally, we provide suggestions for policy, intervention, and service response in light of the gaps and limitations present in our body of knowledge on sibling abuse.

2.1 The State of the Literature on Sibling Abuse

2.1.1 What is Sibling Abuse? Definition and Theoretical Models

In order to provide a review of the literature on sibling abuse, it is imperative to discuss a proper definition for this phenomenon. Sibling abuse is commonly categorized into physical abuse, psychological abuse, and sibling incest/sexual abuse (Haskins, 2003; Relva et al., 2013). Physical aggression includes willful acts between siblings that may result in physical injury, including but not limited to slapping, hitting, biting, kicking, smothering or choking with or without the use of an object or

M. P. Desir (✉) · C. Karatekin
Institute of Child Development, University of Minnesota, Minneapolis, MN, USA
e-mail: mdesir@pennstatehealth.psu.edu

M. P. Desir
Child Abuse Pediatrics, Penn State Hershey Medical Center, Hershey, PA, USA

K. Fitz-Gibbon et al. (eds.), *Young People Using Family Violence*,
https://doi.org/10.1007/978-981-16-1331-9_2

weapon such as a stick, bat, gun, or knife (Haskins, 2003). Psychological/emotional abuse often involves teasing, ridiculing, insulting, terrorizing, belittling, or rejecting one's sibling (Haskins, 2003). Sibling incest includes developmentally inappropriate sexual behavior that may involve physical touching, fondling, attempted penetration, intercourse by coercion or force, oral, or anal sex. Sibling incest may also include non-contact behavior, such as unwanted sexual references in conversation, indecent exposure, forcing a sibling to observe the other's sexual behavior, taking pornographic pictures, or forcing a sibling to view pornography (Haskins, 2003).

More generally, one commonly accepted definition of sibling abuse is a "repeated pattern of aggression directed toward a sibling with intent to inflict harm, and motivated by an internal emotional need for power and control" (Caffaro & Conn-Caffaro, 2005). However, there are limitations to this definition. For example, it may be difficult for children to identify their motivations for inflicting harm on siblings. Thus, establishing such motivations may be subjective. Furthermore, although this definition is frequently referenced in the literature, issues of establishing a consistent or standard definition remain (Phillips et al., 2018), which is partly due to the interchangeable use of various terms (e.g., sibling violence/aggression/conflict/rivalry) to describe the same acts (Eriksen & Jensen, 2009). Additionally, making clear distinctions as to when normal developmental behavior between siblings crosses the barrier into abusive behavior (Kiselica & Morill-Richards, 2007) can be difficult.

One potential objective way of delineating normal behavior from abusive behavior is to consider the seriousness or severity of the act. A few researchers have attempted to do so for physical acts. Eriksen and Jensen (2009) constructed and validated a model of sibling violence severity using items on child-to-child conflict from the Conflicts Tactics Scale (CTS; Straus et al., 1980). They dichotomized physical violence between siblings into severe acts and threats that had potential for injury (e.g., beaten up, threatened with weapons, use of weapons) and less severe forms (e.g., hitting and other less injurious forms of physical contact). Khan and Cooke (2013) explored whether a two-factor model for severe violence developed with an adult offender population (Michie & Cooke, 2006), which conceptualized severe violence into weapon and non-weapon use, could be generalized to deliberate severe inter-sibling violence with juvenile offenders. Using items from the same measure (CTS; Straus et al., 1980) as Eriksen and Jensen (2009), Khan and Cooke (2013) used exploratory factor analysis and validated the use of a two-factor model with a juvenile (ages 10–19 years) offender population (Khan & Cooke, 2013). This model was later validated in a community sample of participants aged 16–55 years (Khan, 2017) and conceptualizes severe sibling violence into lethal (attempts to strangle, threatened with knife, use of knife, threatened with gun, use of gun, hanging/burning) and non-lethal (kicked, bitten, punched, thrown something heavy/sharp, battered/beaten, slapped, pushed, grabbed) acts. Despite these efforts, these models have yet to be adopted by sibling abuse researchers, further highlighting the inconsistencies in definition and categorization.

Discussions of theoretical models of sibling abuse by various researchers also reflect efforts to more fully understand the nature of sibling abuse. To summarize, social learning theory and family systems theory are amongst the most common perspectives adopted and appear to have garnered the strongest support. Specifically, social learning theory suggest that abusive behavior toward siblings is learned via modeling and reinforcement by key adult figures, usually parents (Hoffman & Edwards, 2004; Hoffman et al., 2005). Family systems theory suggests that sibling abuse cannot be examined without an understanding of the family system in which the sibling relationship is embedded. For example, family dynamics such as high levels of parenting stress and frustration, parentification, unclear boundaries, parental dysfunction, and conflict/violence in the marital and/or parent–child relationship may all contribute to abusive behaviors among siblings (Eriksen & Jensen, 2009; Haskins, 2003). An in-depth discussion of these models is beyond the scope of this chapter. However, interested readers may wish to reference other studies for a more complete discussion (Eriksen & Jensen, 2009; Haskins, 2003; Hoffman & Edwards, 2004; Hoffman et al., 2005).

2.1.2 Prevalence of Sibling Abuse

In addition to establishing a proper definition and categorization system, information regarding the scope of the problem is necessary. The literature provides clear indication that the prevalence of this phenomenon is quite high. Nationally representative samples in the U.S. and U.K. have yielded prevalence rates for sibling abuse between 21 and 46%. Specifically, one study of 4237 adolescents participating in a longitudinal study of U.K. households inquired about four subtypes (i.e., physical, verbal, stealing, and teasing) of sibling abuse and reported 46% of participants had been victimized by siblings and 36% had perpetrated aggression. The National Survey of Children's Exposure to Violence (NatSECV), which is a questionnaire periodically administered to different cohorts of U.S. children (ages 0–17) and their parents, has estimated lifetime prevalence of physical assault by a juvenile sibling to be between 29 and 37%, with past year prevalence estimates between 21 and 36% (Finkelhor et al., 2005, 2009, 2013, 2015). Using this same data, a two-year longitudinal study found that 51% of youth experienced victimization (i.e., physical, property, or psychological) by a sibling at one or both waves (Tucker et al., 2018). Similarly, an annual survey conducted in a state public school system with 8th and 11th grade students revealed that 42% of participants reported some form of physical or verbal victimization by a sibling (Button & Gealt, 2010).

In retrospective studies with undergraduates and young adults, prevalence rates are much higher with 48–71% of participants reporting physical violence victimization by a sibling (Hardy, 2001; Khan & Rogers, 2015; Relva et al., 2013). When including acts of emotional or psychological aggression, prevalence rates of sibling victimization jump to 78–95% (Mathis & Mueller, 2015; Relva et al., 2013; Skinner & Kowalski, 2013). For studies that ask undergraduate participants whether they have perpetrated aggressive acts towards siblings, prevalence rates are similar, ranging from 41 to 73% for physical acts (Hardy, 2001; Hoffman et al., 2005; Relva et al.,

2013) and 85 to 95% when psychological aggression is included (Mathis & Mueller, 2015; Relva et al., 2013; Skinner & Kowalski, 2013).

Studies conducted with children and adolescents using community samples, clinic-referred children, and psychiatrically hospitalized children reveal higher rates for physical, but similar rates for psychological aggression, and mostly ask about perpetration of such acts rather than victimization. Specifically, children/adolescents and/or their parents reported a 70–72% rate of perpetrating physical acts towards a sibling (Khan, 2017; Miller et al., 2012). Rates ranged from 76 to 95% when including perpetration of verbal or psychological aggression (Kolko et al., 1996; Phillips et al., 2018; Tompsett et al., 2018).

Across studies that inquire about specific acts, the most common aggressive acts are usually verbal/psychological aggression (e.g., insulting, shouting/yelling, hurtful teasing), followed by physical acts (e.g., pushing, shoving, or grabbing). Regarding sibling incest, 7.4% of undergraduates in one study reported some "sexual behavior" between them and a sibling (Hardy, 2001) and one study of 590 Portuguese university students reported that 11% of males and 5% of females had sexually coerced a sibling (Relva et al., 2017). However, most studies do not include prevalence rates for sibling sexual abuse, and most of the literature on sibling incest only includes participants who have been identified as perpetrators or victims, precluding prevalence estimates.

Some studies have estimated prevalence rates for sibling abuse that may be deemed more severe, albeit using varying definitions or categorizations. In a study utilizing one of the validated severity models referenced above with a nationally representative sample of U.S. families, 14% of participants reported being the victim of severe acts of physical violence by a sibling, such as being beaten up, threatened with weapons, or having weapons used on them (Eriksen & Jensen, 2009). In a study with Head Start participants, 21% of mothers reported an aggressive act by a sibling resulting in injury to another sibling (Miller et al., 2012) and 28% of college students reported "high levels of conflict" with a sibling (Graham-Bermann et al., 1994). There is also some evidence to suggest sibling abuse may be chronic for many children. A two-year longitudinal study using NatSECV data in a nationally representative sample of 1653 youth found that 20% of the sample experienced sibling victimization at both waves of data collection (Tucker et al., 2018). Perpetration of verbal and physical sibling aggression was also moderately stable over a two-year period in one study using a clinic and community sample (Kolko et al., 1996).

There is limited information regarding the association of demographic characteristics to prevalence rates. Multiple studies find that males are more likely to perpetrate sibling abuse (Eriksen & Jensen, 2009; Phillips et al., 2018; Relva et al., 2013; Tippett & Wolke, 2015), but rates among females are high as well. The literature is inconsistent regarding whether males or females are more likely to be victims. Race, socioeconomic status (SES), and cross-cultural differences are rarely examined, and findings are inconsistent across studies regarding which groups are more likely to experience sibling abuse perpetration/victimization. However, a recent longitudinal study of sibling victimization patterns using the NatSECV data with 1653 U.S. youth found that white children/adolescents and those with college-educated parents had the greatest likelihood of belonging to a group ("Persist") who reported sibling victimization at both waves of the study (Tucker et al., 2018).

It is clear that there is wide variability in prevalence rates of sibling aggression due to differences in definition, categorization, methodology, ages of participants, and time frame (e.g., past year versus lifetime experiences). Nevertheless, there are some themes that hold constant. There is substantial evidence that physical and psychological sibling aggression/victimization decline with age, peaking prior to adolescence (Button & Gealt, 2010; Eriksen & Jensen, 2009; Finkelhor et al., 2005, 2009, 2013, 2015; Hoffman & Edwards, 2004; Johnson et al., 2015; Tompsett et al., 2018; Tucker et al., 2013a, 2013b, 2018). Of note, prevalence rates across age are not as available for sibling sexual abuse, but in one exploratory study with 34 young boys who displayed harmful sexual behaviors, the age of onset ranged from 6 to 16 years with a mean of 12.4 years (Yates et al., 2012). Furthermore, sibling abuse is more common in families where children have been exposed to domestic violence or child maltreatment (Bowes et al., 2014; Button & Gealt, 2010; Caffaro & Conn-Caffaro, 2005; Eriksen & Jensen, 2009; Hoffman et al., 2005; Kolko et al., 1996; Relva et al., 2013; Tompsett et al., 2018; Tucker et al., 2014a; Yates et al., 2012). Additionally, even amongst studies that estimate the lowest prevalence rates of sibling abuse, it is universally recognized as the most prevalent form of family violence, far exceeding prevalence estimates for parental childhood maltreatment/abuse, and even peer bullying/victimization (Caffaro & Conn-Caffaro, 2005; Finkelhor et al., 2005, 2009, 2013, 2015; Hoetger et al., 2015; Johnson et al., 2015).

2.1.3 Sibling Abuse Perpetration and Adverse Outcomes

Despite its high prevalence rates and identification as the most common form of family violence, sibling abuse has largely been overlooked in the research literature relative to other types of intrafamilial abuse (Hoetger et al., 2015; Hoffman & Edwards, 2004; Johnson et al., 2015; Tippett & Wolke, 2015). A search using the keywords "sibling aggression" or "sibling abuse" on PsycINFO on 06/28/2019 returned 159 results compared to 29,610 results for "child maltreatment" or "child abuse" and 19,448 results for "domestic violence" or "intimate partner violence." Furthermore, in a 200+ page report on child maltreatment published by the U.S. Department of Health and Human Services, mentions of sibling abuse are practically nonexistent, only referring to foster siblings as one of many potential "other perpetrators" of abuse (U.S. Department of Health and Human Services, Administration for Children and Families, Administration on Children, Youth and Families, Children's Bureau, 2019).

Sibling abuse's infrequent appearances in the research literature compared to these other forms of family violence may lead to a misconception that it is not harmful. However, this small but growing body of research literature suggests that this is far from the truth. Cross-sectional studies of individuals who have used sibling violence have demonstrated associations with lower self-esteem (Graham-Bermann et al., 1994), adult emotional difficulties (Mathis & Mueller, 2015), and externalizing symptoms (Tompsett et al., 2018), even when controlling for demographic characteristics and exposure to other forms of family violence. Longitudinal studies have identified sibling abuse as a risk factor for similar outcomes. One found that sibling verbal aggression predicted internalizing and externalizing symptoms two years later in a clinic and community sample of 6- to 13-year-old children (Kolko et al., 1996). However, it is unclear whether researchers controlled for other forms of family violence measured. Another study using a birth cohort of 6988 individuals found sibling bullying perpetration at 12 years of age to predict antisocial behavior at age 18–20 years, even after controlling for peer bullying and maltreatment by parents. Odds increased with more frequent perpetration (Dantchev & Wolke, 2019).

Perpetrating sibling abuse is also associated with utilizing other forms of aggression and violence, including towards oneself, mothers, and teachers (Phillips et al., 2018). Furthermore, children who fought with siblings were 2.49 times more likely to fight with peers, after controlling for race/ethnicity, sex, school failure, substance use, and caregiver aggression (Johnson et al., 2015) in a school-based sample. Increased odds of perpetrating aggression toward peers for those who perpetrate sibling abuse has also been found in other studies (Dantchev & Wolke, 2019; Tippett & Wolke, 2015) and appears to precede such behavior, with those exhibiting violent behaviors towards children in their school and/or community often having engaged in such behaviors with siblings first (Yates et al., 2012).

2.1.4 Sibling Abuse Victimization and Adverse Outcomes

When considering the nature of sibling relationships, it becomes clear that they are influential. Siblings are typically in a non-voluntary and enduring relationship that outlast all other relationships, including with parents (Hoffman & Edwards, 2004). As a result, such a relationship is often dependent or interdependent, and siblings are unable to avoid each other. Thus, when such relationships are abusive, they have the potential to be the most damaging (Hardy, 2001) and inescapable, as sibling offenders, unlike adult offenders, are more likely to remain in the same home, school, and community as their victims, even if a child welfare services report has been filed (Caffaro, 2011).

The body of research literature on the impact that sibling abuse has on victims has provided substantial evidence to support claims of it damaging effects. Cross-sectional and retrospective studies with grade school students and college undergraduates have linked sibling abuse victimization with emotional difficulties, aggressive behaviors, delinquency, and substance use (Button & Gealt, 2010; Mathis & Mueller, 2015), after controlling for exposure to other forms of family violence and demographic characteristics. Anxiety and low self-esteem are also associated with sibling abuse victimization (Graham-Bermann et al., 1994; Morrill, 2014). Findings from the NatSECV using nationally representative samples of more than 3000 youth have linked the experience of various types (i.e., physical, psychological, property) of sibling aggression, with or without use of weapons, to greater mental health distress (combination of anger, depression, anxiety, dissociative, and post-traumatic stress symptoms) compared to those who had not been assaulted by a sibling (Tucker et al., 2013c, 2014b). This finding holds even after controlling for demographic characteristics and all other forms of non-sibling victimization assessed (e.g., maltreatment, peer victimization, witnessing violence). Furthermore, Tucker et al. (2013c) found a dose–response relationship, in that children and adolescents experiencing more sibling victimization types reported greater mental health distress than those experiencing one type. Large longitudinal, prospective cohort studies have reported similar findings, with children frequently bullied (most commonly name-calling/insulting/made fun of, shouting/yelling, swearing, hitting/kicking/pushing/shoving) by a sibling at age 12 years having increased odds of nicotine dependence (Dantchev & Wolke, 2019) and depression and self-harm (Bowes et al., 2014) at ages 18–20 years compared to those who were not bullied by siblings. Victimization by both peers and parents were controlled for.

Beyond increased risk for negative emotional and behavioral consequences, children abused by siblings are significantly more likely to experience dating violence (Simonelli et al., 2005) and peer victimization (Johnson et al., 2015; Tippett & Wolke, 2015; Tucker et al., 2013c, 2014b). Furthermore, experiencing sibling victimization predicted peer victimization in a two-year longitudinal study (Tucker et al., 2018) and experiencing victimization by both siblings and peers is linked to greater mental health distress than experiencing victimization from one source (Tucker et al., 2013c). Nearly all studies controlled for maltreatment by parents. A couple of studies found the detrimental impact of sibling abuse to be just as harmful as peer victimization (Tucker et al., 2013c, 2014b). With regard to sibling incest, the damaging effects appear to be no different than that of father- or stepfather-daughter incest and, in some aspects, may be even worse (Caffaro & Conn-Caffaro, 2005; Cyr et al., 2002).

2.1.5 Normalization of Sibling Abuse

Despite the high prevalence of sibling abuse, its identification as the most common form of family violence, and evidence of its associations with adverse outcomes for perpetrators and victims, sibling abuse is highly normalized and largely viewed as harmless. This is the case even when it takes the same or similar forms as behaviors perpetrated by others. In one study with 392 U.S. young adults, participants reported bullying behaviors perpetrated by siblings to be more prevalent than and somewhat similar to peer bullying but did not view such behaviors by siblings as aggression or bullying (Hoetger et al., 2015). When asked why bullying is not a good term to describe such behaviors, the most common reason given was that "sibling fighting is normal." Another study involved 605 university students being presented with identical hypothetical scenarios of a young adult male assaulting a young adult female who was either a sibling, dating partner, stranger, or peer. Assault by a sibling was considered to be less severe than assault against a dating partner or stranger (Khan

& Rogers, 2015). Notably, those who had more frequent experiences of childhood sibling violence victimization perceived these hypothetical assaults by siblings as less severe and the victim more culpable than respondents with no experience of sibling violence victimization. Similar findings have been noted in other studies examining views of sibling abuse with undergraduates who have experienced such acts themselves, or who have admitted to perpetrating such acts, including viewing sibling bullying as acceptable, believing it is to be expected, or not considering it to be abusive at the time or in retrospect (Hardy, 2001; Skinner & Kowalski, 2013).

Of additional concern is the lack of action taken regarding sibling abuse by those whom victims would expect to protect them. A retrospective chart review of medical records for 135 children who had been hospitalized for psychiatric reasons revealed that 76% of these children (N = 103) had perpetrated sibling violence but only two were reported to Child Protective Services (CPS) (Phillips et al., 2018). Researchers noted that the sibling violence documented in those two records did not stand out as more frequent or serious than that documented in many other records where no intervention was noted. Sibling abuse is also often normalized by parents. With regard to sibling incest, a qualitative research study based on interviews with adult survivors and practitioners' clinical experiences revealed a pattern of family members' failure to acknowledge and validate the abuse (Caffaro & Conn-Caffaro, 2005). Another study that involved interviews with adult survivors reported a tendency for families to deny its occurrence and minimize its long-term consequences (Morrill, 2014). Beyond sexual abuse, in a case study of a mother identified by social services as being at risk for child abuse and neglect, the mother referred to her youngest child picking on her oldest child for her weight as something that brothers and sisters just do. Additionally, she described her own previous experiences of fighting with her sister growing up as normative, including an incident in which her sister chased her and stabbed her in the back with a fork (Perkins & Shadik, 2018). Even when parents do acknowledge such abusive behaviors as problematic, victims of physical sibling abuse reported that parents' responses were generally ineffective, as they were either unable or unwilling to end the abuse (McDonald & Martinez, 2016).

There are several reasons why sibling abuse may be normalized, including its high prevalence and the general lack of distinction between mild and severe forms when examining potential consequences. Indeed, Gnaulati (2002) cautions that when therapy is being sought to correct undue discord in sibling relationships, thorough assessment is necessary to ascertain to what degree aggressive exchanges are relatively benign and expectable versus noxious. However, due to inconsistencies in the research literature, it is unclear how to make such a determination, which poses difficulties for researchers and policymakers attempting to understand its harmful consequences and for practitioners seeking to determine when intervention may be necessary. Nevertheless, similar to the abuse itself, nonexistent and ineffective responses by parents can have a detrimental impact on victims. Adult victims of sibling abuse reported responses from parents were harmful to their mental health when parents minimized abuse, defended perpetrators, or were ineffective in stopping it (McDonald & Martinez, 2016). Of note, participants in this study self-identified their experiences with sibling victimization as abusive, which may be indicative of more severe experiences. Additionally, parental nonintervention into fights (e.g., yelling, name-calling, pushing, biting, hitting, or kicking) between school-aged siblings was related to less sibling warmth, more sibling conflict/rivalry, and poorer psychosocial functioning (i.e., less prosocial behavior, more depressive affect, and poorer physical health) (Tucker & Kazura, 2013).

2.2 The State of Interventions for Sibling Abuse

2.2.1 Targeted Interventions for Sibling Abuse

Considering the normalization of sibling abuse despite its high prevalence and concerning prognosis for victims and victimizers, as well as the lack of policy to address sibling abuse, it is unsurprising that interventions to address these acts are limited. Additionally, research on interventions for sibling abuse has primarily been conducted with U.S. samples with the exception of one article describing a framework for sibling sexual abuse developed in Australia (Keane et al., 2013). Even within the U.S., there are no intervention programs rated by the California Evidence-Based Clearinghouse for Child Welfare as a 1 ("well supported by research evidence") or 2 ("supported by research evidence") that have any coverage of sibling violence (Shadik et al., 2013). Nevertheless, several researchers and practitioners have contributed some knowledge of potential treatment approaches.

Three studies in particular, informed by behavioral/parent training models, have highlighted the effectiveness of using timeout in reducing sibling aggression (Adams & Kelley, 1992; Allison & Allison, 1971; Olson & Roberts, 1987). One utilized a single case experimental design, which involved a baseline, experimental, reversal, and 2nd experimental condition, each lasting 10 days, with a 26-month old girl who was exhibiting aggressive behaviors (i.e., hitting, kicking, biting, kicking, shoving, taking a toy away) toward her 11-month-old brother. Aggressive behaviors decreased from a relatively high rate during baseline to essentially zero during the first experimental period, partially recovered during reversal, and declined again during the second experimental period. Two additional studies used randomized controlled trial (RCT) designs to compare timeout to other interventions. In one study, 18 clinic-referred sibling pairs (mean ages 5–6 years) with a presenting problem of sibling aggression were randomly assigned to one of three interventions (timeout, social skills training, combination of timeout and social skills training). Each condition involved four sessions over a minimum 3-week treatment period. Analyses of covariance revealed that children in the timeout and combination conditions displayed progressively fewer aggressive episodes (e.g., hitting, pushing, kicking, spitting, biting, throwing objects, struggling over toys). However, children in the social skills condition were significantly more aggressive than children in the timeout and combination groups. Furthermore, rates of aggression in the timeout and combination group were not statistically different from each other, suggesting that the addition of social skills training did not improve results (Olson & Roberts, 1987). In another study, 30 parents seeking assistance with problems of sibling aggression were randomly assigned to a 3-week period of timeout, overcorrection (brief restitution/apology and practicing appropriate behaviors following aggressive acts), or a control condition. Aggressive sibling dyads ranged in age from 1 to 12 years (M = 5.72). Statistical analyses revealed about a 50% reduction in aggression rates (e.g., hitting, pushing, kicking, spitting, biting, throwing objects, struggling over toys, name-calling, hostile arguing, cursing, screaming) from baseline to the last week of treatment and additional decreases at one-month follow-up for both treatment conditions.

Although these studies have contributed to highlighting potential interventions for sibling abuse, they are not without limitations. Each of these studies involved pre-adolescent sibling pairs ranging in age from 1 to 12 years who were engaged in aggressive behaviors that may be considered minor physical acts. Furthermore, sample sizes are small, and these studies are relatively outdated.

A more recent intervention for addressing sibling abuse, informed by both behavioral methods and structural family therapy, referred to as the "task-centered sibling aggression treatment model," involves the formulation of actions, or tasks, to be accomplished (often as homework between sessions) to ameliorate target problems that are individualized to specific families (Caspi, 2008). This time-limited treatment model (6–12 weekly sessions) was utilized in a field study of three families with physically aggressive siblings who ranged in age from 9 to 13 years and their siblings who were the target of aggression (ages 5–9 years). Common sibling aggression themes are addressed, such as perceived favoritism, parents' ignoring claims of injustice, parental reinforcement of antagonistic behaviors, and siblings being put in caretaker roles. Diminished frequency and severity of sibling conflict was reported at the end of 6-week pilot testing for each client according to parent and child report. This treatment method continues to be used with more families (Caspi, 2011).

Additional case studies and practitioner accounts that are more recent and describe treatment approaches for sibling abuse tend to address more severe abusive behaviors, including sibling incest, with both younger children and adolescents, and are mostly informed by family systems theory. These case studies and practitioner accounts describe treatment modalities that involve a combination of individual, subsystem (e.g., siblings, parent–child) and family/group sessions (Caffaro, 2011; Caffaro & Conn-Caffaro, 2005; Haskins, 2003; Keane et al., 2013). The abusive siblings in these accounts and studies range in age from 6 to 14 years, and victims of their abuse are 5–11 years old. Session content includes thoroughly assessing and treating family dynamics that contribute to sibling abuse, strengthening boundaries, and improving parent–child bonds.

An additional approach is SAFE, a family-oriented problem-solving intervention that involves "Stopping the action," "Assessing what is happening," "Finding out what will work," and "Evaluating the outcome" (SAFE; Wiehe, 1998). Gnaulati (2002) describes extending sibling therapy—a distinct treatment modality for child and adolescent problems focused on strengthening siblings' connection without the involvement or oversight of parents—to destructive sibling aggression using a case example of 7- and 11-year-old brothers who frequently "bickered" with each other.

2.2.2 Other Potential Interventions to Address Sibling Aggression

In addition to RCTs, experimental case designs, and case studies/practitioners accounts of treatment modalities for sibling abuse, a few studies have described potential interventions designed for alternative purposes that could target sibling aggression. One such study included 22 maltreated elementary school-aged sibling pairs (ages 5–11 years) and their foster parents. Due to previous experiences of maltreatment, these children were considered to be at risk for sibling abuse. The families were randomly assigned to participate in an 8-week preventive intervention aimed at increasing positive sibling interaction, reducing conflict during play, and promoting conflict mediation (Linares et al., 2015). Participants who completed this 3-component intervention (including sibling pair, parent, and joint sibling pair-parent sessions) demonstrated significantly higher positive interaction quality, less sibling conflict during play, a higher number of conflict mediation strategies, and less physical aggression from older to younger siblings compared to a control group (rates decreased by about 50%). However, intervention pairs showed less reduction in negative interaction quality (e.g., unsuccessful exchanges, ignoring, bossiness) at post-intervention than control pairs.

Additionally, Tucker and Finkelhor (2017) completed a systematic review of interventions for sibling conflict and aggression. They described five RCTs (distinct from the ones previously described) using community samples of 20–95 children who were mostly between 5 and 9 years of age. Of note, although described as a review of interventions for sibling conflict/aggression, authors noted that the studies reviewed were aimed at general populations with typically developing children likely dealing with normal levels of sibling conflict, and none included parents who identified sibling conflict and aggression as the problem for which they were seeking help. Instead, these 2–7 session RCTs were aimed at either directly improving children's social skills with siblings or training parents to use mediation techniques during conflicts. Children's social skills were improved in the four studies that assessed them, and sibling relationship quality improved in two of three studies. Effect sizes for outcomes were small to large.

Taken together, the literature on treatment approaches for sibling abuse includes interventions mostly informed by family systems and/or behavioral models that have been utilized in case studies, single case experimental designs, and small RCTs. Although these methods appear to be effective in reducing abusive and/or aggressive sibling behaviors in the studies described, these treatment models have yet to be implemented on a wide scale or compared to existing evidence-based interventions for aggressive behaviors.

2.3 Suggestions for Future Research

The growing body of literature on sibling abuse provides ample opportunity for additional research efforts. Of primary importance is for future research studies to address the definitional, methodological, and categorical issues present, which pose significant limitations to the study of sibling abuse and its implications. Specifically, establishing the appropriate terminology to use and determining which behaviors constitute sibling abuse by taking intent, chronicity, and severity into consideration have yet to be resolved (Tippett & Wolke, 2015), which directly influences prevalence estimates. Other strategies include the use of multiple raters (parents and children), as prevalence rates may be influenced by parents who are not aware of all aggressive acts siblings engage in and children who may not consider such acts as aggressive (Tompsett et al., 2018). Research efforts to address severity could be advanced by utilizing the 2-factor model of sibling abuse severity established and validated in juvenile offender and community populations (Khan, 2017). Furthermore, definitions of and prevalence rates for sibling sexual abuse should be included in these research efforts. Taken together, these efforts can help to inform a more in-depth understanding of the long-term physical, emotional, and psychological consequences of the different forms that sibling abuse perpetration and victimization may take (Phillips et al., 2018).

Furthermore, understanding various dynamics of abusive relationships between siblings is key to strengthening this research area. For example, research must take into account the dual role that children involved in sibling abuse often have. Specifically, many studies have found that a large percentage of children are bully-victims, or engage in sibling abuse/aggression both as the victim and the victimizer (Dantchev & Wolke, 2019; Hardy, 2001; Mathis & Mueller, 2015; Phillips et al., 2018; Skinner & Kowalski, 2013; Tippett & Wolke, 2015), despite the majority of studies focusing on either perpetration or victimization. Furthermore, investigating the functions (e.g., proactive vs. reactive aggression) and motivations (e.g., jealous anger) behind sibling aggression may play a key role in understanding causes and potential prevention avenues for continued sibling aggression or perpetration of aggression against others (Tucker et al., 2013a; Yates et al., 2012). In the search for more in-depth understanding of the causes, functions, and motivations behind sibling abuse, research should continue to be informed by theoretical models such as social learning theory and family systems theory, which have both been supported in a couple of empirical studies (Eriksen & Jensen, 2009; Hoffman et al., 2005) and informed many of the treatment approaches described.

Prospective longitudinal research studies that control for the influence of other forms of victimization (e.g., domestic violence, child maltreatment, peer bullying) are imperative for examining the stability and prevalence of sibling abuse over time, testing theoretical models of sibling abuse, and building on findings regarding the detrimental impact of sibling abuse on emotional and behavioral outcomes for perpetrators and victims. Such studies can delineate the impact of various sibling abuse types and levels of severity on later functioning, as well as determine whether sibling abuse perpetration precedes similar behaviors toward peers, as suggested by an exploratory study of young boys displaying harmful sexual behaviors (Yates et al., 2012). Examination of potential moderators in influencing these relationships would be informative as well. Notably, one study of adults did not find a moderating effect of sibling relationship quality or gender on the relationship between sibling abuse and later functioning (Mathis & Mueller, 2015). However, this was a cross-sectional, retrospective study conducted with adults. The role of parental intervention or nonintervention in sibling abuse could also be tested over time to provide further support for the detrimental impact that ineffective parental responses may have on the mental-health of sibling abuse victims (McDonald & Martinez, 2016).

Finally, more intervention research is sorely needed. Future research on interventions should focus on determining which theoretical frameworks for intervention with sibling abuse are more effective (Caffaro, 2011) and comparing these treatments to widely used evidence-based interventions informed by the same theoretical frameworks. For example, behaviorally-based sibling abuse interventions could be evaluated against established interventions for oppositional, aggressive, disruptive, and/or antisocial behaviors such as Parent Management Training—Oregon Model (PMTO; Forgatch & Patterson, 2010) and Parent Child Interaction Therapy (PCIT; Zisser-Nathenson et al., 2017). Comparison to interventions that address aggressive behaviors in general is critical to understanding whether interventions that specifically target sibling abuse are needed. Studies suggest sibling abuse involves special circumstances because of the nature of the sibling relationship and what the behaviors may be motivated by such as jealousy or perceived favoritism (Caspi, 2008). However, the unique nature of sibling abuse compared to other forms of aggression and thus, the need for targeted interventions to address it, has not been demonstrated, especially considering its association with perpetration of other aggressive behaviors. Based on findings, determinations could be made as to whether targeted interventions for sibling abuse should be implemented or existing well-supported and evidence-based interventions and/or popular parent education programs and classes could be modified to incorporate sibling abuse (Shadik et al., 2013; Tucker & Finkelhor, 2017; Tucker et al., 2013c). Longitudinal and follow-up studies should also be utilized in intervention research to examine whether there are lasting effects in reducing abusive behaviors towards siblings.

2.4 Suggestions for Policy, Intervention, and Service Response

Although greater research efforts are needed to further understand the phenomenon of sibling abuse and how to treat it, this cannot be accomplished in isolation of policy. Kiselica and Morill-Richards (2007) report that funding for research on sibling abuse has been reduced since the mid-1980s, while funding for other forms of maltreatment has not. Indeed, a search for the keyword "sibling" in the grant database of the National Institutes of Health (https://grants.nih.gov/grants/oer.htm) on 7/10/19 brought up only five items, none of which was related to sibling abuse. This is likely one of the many underlying reasons for the paucity of research on the topic and the lack of national policies related to sibling abuse in the child welfare field (Perkins et al., 2017), despite its overlap with other forms of family violence and peer bullying.

Furthermore, it is necessary to ensure that conceptualizations of sibling abuse in research match up with how it is classified in policy. Federal guidelines in the U.S. place sibling abuse under parental neglect (Perkins et al., 2017), and each state has its own specific definitions of maltreatment. In Minnesota, for example, the definition of sexual abuse includes abuse by siblings, regardless of the age difference, and parental neglect includes "reports of ongoing abuse between siblings that results in physical injury and the parent(s) or caretaker(s) do not act to protect a child" (https://edocs.dhs.state.mn.us/lfserver/Public/DHS-5144-ENG). However, there is no provision for psychological abuse by siblings, and it may be very hard to determine when parents do not act adequately to protect children. This definition also makes it impossible to extract sibling abuse statistics from other kinds of parental neglect reported by child welfare agencies.

Given the conceptualization of sibling abuse under policy as parental neglect, the exceedingly high prevalence rates per the literature, and notable gaps in our present body of knowledge about sibling abuse, policy-makers and researchers seeking to inform them need to walk a fine line between increasing awareness and protecting children and others versus over-reacting and unnecessarily getting more families involved with the child welfare system. Thus, we suggest that the greatest policy need at this point is for more research funding to increase understanding of the phenomenon and to build the foundation for effective interventions. Kiselica and Morill-Richards (2007) urge professional organizations to advocate for more funding, which could push agencies that provide research funds, especially those concerned with public health and violence prevention, to elevate sibling abuse on their list of funding priorities. Additionally, public agencies can include questions on sibling abuse in community surveys, such as the Behavioral Risk Factor Surveillance System surveys administered annually in all states in the U.S. in collaboration with the Centers for Disease Control (https://www.cdc.gov/brfss/index.html). Prioritizing sibling abuse in research funding could also incentivize professional societies and widely circulated scientific journals to increase awareness and highlight gaps in research through workshops, conferences, and special issues.

Second, research on sibling abuse should be incorporated into the education and training of professionals likely to encounter perpetrators and/or victims of sibling abuse, including case workers, social workers, child and family therapists, health care providers, legal professionals, law enforcement personnel, teachers, and other mandated reporters (Kominkiewicz, 2004; Meyers, 2014). This increased awareness of professionals, combined with more research funding, could empower service providers to feel comfortable providing psychoeducation about sibling abuse to families either when they come into contact with families facing sibling abuse or through the provision of more general education to families about sibling violence (McDonald & Martinez, 2016) via workshops and other services (Perkins & Shadik, 2018).

Considering the lack of awareness in the general population about sibling abuse and its harmful consequences, we agree with recommendations by other researchers that screening for sibling abuse perpetration or victimization be incorporated into standard pediatric health visits that could enable identification of abusive behaviors and facilitate discussion that involves psychoeducation (Phillips et al., 2018; Tucker et al., 2013c). Screening could even be targeted to populations at increased risk for sibling abuse, including children hospitalized for psychiatric problems (Phillips et al., 2018), clinic-referred children (Tompsett et al., 2018), children participating in programs aimed at reducing school bullying (Tucker et al., 2013c, 2014b), or children exposed to domestic or intimate partner violence (Desir & Karatekin, 2018).

For more thorough assessments, several additional factors associated with sibling abuse can be taken into account. Specifically, considering sibling abuse's high co-occurrence with domestic violence and child maltreatment, families reporting the presence of sibling abuse should be assessed for exposure to these forms of family violence as well, which may warrant a referral for treatment for parents and/or a report to child protection agencies (Kiselica & Morill-Richards, 2007). Beyond family violence, family systems theory perspectives suggest several characteristics of the family environment (e.g., parental warmth, supervision, high stress, parental dysfunction) that may contribute to sibling abuse as well and have been confirmed in a few empirical studies (Eriksen & Jensen, 2009; Tucker et al., 2014a). Clinicians can reference Kiselica and Morill-Richards (2007) for a more complete discussion on the types of family environments and other environmental circumstances that sibling abuse often occurs in. Similarly, assessing victimizers' engagement in other forms of violence, including aggression directed toward parents and peers (Desir & Karatekin, 2018), and considering many children's dual roles as both victim and offender (Caffaro & Conn-Caffaro, 2005; Hardy, 2001) can delineate a more complete picture. Clinicians may wish to utilize the Conflict Tactics Scale (CTS; Straus, 2017), which is a widely used reliable and valid tool for assessing various forms of family violence.

Third, we suggest that existing research on sibling abuse should be incorporated into CPS practices and maltreatment reporting guidelines so that sibling abuse is not overlooked (Hoetger et al., 2015; Meyers, 2014; Perkins et al., 2017). In particular, clearer definitions are needed for CPS workers, who are otherwise likely to use subjective and inconsistent criteria for making decisions (Kominkiewicz, 2004). Furthermore, greater familiarity with research on sibling abuse can help with making more informed decisions about whether to keep siblings together as they go through the child welfare system.

Finally, in the absence of well-established, evidence-based interventions for sibling abuse, schools and service agencies could incorporate modules on sibling abuse into existing interventions for bullying (Hoetger et al., 2015), family conflict and parenting skills (Shadik et al., 2013), and interpersonal and self-regulation skills and externalizing behaviors (Wolke et al., 2015). Professional societies and peer-reviewed journals could also contribute to this effort by developing best-practice guidelines for sibling abuse. For children and family therapists working with families for which sibling abuse is the primary referral problem, increased understanding of sibling abuse and knowledge of how to implement evidence-based behavioral and family interventions are likely to equip clinicians with the tools and framework to work with these families.

References

Adams, C. D., & Kelley, M. L. (1992). Managing sibling aggression: Overcorrection as an alternative to time-out. *Behavior Therapy, 23*(4), 707–717. https://doi.org/10.1016/S0005-7894(05)80230-8

Allison, T. S., & Allison, S. L. (1971). Time-out from reinforcement: Effect on sibling aggression. *The Psychological Record, 21*(1), 81–86.

Bowes, L., Wolke, D., Joinson, C. J., Lereya, S. T., & Lewis, G. (2014). Sibling bullying and risk of depression, anxiety, and self-harm: A prospective cohort study. *Pediatrics, 134*(4), 1–8. https://doi.org/10.1542/peds.2014-0832

Button, D. M., & Gealt, R. (2010). High risk behaviors among victims of sibling violence. *Journal of Family Violence, 25*(2), 131–140. https://doi.org/10.1007/s10896-009-9276-x

Caffaro, J. (2011). Sibling violence and systems-oriented therapy. In J. Caspi (Ed.), *Sibling development: Implications for mental health practitioners* (pp. 245–272). Springer Publishing Company.

Caffaro, J. V., & Conn-Caffaro, A. (2005). Treating sibling abuse families. *Aggression and Violent Behavior, 10*(5), 604–623. https://doi.org/10.1016/j.avb.2004.12.001

Caspi, J. (2008). Building a sibling aggression treatment model: Design and development research in action. *Research on Social Work Practice, 18*(6), 575–585.

Caspi, J. (2011). *Sibling aggression: Assessment and treatment*. Springer Publishing Company.

Cyr, M., Wright, J., McDuff, P., & Perron, A. (2002). Intrafamilial sexual abuse: Brother–sister incest does not differ from father–daughter and stepfather–stepdaughter incest. *Child Abuse & Neglect, 26*(9), 957–973.

Dantchev, S., & Wolke, D. (2019). Sibling bullying at 12 years and high-risk behavior in early adulthood: A prospective cohort study. *Aggressive Behavior, 45*(1), 18–32. https://doi.org/10.1002/ab.21793

Desir, M. P., & Karatekin, C. (2018). Parent- and sibling-directed aggression in children of domestic violence victims. *Violence and Victims, 33*(5), 886–901. https://doi.org/10.1891/0886-6708.VV-D-16-00219

Eriksen, S., & Jensen, V. (2009). A push or a punch: Distinguishing the severity of sibling violence. *Journal of Interpersonal Violence, 24*(1), 183–208. https://doi.org/10.1177/0886260508316298

Finkelhor, D., Ormrod, R., Turner, H., & Hamby, S. L. (2005). The victimization of children and youth: A comprehensive, national survey. *Child Maltreatment, 10*(1), 5–25.

Finkelhor, D., Turner, H., Ormrod, R., & Hamby, S. L. (2009). Violence, abuse, and crime exposure in a national sample of children and youth. *Pediatrics, 124*(5), 1411–1423. https://doi.org/10.1542/peds.2009-0467

Finkelhor, D., Turner, H. A., Shattuck, A., & Hamby, S. L. (2013). Violence, crime, and abuse exposure in a national sample of children and youth: An update. *JAMA Pediatrics, 167*(7), 614–621. https://doi.org/10.1001/jamapediatrics.2013.42

Finkelhor, D., Turner, H. A., Shattuck, A., & Hamby, S. L. (2015). Prevalence of childhood exposure to violence, crime, and abuse: Results from the National Survey of Children's Exposure to Violence. *JAMA Pediatrics, 169*(8), 746–754. https://doi.org/10.1001/jamapediatrics.2015.0676

Forgatch, M. S., & Patterson, G. R. (2010). Parent management training-Oregon model: An intervention for antisocial behavior in children and adolescents. In J. R. Weisz & A. E. Kazdin (Eds.), *Evidence-based psychotherapies for children and adolescents* (pp. 159–177). The Guilford Press.

Gnaulati, E. (2002). Extending the uses of sibling therapy with children and adolescents. *Psychotherapy: Theory, Research, Practice, Training, 39*(1), 76–87. https://doi.org/10.1037/0033-3204.39.1.76

Graham-Bermann, S. A., Cutler, S. E., Litzenberger, B. W., & Schwartz, W. E. (1994). Perceived conflict and violence in childhood sibling relationships and later emotional adjustment. *Journal of Family Psychology, 8*(1), 85–97.

Hardy, M. S. (2001). Physical aggression and sexual behavior among siblings: A retrospective study. *Journal of Family Violence, 16*(3), 255–268. https://doi.org/10.1023/A:1011186215874

Haskins, C. (2003). Treating sibling incest using a family systems approach. *Journal of Mental Health Counseling, 25*(4), 337–350. https://doi.org/10.17744/mehc.25.4.r0vm1whayctmlmww

Hoetger, L. A., Hazen, K. P., & Brank, E. M. (2015). All in the family: A retrospective study comparing sibling bullying and peer bullying. *Journal of Family Violence, 30*(1), 103–111.

Hoffman, K. L., & Edwards, J. N. (2004). An integrated theoretical model of sibling violence and abuse. *Journal of Family Violence, 19*(3), 185–200. https://doi.org/10.1023/B:JOFV.0000028078.71745.a2

Hoffman, K. L., Kiecolt, K. J., & Edwards, J. N. (2005). Physical violence between siblings: A theoretical and empirical analysis. *Journal of Family Issues, 26*(8), 1103–1130.

Johnson, R. M., Duncan, D. T., Rothman, E. F., Gilreath, T. D., Hemenway, D., Molnar, B. E., & Azrael, D. (2015). Fighting with siblings and with peers among urban high school students. *Journal of Interpersonal Violence, 30*(13), 2221–2237. https://doi.org/10.1177/0886260514552440

Keane, M., Guest, A., & Padbury, J. (2013). A balancing act: A family perspective to sibling sexual abuse. *Child Abuse Review, 22*(4), 246–254. https://doi.org/10.1002/car.2284

Khan, R. (2017). Sibling violence: Validating a two-factor model of severity in nonoffender populations. *Psychology of Violence, 7*(4), 498–507.

Khan, R., & Cooke, D. J. (2013). Measurement of sibling violence: A two-factor model of severity. *Criminal Justice and Behavior, 40*(1), 26–39.

Khan, R., & Rogers, P. (2015). The normalization of sibling violence: Does gender and personal experience of violence influence perceptions of physical assault against siblings? *Journal of Interpersonal Violence, 30*(3), 437–458. https://doi.org/10.1177/0886260514535095

Kiselica, M. S., & Morill-Richards, M. (2007). Sibling maltreatment: The forgotten abuse. *Journal of Counseling & Development, 85*(2), 148–161.

Kolko, D. J., Kazdin, A. E., & Day, B. T. (1996). Children's perspectives in the assessment of family violence: Psychometric characteristics and comparison to parent reports. *Child Maltreatment, 1*(2), 156–167. https://doi.org/10.1177/1077559596001002007

Kominkiewicz, F. B. (2004). The relationship of Child Protection Service caseworker discipline-specific education and definition of sibling abuse. *Journal of Human Behavior in the Social Environment, 9*(1–2), 69–82. https://doi.org/10.1300/J137v09n01_06

Linares, L. O., Jimenez, J., Nesci, C., Pearson, E., Beller, S., Edwards, N., & Levin-Rector, A. (2015). Reducing sibling conflict in maltreated children placed in foster homes. *Prevention Science, 16*(2), 211–221. https://doi.org/10.1007/s11121-014-0476-0

Mathis, G., & Mueller, C. (2015). Childhood sibling aggression and emotional difficulties and aggressive behavior in adulthood. *Journal of Family Violence, 30*(3), 315–327. https://doi.org/10.1007/s10896-015-9670-5

McDonald, C., & Martinez, K. (2016). Parental and others' responses to physical sibling violence: A descriptive analysis of victims' retrospective accounts. *Journal of Family Violence, 31*(3), 401–410. https://doi.org/10.1007/s10896-015-9766-y

Meyers, A. (2014). A call to child welfare: Protect children from sibling abuse. *Qualitative Social Work, 13*(5), 654–670. https://doi.org/10.1177/1473325014527332

Michie, C., & Cooke, D. J. (2006). The structure of violent behavior: A hierarchical model. *Criminal Justice and Behavior, 33*, 706–737.

Miller, L. E., Grabell, A., Thomas, A., Bermann, E., & Graham-Bermann, S. A. (2012). The associations between community violence, television violence, intimate partner violence, parent–child

aggression, and aggression in sibling relationships of a sample of preschoolers. *Psychology of Violence, 2*(2), 165–178.
Morrill, M. (2014). Sibling sexual abuse: An exploratory study of long-term consequences for self-esteem and counseling considerations. *Journal of Family Violence, 29*(2), 205–213. https://doi.org/10.1007/s10896-013-9571-4
Olson, R. L., & Roberts, M. W. (1987). Alternative treatments for sibling aggression. *Behavior Therapy, 18*(3), 243–250. https://doi.org/10.1016/S0005-7894(87)80018-7
Perkins, N. H., & Shadik, J. A. (2018). A parent's perceptions of physical and emotional sibling violence. *Families in Society, 99*(1), 78–86. https://doi.org/10.1177/1044389418756638
Perkins, N. H., Coles, D. C., & O'Connor, M. K. (2017). Physical and emotional sibling violence and policy: An examination of Fox-Harding's child care value perspectives. *Child & Youth Services, 38*(1), 4–23. https://doi.org/10.1080/0145935X.2016.1166947
Phillips, D. A., Bowie, B. H., Wan, D. C., & Yukevich, K. W. (2018). Sibling violence and children hospitalized for serious mental and behavioral health problems. *Journal of Interpersonal Violence, 33*(16), 2558–2578. https://doi.org/10.1177/0886260516628289
Relva, I. C., Fernandes, O. M., & Mota, C. P. (2013). An exploration of sibling violence predictors. *Journal of Aggression, Conflict and Peace Research, 5*(1), 47–61. https://doi.org/10.1108/17596591311290740
Relva, I. C., Fernandes, O. M., & Alarcão, M. (2017). Dyadic types of sibling sexual coercion. *Journal of Family Violence, 32*(6), 577–583. https://doi.org/10.1007/s10896-017-9918-3
Shadik, J. A., Perkins, N. H., & Kovacs, P. J. (2013). Incorporating discussion of sibling violence in the curriculum of parent intervention programs for child abuse and neglect. *Health & Social Work, 38*(1), 53–57. https://doi.org/10.1093/hsw/hls066
Simonelli, C. J., Mullis, T., & Rohde, C. (2005). Scale of negative family interactions: A measure of parental and sibling aggression. *Journal of Interpersonal Violence, 20*(7), 792–803. https://doi.org/10.1177/0886260505277102
Skinner, J. A., & Kowalski, R. M. (2013). Profiles of sibling bullying. *Journal of Interpersonal Violence, 28*(8), 1726–1736. https://doi.org/10.1177/0886260512468327
Straus, M. A. (2017). Measuring intrafamily conflict and violence: The Conflict Tactics (CT) Scales. In M. A. Straus & R. J. Gelles (Eds.), *Physical violence in American families* (pp. 29–48). https://doi.org/10.4324/9781315126401-4
Straus, M. A., Gelles, R. J., & Steinmetz, S. K. (1980). *Behind closed doors: Violence in the American family*. Anchor Press/Doubleday.
Tippett, N., & Wolke, D. (2015). Aggression between siblings: Associations with the home environment and peer bullying. *Aggressive Behavior, 41*(1), 14–24. https://doi.org/10.1002/ab.21557
Tompsett, C. J., Mahoney, A., & Lackey, J. (2018). Sibling aggression among clinic-referred children and adolescents. *Journal of Clinical Child & Adolescent Psychology, 47*(6), 941–953. https://doi.org/10.1080/15374416.2016.1138409
Tucker, C. J., & Finkelhor, D. (2017). The state of interventions for sibling conflict and aggression: A systematic review. *Trauma, Violence, & Abuse, 18*(4), 396–406.
Tucker, C. J., & Kazura, K. (2013). Parental responses to school-aged children's sibling conflict. *Journal of Child and Family Studies, 22*(5), 737–745.
Tucker, C. J., Cox, G., Sharp, E. H., Van Gundy, K. T., Rebellon, C., & Stracuzzi, N. F. (2013a). Sibling proactive and reactive aggression in adolescence. *Journal of Family Violence, 28*(3), 299–310. https://doi.org/10.1007/s10896-012-9483-8
Tucker, C. J., Finkelhor, D., Shattuck, A. M., & Turner, H. (2013b). Prevalence and correlates of sibling victimization types. *Child Abuse & Neglect, 37*(4), 213–223.
Tucker, C. J., Finkelhor, D., Turner, H. A., & Shattuck, A. M. (2013c). Association of sibling aggression with child and adolescent mental health. *Pediatrics, 132*(1), 79–84. https://doi.org/10.1542/peds.2012-3801
Tucker, C. J., Finkelhor, D., Turner, H., & Shattuck, A. M. (2014a). Family dynamics and young children's sibling victimization. *Journal of Family Psychology, 28*(5), 625–633.

Tucker, C. J., Finkelhor, D., Turner, H., & Shattuck, A. M. (2014b). Sibling and peer victimization in childhood and adolescence. *Child Abuse & Neglect, 38*(10), 1599–1606.

Tucker, C. J., Finkelhor, D., & Turner, H. (2018). Patterns of sibling victimization as predictors of peer victimization in childhood and adolescence. *Journal of Family Violence*. https://doi.org/10.1007/s10896-018-0021-1

U.S. Department of Health and Human Services, Administration for Children and Families, Administration on Children, Youth and Families, Children's Bureau. (2019). *Child maltreatment 2017*. https://www.acf.hhs.gov/cb/research-data-technology/statistics-research/child-maltreatment

Wiehe, V. R. (1998). *Understanding family violence: Treating and preventing partner, child, sibling and elder abuse*. Sage.

Wolke, D., Tippett, N., & Dantchev, S. (2015). Bullying in the family: Sibling bullying. *The Lancet Psychiatry, 2*(10), 917–929. https://doi.org/10.1016/S2215-0366(15)00262-X

Yates, P., Allardyce, S., & MacQueen, S. (2012). Children who display harmful sexual behaviour: Assessing the risks of boys abusing at home, in the community or across both settings. *Journal of Sexual Aggression, 18*(1), 23–35. https://doi.org/10.1080/13552600.2011.634527

Zisser-Nathenson, A. R., Herschell, A. D., & Eyberg, S. M. (2017). Parent-child interaction therapy and the treatment of disruptive behavior disorders. In J. R. Weisz & A. E. Kazdin (Eds.), *Evidence-based psychotherapies for children and adolescents* (pp. 103–121). The Guilford Press.

Michelle Patrice Desir Ph.D. is a Postdoctoral Fellow in Child Abuse Pediatrics at Penn State Milton S. Hershey Medical Center. She completed her Ph.D. in Child Psychology at the University of Minnesota Institute of Child Development, where she received joint training in developmental and clinical psychology. Dr. Desir studies how modifiable risk and protective factors influence the developmental trajectory of individuals who have experienced childhood maltreatment and other forms of victimization. In the future, she intends to translate knowledge gleaned from this work into evidence-based interventions with this population.

Canan Karatekin Ph.D. is an Associate Professor at the Institute of Child Development, University of Minnesota. She completed her Ph.D. in Clinical Psychology at the University of California, Los Angeles. Dr. Karatekin's main focus of research is adverse childhood experiences (ACEs), and she is currently conducting a broad review of the research in this area.

Chapter 3
Barriers to Help Seeking for Women Victims of Adolescent Family Violence: A Victorian (Australian) Case Study

Kate Fitz-Gibbon, JaneMaree Maher, and Karla Elliott

Abstract Adolescent family violence (AFV) has been the subject of little scholarly inquiry within Australia. Recent reviews undertaken at the state and national level reveal limited understandings of the experiences of victims alongside a failure of the system to provide effective responses both within the service system and the justice sector. Acknowledging the need for greater understandings of this complex form of family violence, this chapter draws on the findings of a qualitative Victorian study that collected practitioner views alongside first person accounts from people who had experienced AFV. It focuses specifically on the barriers women experience when seeking help for adolescent family violence, including the need for future reform to policy and practice. The analysis provides insights into the impact of AFV, experiences of shame and fear of stigma and why women report a reluctance to engage police as primary responders. The second half of the chapter explores the perceived inadequacy of existing support services and referral pathways as well as the opportunities for school-based interventions. Consistent with previous research, the chapter demonstrates that the complex needs of adolescents who use violence in the home and those caring for them may require specialist service responses outside of the criminal justice system and argues that existing paradigms of family violence need to be extended to better capture and address the impacts of AFV.

3.1 Introduction

To date, there is limited research examining adolescent family violence (AFV) in Australia and elsewhere. Very few tailored service responses and programs are available for those who use or those who are affected by this unique form of family violence (RCFV, 2016; McCulloch et al., 2016). In 2016, the Report and Recommendations of the Victorian Royal Commission into Family Violence (RCFV, 2016, Chap. 23, p. 149) described AFV as a 'distinct form of family violence' that occurs

K. Fitz-Gibbon (✉) · J. Maher · K. Elliott
Faculty of Arts, School of Social Sciences, Monash Gender and Family Violence Prevention Centre, Monash University, Melbourne, Australia
e-mail: kate.fitzgibbon@monash.edu

K. Fitz-Gibbon et al. (eds.), *Young People Using Family Violence*,
https://doi.org/10.1007/978-981-16-1331-9_3

in all communities and geographic areas of the state. In examining what is known about this form of family violence, the RCFV (2016, Chap. 23, p. 150) heard that there is currently 'no systemic response to the needs of these young people and their families'. Compounding this the RCFV identified a:

> lack of awareness and understanding of this particular type of family violence among the community, family violence prevention and support services, youth services, and the justice system … Most devastating of all are the stigma and shame associated with those forms of violence, which arises from unfair assumptions about the victim's ability to be a good parent … Shame is exacerbated by lack of community awareness about this form of violence. All these factors create enormous barriers to seeking help. (RCFV, 2016, Chap. 23, p. 150)

In response to these findings, this chapter seeks to contribute specifically to knowledge of the barriers experienced by women victims of AFV, who are mothers. In order to do so it draws on the findings of a qualitative Victorian study that collected practitioner views alongside first person accounts from people who had experienced AFV. It focuses specifically on the barriers mothers experience when seeking help for AFV, including the need for future reform to current policy and practice. This focus on mothers is informed by increasing recognition of the responsibiliation of, and often blame directed towards, mothers in the context of all forms of family violence including AFV (Maher et al., 2020). The chapter is structured into five parts. Part one provides an overview of the study upon which this chapter draws. Part two examines the impacts of AFV, with a focus on impacts that minimise a person's ability to seek help. Building on this, part three briefly details the reasons why parents, and mothers in particular, are reluctant to engage police as primary responders when their adolescent uses violence in the home. The second half of the chapter outlines the inadequacy of existing support services and referral pathways (part four), as well as the opportunities for school-based interventions (part five). The chapter argues that the complex needs of adolescents who use violence in the home and those caring for them may require specialist service responses outside of the criminal justice system. The existing paradigms of family violence need to be extended to better understand and address the impacts of AFV.

3.2 Adolescent Family Violence in Victoria (Australia): Our Study

This chapter presents the findings of an Australian qualitative study, *Investigating Adolescent Family Violence in Victoria* (Fitz-Gibbon et al., 2018) as they relate to help seeking behaviours and challenges for victims of AFV. In that study, a multimethods approach was adopted. In the first phase of the research, six focus groups and 14 interviews were completed with 45 experts, family violence specialist and youth service providers, legal practitioners, health service providers, and general practitioners (GPs). Given the range of professional experience and expertise of participants, broad open-ended questions were used to guide focus group and interview discussions. All focus groups and interviews were audio recorded and professionally transcribed in full before a thematic analysis of the data was completed.

In phase two, an online anonymous survey was utilised to gain insights from individuals who have experienced AFV. The survey was hosted using Qualtrics (a survey development software program) and distributed through Twitter, email promotion, and circulation by relevant service providers and experts. It included a range of closed demographic questions alongside open ended questions that asked participants about their experiences of AFV, whether they sought help from a support service and/or whether they reported the AFV to the police. 138 survey responses were received, of which 120 were included in the survey sample as they met the criteria: i.e. an individual who had experienced AFV. Of these responses, 81 surveys were completed by mothers of an adolescent using violence, 22 by siblings of an adolescent using violence, and four by a father (including step) of an adolescent using violence. This chapter focuses on the 81 responses received from mothers; identified in existing research as the primary and predominant victims of AFV (Condry & Miles, 2014).

Anonymity was assured for all participants. Where quoted, focus group and interview participants are assigned a pseudonym that indicates their professional role only (i.e. Expert Interview A, Health Interview A, OpenFG-A). Survey participants were each assigned a pseudonym followed by an indication of their relationship to the young person using violence in the home (i.e. Brooke, mother).

3.3 The Impacts of AFV and Recognising the Need for 'Help'

In examining the degree to which persons who experience AFV seek help and the adequacy of the responses they received, the question arose at the outset of our research as to the 'need' for help. This study sought to document the harms experienced and possible pathways for AFV victim/survivors for help through specialist, generalist and/or criminal justice systems. In looking at the first of those two questions, the survey revealed a range of harms and impacts on the lives of families experiencing AFV. Victim/survivors detailed diverse and high impact experiences of physical violence, as captured in the following three survey excerpts:

> Having doors broken in my home either through continuous banging, punching or throwing bricks through the glass. Having a teenager scream and yell at me, swear and belittle me. Being spat on. Having a teenager stand over me and using threatening behaviour to get what he wanted such as money or other items of value. Having no control over how my home is treated, being expected to just put up with any type of behaviour and when setting boundaries being physically and emotionally abused. Having things thrown at me including bags, books, clothes racks. Being threatened with knives and pieces of wood. Having my son threaten to harm himself with knives and through banging his head on the floor if I didn't give him what he wanted. Having my possessions stolen in the home. (Mary, mother)

> Being hit with lumps of wood. Heavy objects thrown in the face e.g. metal trophies. Punching, kicking, spitting. Verbal abuse, belittling. Damage to car e.g. glove box door removed. Swear words written on ceiling. Holes in the wall. Pulling hair and hitting while driving. (Phillipa, mother)

> It's a nightmare. My son (now 13) has cracked my windscreen, broken windows (then cut himself on the face in front of the entire family), punched so many holes in walls and doors that I've lost count, kicked a number of us hard, tried to punch me, thrown a full bowl of water (the dog's) over me, thrown furniture, held a knife to my daughter's throat, threatened me with a knife … not to mention the unbelievable verbal abuse. He's called me every horrific word that exists and said the most devastatingly cruel things (for instance, that I'm the reason my mum died). It's seriously a living nightmare and sometimes I feel like I cannot possibly go on. (Sarah, mother)

Beyond the impacts of physical violence and property damage, participants described depression, high levels of stress and anxiety and consequent impacts such as social isolation, financial impacts, and having to take leave from work. The violence impacted all aspects of their lives. Mothers responding to our survey explained:

> Often, I am walking on eggshells within the family home, waiting for the next episode to occur. I am stuck as a victim in a cycle of violence, usually attributable to that of adult perpetrated family violence. Align[ing] that with the guilt and self-doubt of being a parent who should be able to 'fix' these things can often be an emotionally challenging roller coaster ride. I am spat at, hit, struck, kicked, emotionally and verbally abused. My property is damaged, personal items in the home are destroyed and every day household items are used as weapons or missiles aimed at me. I am often faced with the decision of trying to maintain my safety, that of the other children in the home and that of the adolescent perpetrator himself. I am also often torn between trying to address the behaviour so that the boundaries are not further extended but also trying not to escalate matters. Being a victim of adolescent family violence is difficult to explain, difficult to talk about and difficult to deal with. It is an isolating, emotionally damaging experience that leaves you numb, hollow and negatively fraught at all times. (Tiffany, mother)

> I ended up on antidepressants to help me cope with it. Our now 16-year-old son has ongoing problems with mental health, substance abuse and school refusal. The violence has all but stopped, thankfully, apart from the occasional verbal attack. If he wants to punch a wall he'll go outside and do it. Our daughter, who was 16 when this all started, suffers from anxiety and panic attacks and moved out of home because she could no longer live with the brother she once was very close to. Overall it's had a huge impact on the family and although it's improved, there are still deep wounds. It put a lot of strain on the relationship between my husband and I, particularly in the beginning. (Amelia, mother)

Survey participants recounted many different types of family relationship breakdown, including estrangement between parents and the adolescent child, parental separations, and estrangement between parents and other siblings who did not feel supported or safe (on sibling violence, see further, Elliott et al., 2020). These effects were identified as long-term—'it goes on and on' (OpenFG-P)—impacting family relationships for many decades. Additionally, several survey respondents described the loss of extended family relationships as a consequence of AFV, indicating that visits to grandparents had become too difficult, resulting in the loss of these supports and networks. Similarly, friends were lost to these participants because they either could not invite them into their home or were unable to visit others given the perceived constant need to supervise the adolescent and/or siblings.

Parental work patterns were also affected, as regular attendance became difficult due to the need to care for a child or children, or simply because of the impact of the behaviours or violence. One mother described her decision to stop going into work as a result of the AFV she was experiencing:

> I have had to change the way I work. I now do consulting work from home so that my house is not left unattended. I was also getting abusive calls from my son in the workplace if he couldn't find things. I have had bouts of depression and [have] become socially isolated. I avoid places where I meet people known to my son such as the school, shopping centres and cafes. I don't invite people into my home because of the damage and because my home environment is very unpredictable. I have lost a lot of confidence in my abilities and feel like a failure as a parent. I don't get much sleep as I am constantly worried for my son's wellbeing. (Amelia, mother)

As captured here, the impacts of AFV affected all aspects of this mother's life—her employment, socialisation, home environment, and her own personal confidence and well-being. These findings build on previous work by Daly and Wade (2016), Walsh and Douglas (2018) and the RCFV (2016), which found that AFV can have a detrimental impact on the health and wellbeing of families, including parental depression, and feelings of shame, sadness, powerlessness, isolation, frustration and anger. Research has similarly shown that AFV can cause economic pressures, with McKenna et al. (2010) reporting that 24% of parents in their study suffered financial strain as a result of AFV.

An extension of these impacts was the almost universal experience of shame and the fear of stigma experienced by parents as well as by siblings affected. One mother described living in a spiral of shame and secrecy that prevented her from telling anyone what she was going through or from seeking help:

> Frightening and shameful. The violence is pervasive and when it comes into your home you can't get it out. I didn't grow up in a violent home and wasn't in a violent relationship with my son's father so I had never experienced anything like this before. Soon, it becomes a way of interacting, a default position and the shame and secrecy stops you from telling people or seeking help. You become a victim and are in a cycle of violence believing that it will stop; so much so that when it happens again, the shame goes deeper. (Janet, mother)

Interestingly, what this mother also described was the shame associated with the continuation of the violence: each time there was an episode her shame worsened. These experiences of shame and the fear of being stigmatised if people beyond the family were to find out their children were using violence against them were pivotal in decisions of whether to seek help and contact a support service or not. Feelings of self-blame, shame and stigma are then compounded by the lack of services readily available for those parents who do try and seek help.

3.4 A Reluctance to Engage Police as Primary Responders

An overwhelming number of survey participants described an unwillingness to report their victimisation to the police. Survey respondents identified the risk of criminalisation and the impact this had on their decision not to report ongoing patterns of abuse. This fear was captured in the following survey comments of two affected parents:

> We threatened to call the police on many occasions. But could not pull it off … we were scared of contacting police. … A terrible dilemma. … We wanted to involve police at times but couldn't because of effects and ramifications for [the] whole family. (Katrina, mother)

> I don't think I could trust the police. I would want them [the adolescent] to be educated rather than arrested. (Taylor, mother)

These parental viewpoints align with the results of UK-based research conducted by Miles and Condry (2015, p. 1086), which found that:

> while parents do want their victimisation to be taken seriously and often require emergency help from police, most parents do not want their children prosecuted, but rather, want to receive long term help and support in order to facilitate a non-violent child–parent relationship.

Other national and international research has noted a range of reasons why parents may be hesitant to involve the police in cases of AFV, including feelings of shame, denial, social isolation and self-blame; fear of estrangement from the child; and fear of how the adolescent will react to the AFV being reported to police (Cottrell & Monk, 2004; DVRCV, 2010; Thomas et al., 2019; Holt, 2009; Howard, 2014; RCFV, 2016). As Howard (2014, p. 26) explains:

> Some [parents] were fearful that police involvement would deprive them of parental autonomy and decision making. This concern, together with lack of awareness and understanding about the legal options available, meant parents accessed the criminal justice system as a last resort.

The desire to avoid criminal justice intervention, and an adolescent possibly thereby gaining a criminal record, has also been noted by Howard and Abbott (2013), who argue that, wherever possible, responses to AFV should aim to reduce the likelihood of an adolescent receiving a criminal record as a result of their violence.

Survey respondents whose adolescents had complex needs, in particular those with Asperger's Syndrome and Autism, were very hesitant to engage the police, believing that police officers were ill equipped to deal with the needs of their adolescents. One respondent said, 'I never reported it to the police and never would as I don't believe the justice system would treat a child with Asperger's fairly' (Rose, mother). While some research has been undertaken internationally looking at the ways in which standard criminal justice system responses are inadequate for children with such complex needs (see Omer, 2016), there is very limited understanding in this area in Australia and a definite need to develop greater knowledge on what interventions would be best suited in such cases. The recent AFV Issues Paper by Walsh and

Douglas (2018) identifies the importance of these factors in AFV, reinforcing the need for targeted and appropriate responses.

Beyond policing, one of the other points of justice system interaction in cases of AFV frequently referenced by study participants were civil intervention orders. While it is beyond the scope of this chapter to examine the use of protection orders in cases of AFV (on this see Thomas et al., 2019), our study highlighted how the justice system is ill-suited to respond to AFV. While criminal justice system options may be necessary in the small number of cases where physical threats or acts of violence present immediate safety concerns, the majority of those in our study refused to engage the justice system or had engaged with it but were left feeling it was unable to offer any effective long-term solutions or to increase security in a meaningful way (see further Fitz-Gibbon et al., 2018).

3.5 The Lack of Targeted Services and Programs for AFV

There was consistent acknowledgement among those experiencing AFV and those working in the integrated family violence system, that in Victoria specifically and Australia more broadly there is a lack of targeted services and programs for persons experiencing AFV and for adolescents using violence in the home. There are few Australian programs that address AFV, although considerable resources have been targeted at preventing and responding to adult family violence (DVRCV, 2010; RCFV, 2016). This gap persists despite the significant resource commitments towards improving responses to family violence in Victoria over the last five years, including a Royal Commission and a billion-dollar political investment at state level. Despite this, our research revealed that there are few funded programs or services that are specifically tailored to respond to adolescents and their families, and four years following the RCFV (2016) the recommendations relating to AFV are yet to be fully implemented.[1]

Integrated service responses for vulnerable children and young people therefore require development and greater funding in Australia (DHS, 2013; Howard, 2015). Such programs would reduce 'the likelihood that the young person will use family violence in their future relationships as well as increasing the immediate safety of family members and strengthening family relationships' (DHS, 2014, p. 3).

Many survey participants and experts identified the limited number of targeted services available for families experiencing AFV, the difficulty of accessing services that might meet the complex needs generated by this type of violence, and the gaps in effective responses. As captured in the following quotes:

[1]At the time of writing this chapter, responses to AFV are undergoing significant development within Victoria and we note that the discussion below may not reflect the delivery of new pilots and services. It does, however, affirm the findings of the RCFV that at present there is a significant dearth of targeted resources and specialist responses for AFV.

> When you got those queries about, 'Where do you send a young person?' it was kind of like, at the time, you kind of do your bit of research and find there's one boys program somewhere down Woop Woop somewhere. There wasn't even anything kind of within a local area. (OpenFG-A)

> I'm a family doctor. People come to me for help but I don't have anything to offer. There are no services available to help with the child's complex needs. The families feel dismissed by the mental health service, especially for violent girls. The families do end up going to the police which may then get MH [mental health] services to take it more seriously, but the child then loses trust and may gain a police record. (Charlotte, mother)

The need for early intervention was often raised; both service providers and family members described behaviours of pre-adolescent children (below 12 years) that made them fearful or that the younger child required redirection or reorientation. There were, however, no clear avenues for accessing effective support or responses for those in this younger age group. Other consistently noted issues were the lack of interim or short-term respite for families, and the lack of care options for adolescents beyond state intervention through Child Protection services or residential care—and most often families did not want to pursue the latter two options. As one health provider explained:

> The challenges that would come with that, I guess, is when the violence is precipitated by other, you know, if it is a child that has developmental, you know, whether it's autism or like [another focus group participant] mentioned, it's quite common for our patients who are here with eating disorders to be physically acting out and aggressive towards parents, and that's around the battle to feed them and keep them alive. So instead of putting someone on a treatment order to deal with, you know, you'd have to have some fairly clear boundaries around that. (HealthFG-D)

For some participants the difficulty of accessing a specialised service response was intensified by geographical factors because of the chronic lack of rural and regional services. As captured in the following survey excerpt:

> We live in the country. There is so little support it is almost non-existent. We were seeing a psychologist with him and she advised us to call the police if he got violent. But after waiting 10 hours for a response the first time we tried calling we asked what to do next. Next time we called the ambulance. As he was under 13 he was kept in casualty sedated for two days. There was nowhere that could take him. There was no help anywhere. He was sent home and we were left to deal with it on our own and wondering which one of us would end up dead before anything was done. We have spent lots of money seeing any available doctors, psychologists, councillors and even the adolescent psychiatrist. We have tried numerous medications all with little success. (Faith, mother)

Service provider remits, and the potential for service siloes in relation to this, were also cited as creating difficulties. As service providers and parents commented, being caught between system borders and protocols was a commonplace experience in the context of AFV. This also impacted opportunities for early intervention, as described by one expert:

> the services for young people have tended to be located at the risky end, so where the young person was at risk of harming themselves, or harming others, doing damage to property, risk of escalating into prison. So it's all about – it's all far too late really in the equation.

> There certainly has not been any interest in early intervention in that space. I'm sure there are pockets of programs that are very successful, I don't know about them but I'm sure they're out there, where people have been trying to do good work with young people. (Expert Interview D)

While youth offending may intersect with the use of violence in the home context, the use of violence by young people within the home is often not the presenting issue. This may mean that parents seeking help are asked to take greater care of their adolescent, rather than the violent behaviour being addressed, effectively reinforcing isolation and risk for affected families. The gaps that emerge in practice were identified and described by experts and service providers and are well captured in the following excerpt:

> There are still significant policy gaps but I know there actually is a lot of work happening, bubbling away about improving a response where young people come to the attention of the police and justice system because of their violence. So I feel hopeful that's developing but yet, there's still a long way to go. I think in terms of practice, there's a lack of an evidence-based or research-based practice about what really works. So it's a bit of a hodgepodge at the moment. (Expert Interview A)

As a number of participants observed, by the time families had reached 'the pointy end', the likelihood of successful engagement through a service system response, especially for the young person, was significantly diminished. This was particularly emphasised by the health providers in our study:

> But if the young person goes, 'Well I don't want to engage in that, I'm not going to do that'. It's not mandated … things could have been offered over the years that could have been proactive to help prevent us from getting to this point but they haven't been taken on board. (HealthFG-F)

> I wonder whether it's not the parents, particularly the mothers, who are presenting to GPs saying, 'By the way, can I just ask your advice about …?' or, 'I've got a bit of a problem with', or, 'I wonder if you can help me with some advice for', and they're describing a situation of having difficulty managing a son, a daughter even, because we're seeing a lot of violent teenage girls too. 'How do I manage?' or, 'I'd really like', so and so, my son, my daughter, 'to come and see you, but they've refused'. The red flags for me are: the kid won't come, so if they're effectively defiant and won't present with a parent who's saying, 'I'd really like you to come with me to the GP. I'm concerned about how we're getting on. It's not you. It's me', kind of approach, but then the child refuses. (Health Interview G)

As the quotes above indicate, the problem of a lack of pathways and inadequate responses arose in many different contexts. One concern that was consistently raised related to the lack of options in state-based residential care (on this, see Gerard et al., 2019), and potentially a lack of safety for those placed in such care. While charting the range of current responses and their application to different family settings and home environments was not within the scope of the current project, this issue was identified by several focus group participants. One practitioner commented:

> It may also come out, for example, and I'm interested to see how you're defining, for example, violence in the home, through the out-of-home care system. A huge issue with resi [residential] care, for example, is concerns around violence in residential care units that may not be particularly well run to begin with. I know there's been a lot of reform in that space

> lately, and a lot more reform that's being planned, but certainly, traditionally, one problem that presents within the out-of-home care system is if you have a young person who has used violence or been involved in a conflictual incident or had the police called to the unit, sometimes for quite minor things, I would add, and sometimes with very young kids, the question of where that young person is placed after. (OpenFG-B)

Beyond out of home care, for those services working directly with parents, survey participants expressed concern about services that focused only on parenting and/or the adults involved with the adolescent, without providing targeted support for the adolescents themselves. This often intensified the sense of isolation and lack of support for the affected parent/s more generally, as one mother described:

> Our experiences with services have not been positive. The lack of communication and progress has made our journey very difficult and our child is often put in the 'too hard basket'. We are repetitively told that he is too young (10) to work with individually and that all support and intervention will be given to us as parents. Although this makes sense therapeutically in some sense, it leaves us disheartened and without answers. (Erica, mother)

A number of the responses from service providers indicated that they did often focus on parents as a key point of intervention, however, this viewpoint was not reflected in the survey findings.

3.6 The Role of Schools

During the interviews and focus groups, service providers and experts identified schools as a key interface and potential point of intervention between adolescents, families and support services. While we recognise schools are not the only social institutions that could offer support and intervention for young people, schools were consistently raised by participants as critical, in part due to mandatory schooling provisions (Department of Education (Victoria) 2018). As places where adolescents under 17 years of age are required to spend a considerable amount of time each week, schools were seen as potentially useful sites for identifying, addressing and even preventing AFV. A small number of service providers noted that some schools in Victoria were already responding well to cases of AFV, but that there was considerable scope for enhancing and coordinating school responses, and improving consistency across schools and areas.

Service providers involved in the study described school disengagement as a significant factor in identifying problematic adolescent behavior, and potentially AFV at an early stage. Howard (2015) identifies disengagement as a common issue in her research on adolescents who use violence in the home. Several service providers explained that offering support through the school system to assist with and address such disengagement would provide a meaningful intervention for these adolescents. As one service provider described:

> Yeah boredom, absolutely; potentially start drug using or alcohol. … And then the violence comes about. So if we can target and bring things back into the picture, re-engage in school or education, eventually that has an effect on the violence. (OpenFG-O)

The opportunities and benefits arising from school involvement in responding to AFV were discussed at some length by participants during the interviews and focus groups, as captured in the following excerpts:

> It's about engaging with the schools and maybe modifying their working plan, or letting their teachers know this is why they've been away for a term; this is some of the family dynamics. Can we potentially even start on two or three days a week, or a modified learning plan? And just make them aware that the child is really struggling to re-engage. (OpenFG-O)

> if we could connect with teachers … who might notice changes in an adolescent, or potentially mum comes in … and that might just be enough for a teacher to think, 'I might refer them to this program'. … If sort of working with parents directly might be a bit confronting, if we can work with the teachers, they are the gateway I think, to the parents. (OpenFG-O)

Survey participants and service providers described varied responses from schools and individual educators in responding to adolescent behaviour. Some parents reported difficult interactions with schools, while others recounted positive experiences of social inclusion and connection arising through schooling that was responsive to cases of AFV and supportive of both adolescents and their families. Several parents recounted instances of difficult school behaviour experienced simultaneously to violence being used in the home:

> His school also struggles with him, and we're being constantly contacted [about] his noncompliance and poor behaviour. He has been expelled from one school. He's had multiple suspensions at his current school. (Heather, mother)

> She was expelled from school in Year 11 for threats and verbal abuse of a teacher. She was often in trouble at school for bullying other students. (Courtney, mother)

> When my daughter was around 13, her behaviour started to change, and she became verbally abusive towards me [her mother], and father. She would not obey rules in the house, and when challenged would act out, both at home and at school. Basically, she would not obey any authority. (Trish, mother)

Some parents recounted positive experiences with schools. They described how schools provided appropriate support and understanding to both families and violent adolescents. For example, one survey participant whose son who had used violence at home had been bullied at a previous school recounted:

> I took him out of school … and home-schooled him for three terms while he recovered from the trauma of being at school and the bullying. He is now at a [specialist] school, receiving excellent support and doing very well. (Amanda, mother)

Another mother described her positive experience with her son's school, reflecting the importance of positive mentors and role models:

> Our eldest son is functioning well now and not violent due to a new psychiatrist giving him the right diagnosis and medication and counselling. He also has an incredible school principal and respite carer as mentors. (Katrina, mother)

Mirroring these survey responses, during the interviews and focus groups, some Victorian service providers and experts felt schools could be positive places for addressing AFV. This viewpoint is captured in the following three interview and focus group excerpts:

> Socialisation – I would say, particularly for some of the kids I work with. Socialisation and the social skills and stuff that they get at school is, that's so vital, and consequences. They learn, whether they like it or not, they do learn about the importance of consequences at school. (Expert Interview E)

> I had a client who attached really strongly to a male teacher, and he would disclose everything to this teacher. So the teacher kind of became the key worker, but would feed all that back to me. And if the young person had an appointment, or had to go to court or something, if that teacher was willing and available, he would go with him as a bit of support, and then feed back to me. (OpenFG-0)

> Linking into the school welfare, I mean, they're amazing if you can work well with them, they're really, really good in the schools. (OpenFG-Q)

In contrast, during the focus groups some service providers reflected on what they considered to be 'bad practice' among teachers in responding to AFV:

> Some schools don't have enough awareness of remembering that this child's got trauma, and I guess their focus is on 'but what about our other students? We can't have that behaviour in our school', and stuff. So it's just having a really strong care team, getting the Department of Education on board within the care team, getting them to come to meetings. (OpenFG-P)

One survey participant detailed her experiences with her daughter's school:

> Her school was very unhelpful and did not want her back without an assurance that she would not speak to other students about the incident. They were only concerned about the reputation of the school. (Susan, mother)

Others reported similarly difficult or unhelpful interactions with staff of the school that their adolescent attended:

> School makes matters worse by sending students home for minor behaviours, which places extra burden on families. (Isabelle, mother)

> Ultimately, the school counsellor did see him, but from our son's point of view what he gained from the encounter was information about how to 'emancipate' himself from his family, which he repeatedly threatened to do but didn't follow through with. (Vicki, mother)

> We had counselling from a number of services and many discussions with teachers at the schools she attended. The counselling was ineffective and the school disciplinary measures didn't work either. (Courtney, mother)

> Schools and government authorities have forced me to have my son back home. (Molly, mother)

Regardless of their experience, common across participants and service providers was an acknowledgement of the need for targeted AFV training for those working within the education system to ensure they are adequately equipped to identify and provide support in response to problematic adolescent behaviours, including incidences of AFV. While the burden of responding to AFV cannot fall solely on schools and those working within them, given that teachers are most likely—second perhaps only to parents—to be exposed to the problematic behaviours of an adolescent, the school environment does provide an important opportunity for identification and intervention. As one service provider commented:

> I think it's fair to say that all of the services will be called upon to respond at some point, as will the education system, being the other big player. So I think it's probably about making sure they've all got the capacity, but also that they're well networked with each other and that they have the ability to work well together. In some communities I think there's a really strong history of collaboration between those sectors. (OpenFG-B)

As shown in this quote, targeted training combined with collaboration and coordination of different services and departments was viewed as critical to achieving an effective response to AFV.

In addition to training, service providers suggested a range of ways to foster school responses to AFV, such as providing communication and outreach to schools from service providers, and supporting the ability of schools to act as interfaces between services and families. Regardless of the specific intervention proposed, the need to better equip educators as well as to support educators with well-resourced counselling departments and/or referral pathways, was viewed by many providers as critical. As one service provider described:

> I think it comes back to their [teachers'] lack of, you know, like they don't learn enough at uni[versity] about some of the families that they'll come across … [They] just point the finger, like 'This isn't good enough'. I'm like, 'Yeah, but what's going on?' Or little Johnny's just missing class – they're not thinking, 'Well, why is he doing it?' and looking back into it. Like I don't think their education covers enough of like dealing with families. (Service Provider)

This connects to the findings of the RCFV (2016) which identified the need for all those within the integrated family violence system in Victoria—specialist and generalist workers included—to receive family violence training and a relevant formal educational qualification. While there are significant challenges as well as opportunities in relation to achieving such a workforce transformation, the reflections here point to the need for and benefits of family violence education for persons working in schools and whose close interactions with adolescents provide numerous opportunities to identify harmful behaviours and provide earlier interventions.

3.7 Conclusion: The Need for Specialist Service Responses

> We are very isolated and do not ask people to come over to our house. Family very rarely visits – maybe once a year for a short visit. After a bad morning before school, this affect[s] me psychologically whereby I think about what happened and what I could do differently. There is [sic] not many answers, so history tends to repeat itself. (Brooke, mother)

Brooke's experience, as quoted here, succinctly captures the isolation experienced on multiple levels by mothers who responded to our survey and described having to manage an adolescent using violence in the home with limited or no service system support. Descriptions like these were common from the 81 mothers who responded to our survey illuminating the difficulties they faced surviving and seeking help in the midst of confronting, and often deeply traumatic, experiences of AFV. These accounts revealed long-term patterns of violence, a lack of readily available resources for familial assistance and/or programs for young people involved in the offending. The views of those experiencing AFV were supported by the insights of family services and family violence service providers, who concurred with familial assessments that there are few opportunities for early intervention or pathways for non-punitive rehabilitative responses to young people using violence against family members. Service providers identified a paucity of services, lack of knowledge about any existing programs and difficulty in securing effective family-based service provision.

In recent years, the findings of successive government reviews and research have led to the conclusion that AFV has 'unique characteristics [that require] different responses' from those needed for other forms of family violence (see, inter alia, RCFV, 2016, p. 165; Howard, 2015). The study underpinning this chapter supports that viewpoint and lends further support to the argument for specialised legal, health and social responses to AFV. But we also acknowledge that research on this topic is in its infancy and there is a need for significantly more research into this form of family violence. One of the opportunities identified for reform through this research related to the critical role schools can play in operating as an interface between families and services, and providing support for families. Improving the response to AFV across schools and the education system more widely was considered necessary. In particular, service providers and experts emphasised the need for a coordinated response to AFV between various sites and services interacting with adolescents and their families, including schools. Survey participants who had experienced supportive schools and teachers who were willing to address AFV reported positive outcomes for adolescents and their families. Service providers and experts involved in our research recommended more training for schools around AFV, as well as more support for teachers in identifying AFV and addressing the problem with adolescents and parents.

References

Condry, R., & Miles, C. (2014). Adolescent to parent violence: Framing and mapping a hidden problem. *Criminology and Criminal Justice, 14*(3), 257–275.

Cottrell, B., & Monk, P. (2004). Adolescent-to-parent abuse: A qualitative overview of common themes. *Journal of Family Issues, 25*(8), 1072–1095.

Daly, K., & Wade, D. (2016). Gender and adolescent-to-parent violence: A systematic analysis of typical and atypical cases. In A. Holt (Ed.), *Working with adolescent violence and abuse towards parents: Approaches and contexts for intervention* (pp. 148–168). Routledge.

Department of Education (Victoria). (2018). *If your child wants to leave school early*. State of Victoria.

Department of Human Services (DHS). (2013). *Assessing children and young people experiencing family violence: Practice guide for family violence practitioners*. State of Victoria.

Department of Human Services (DHS). (2014). *Adolescent family violence program service model*. State of Victoria.

Domestic Violence Resource Centre Victoria (DVRCV). (2010). *A coordinated response to adolescent violence in the home*. Domestic Violence Resource Centre Victoria.

Elliott, K., Fitz-Gibbon, K., & Maher, J. M. M. (2020). Sibling violence: Understanding experiences, impacts and the need for nuanced responses. *British Journal of Sociology, 71*(1), 168–182.

Fitz-Gibbon, K., Elliott, K., & Maher, J. M. M. (2018). *Investigating adolescent family violence in Victoria: Understanding experiences and practitioner perspectives.* Monash Gender and Family Violence Research Program, Faculty of Arts, Monash University.

Gerard, A., McGrath, A., Colvin, E., & McFarlane, K. (2019). 'I'm not getting out of bed!' The criminalisation of young people in residential care. *Australian and New Zealand Journal of Criminology, 52*(1), 76–93.

Holt, A. (2009). Parent abuse: Some reflections on the adequacy of a youth justice response. *Internet Journal of Criminology,* 1–9.

Howard, J. (2014). Addressing adolescent violence. *DVRCV Advocate*, p. 24.

Howard, J. (2015). *Adolescent violence in the home: How is it different to adult family violence?* Australian Institute of Family Studies.

Howard, J., & Abbott, L. (2013). *The last resort: Pathways to justice—Adolescent violence in the home.* Peninsula Health in Partnership with Victoria Legal Aid and City of Greater Dandenong—Youth Services, Digital Reprographics.

Maher, J., Fitz-Gibbon, K., Meyer, S., Roberts, S., & Pfitzner, N. (2020). Mothering through and in violence: Discourses of the 'good mother.' *Sociology.* https://doi.org/10.1177/0038038520967262.

McCulloch, J., Maher, J., Fitz-Gibbon, K., Segrave, M., & Roffee, J. (2016). *Review of the family violence risk assessment and risk management framework (CRAF).* Prepared for the Department of Health and Human Services by the School of Social Sciences, Focus Program on Gender and Family Violence: New Frameworks in Prevention, Monash University.

McKenna, M., O'Connor, R., & Verco, J. (2010). Exposing the dark side of parenting: A report of parents' experiences of child and adolescent family violence. In *The regional alliance addressing child and adolescent violence in the home*, South Australia.

Miles, C., & Condry, R. (2015). Responding to adolescent to parent violence: Challenges for policy and practice. *British Journal of Criminology, 55*(6), 1076–1095.

Omer, H. (2016). Helping abused parents by non-violent resistance. In A. Holt (Ed.), *Working with adolescent violence and abuse towards parents: Approaches and contexts for intervention* (pp. 47–63). Routledge.

Royal Commission into Family Violence (RCFV). (2016). *Report and recommendations.* Royal Commission into Family Violence.

Thomas, K., Fitz-Gibbon, K., & Maher, J. M. M. (2019). The use of protection orders in response to adolescent family violence: Mapping divergent Australian approaches and the merits of this criminal justice intervention. *Current Issues in Criminal Justice, 31*(4), 461–475.

Walsh, T., & Douglas, H. (2018). *Adolescent family violence issues paper.* University of Queensland.

Kate Fitz-Gibbon is Director of the Monash Gender and Family Violence Prevention Centre and an Associate Professor in Criminology in the Faculty of Arts at Monash University (Victoria, Australia). She is also an Honorary Research Fellow in the School of Law and Social Justice at University of Liverpool (UK) and a Research Associate of the Research Centre of Violence at West Virginia University (US). Her research examines family violence, femicide, the law of homicide and the impact of criminal law reform across Australian and international jurisdictions. Kate has advised on homicide law reform reviews and family violence inquiries in several Australian and international jurisdictions. Her recent publications include *Towards a Global Femicide Index: Counting the costs* (2020, Routledge) and *The Emerald Handbook on Femicide, Criminology and Social Change* (2020, Emerald), both with Sandra Walklate, Jude McCulloch and JaneMaree Maher.

JaneMaree Maher is Professor in the Centre for Women's Studies and Gender Research, Sociology, in the School of Social Sciences at Monash University. Her research two key areas of gendered social science: women's work, mothering and family, and gendered violences. Current research projects are focused on the impacts of family violence on mothering and intimate partner homicide. She is the author of over 60 peer-reviewed journal articles and five books: most recently *Towards a Global Femicide Index: Counting the costs* (2020, Routledge) with Sandra Walklate, Kate Fitz-Gibbon and Jude McCulloch and *Policing Hate Crime: Understanding Communities and Prejudice* (Routledge 2017) with Gail Mason, Jude McCulloch, Sharon Pickering, Rebecca Wickes and Carolyn McKay.

Karla Elliott is a Lecturer in Sociology in the School of Social Sciences at Monash University (Victoria, Australia). Her research explores shifting expressions of masculinity in late modernity and the intersection of masculinity with gender and family violence. She has research interests in men's alcohol consumption cultures, feminist theory, critical studies on men and masculinities and narrative methods.

Chapter 4
Adolescent-to-Parent Violence and the Promise of Attachment Based Interventions

David Burck

Abstract Adolescent-to-parent violence (APV) is a social issue, which has long term impacts for both families experiencing the violence and young people using violence. One group therapy intervention program for families experiencing APV, where there is a history of domestic violence in the family, is the ReNew program in Queensland, Australia. This chapter presents a brief overview of the ReNew program, a discussion of a number of key risks for young people and mothers experiencing violence and an overview of working with young people using violence. Critically, this chapter highlights how attachment based interventions, like the ReNew program, may provide a new direction for APV interventions in the future. In essence, the ReNew program, and the research underpinning the program, attempts to reduce violence through strengthening attachments between mothers and sons. Attachment based interventions target the core issue, which lies behind adolescent violence in the home and may provide an alternative to behaviour based programs. Finally, reflections from the ReNew program highlight hope for the future and illuminate opportunities to work with young people, and mothers, in a powerful and innovative manner.

4.1 Origins of ReNew and Its Connection to APV

The ReNew program was a co-facilitated twenty session group therapy program with mothers and sons who experienced domestic violence and the sons were currently using violence towards their mothers. I was inspired to create the ReNew program when I was working at a domestic violence support service, Carinity Communities-Talera in Queensland, as a children's counsellor. There was an influx of mothers seeking support, but not for their experience of intimate partner violence, they were concerned about their sons' use of violence at home. Through working with these

D. Burck (✉)
Youth and Family Services (YFS) Queensland, Logan/Jimboomba, Australia
e-mail: david.burck@uqconnect.edu.au

School of Nursing, Midwifery and Social Work, University of Queensland, Brisbane, Australia

K. Fitz-Gibbon et al. (eds.), *Young People Using Family Violence*,
https://doi.org/10.1007/978-981-16-1331-9_4

young people I found that traditional behavioural interventions were not reducing the violence. In response to this finding, I worked in partnership with Andrea Edwards, from the Domestic Violence Action Centre in Ipswich, Queensland, to write ReNew incorporating domestic violence, trauma, attachment and APV literature. Ultimately, the Queensland government funded ReNew as a pilot program, which ran from 2016 to 2018. Two facilitators were employed in the pilot project described in the chapter, along with a women's advocate to support all mothers engaged in the program. During this time, I learned many lessons about the impact of intimate partner violence (IPV) and APV on families, as well as the power of the relationships between mothers and sons.

One key aspect of IPV is how it erodes the attachment between mothers and their children. Research indicates that children and young people who witness IPV possess weakened attachments towards their mothers specifically (Sternberg et al., 2005; Lee et al., 2014; Evans et al., 2008). Moreover, low attachment scores between mothers and their children are evident in families where adolescent-to-parent violence (APV) is present and may lead to adolescents using violence as adults (Simmons et al., 2018). Therefore, APV, especially where there is a history of IPV, is an aspect of family violence that not only destroys the core of the mother/child dyad, but also has long lasting ramifications on how adolescents construct intimate partner relationships (Izaguirre & Calvete, 2017). Often in the ReNew program, mothers commented that ReNew was the last chance for the family and the violence levied at them from their adolescent sons was at a level where they were close to telling their sons to leave the home. Mothers often cried and wondered "what went wrong," while grieving about how violence had taken away their ability to be the mother they wanted to be and have the relationship with their son that they cherished when he was a toddler.

4.2 ReNew's Structure; Similarities and Differences to Step Up

The ReNew program was a group therapy program, which worked with mothers and sons (ages 12–17) who have experienced/witnessed IPV and now are in an environment where sons are using violence towards their mothers. Designing a group therapy program, which worked with both the young person using violence and the victim of the violence simultaneously within the same group environment, created many challenges. First, the program's success hinged on both mothers and young people engaging in difficult subject matter together within a safe, therapeutic, environment. Mothers and sons were tasked with addressing violent behaviour occurring at home, understanding the impact of that behaviour on others, working through how IPV impacted each of them, rebuilding their attachment and challenging gender beliefs all within a group environment. Some families had never engaged in any therapeutic intervention before. Facilitators were faced with how to engage in these conversations and activities, while ensuring mothers' safety within, and outside of, the group environment.

The program Andrea and I turned to for guidance was the Step Up program developed by Routt and Anderson (2011). The Step Up program is a 20 week group adolescent-to-parent violence (APV) intervention based in King County in the United States. Step Up's focus on working through APV in an inclusive process involving both adolescents and parents, while still holding parents' safety paramount, made it an ideal intervention to use as a template (Buel, 2004). Early in ReNew's development, Lily Anderson was briefed on how we wanted to work with mothers and sons on the intersection between intimate partner domestic violence and APV. She allowed us to draw upon Step Up's structure for information and her support was crucial in ReNew's development. The key similarity between the two programs is the young person group, parent group and joint group structure. These three subgroups worked together to effectively address violence/gender beliefs in young people, challenge/monitor violence use by young people, increase mothers' parental capacity, breakdown mothers' feelings of shame and rebuild the attachment within the mother/son dyad (Routt & Anderson, 2011). This three sub-group structure nestled within the larger 20 session group program, is the core element of ReNew that enabled mothers and sons to work through challenging subject matter in a safe and therapeutic manner; therefore, it is important to briefly unpack how they complimented each other.

Research has identified how IPV targets mothers' parenting and attachments with children (Fish et al., 2009). Therefore, above all else, ReNew is an APV program geared to reduce violence within the home, through strengthening the mother/son attachment after experiencing IPV. Research also indicates that domestic violence therapeutic interventions involving both mothers and children/adolescents have positive outcomes and increase both mothers' and children's readiness for change (Humphreys et al., 2006, 2011). An Australian study of mothers' perception of APV support programs, where there is a history of IPV, found that mothers felt further marginalised and blamed when engaged in interventions which worked solely with the young person and did not include mothers (Jackson, 2003). It was crucial for us to work with both mothers and young people in order to effectively rebuild attachments and avoid inadvertently reinforcing maternal shame.

Joint sessions with mothers and young people gave Leia Mackie, the ReNew co-facilitator, and I an opportunity to rebuild these damaged attachments. Similar to Step Up, we worked with both sons and mothers within the same two hour session. Over the period of two years we worked with roughly 27 mother/son dyads. However, some mothers completed the program with more than one son, which means we worked with roughly 33 young people. These sessions focused on developing non-violence plans for young people to adhere to, both within session and outside of session, to ensure a base level of safety. Moreover, joint activities focused on what mothers and sons appreciated about each other, goals for the family to work on, communication skills and games that increased safe attachment behaviours, which all are based on Step Up joint activities. One crucial difference between Step Up and ReNew is ReNew's focus on processing the family's violence experience. Unlike the Step Up cohort, all mothers and young people engaged in ReNew experienced/witnessed IPV. Therefore, other joint session activities focused on discussing the impact of violence on the family and what mothers and sons wanted their home environment to become now that they no longer have the adult IPV perpetrator in the house. These activities gave mothers an opportunity to see sons as victims of violence, as opposed to perpetrators of violence, and gave sons the opportunity to see the impact of violence on their mothers. Unpacking this shared experience in a safe and supportive environment helped strengthen the attachment between mothers and sons throughout the 20 session program.

Similar to Step Up, ReNew employed a number of parent only sessions to discuss challenges and increase parental capacity; however, due to mothers experiencing IPV, ReNew's sessions were mother only sessions. One key barrier to mothers engaging in a support program is the shame associated with experiencing APV (Edenborough et al., 2008; Gallagher, 2016). Holt (2011) describes the intersection of IPV and APV as a "double stigma" where women feel that they have both failed as a partner and now failed as a mother. A number of mothers in ReNew reflected that they believed that they "deserved" the violence from their sons due to not leaving the abusive relationship with their partner earlier, or not caring for their children enough when they were in the midst of violence from their partner. In order to help mothers overcome overwhelming feelings of shame, Leia and I spent these mothers' sessions unpacking how IPV impacted their parenting and would not allow them to be the mothers they wanted to be. In a sense, we moved the responsibility for these impacts back onto the male partner perpetrator of violence and reframed mothers' decisions as protective and necessary in order to survive such an abusive, terrifying and unsafe environment. The ability to recast mothers' decisions in this manner highlights their capacity and strength, which is crucial in their ability to support their sons to reduce their use of violence in the home.

Another key aspect of ReNew is how we adapted the women's advocate model from the Duluth Domestic Abuse Intervention Program (DIAP) (Pence & Paymar, 1993). One major challenge for any therapeutic intervention involving both young people using violence and victims of that violence is ensuring safety both in session and between sessions. To better monitor mothers' safety and react more effectively, we adapted the women's advocate role from DIAP. A women's advocate is a counsellor/support worker who contacts women during the length of the program to monitor violence use at home and react if a woman's safety becomes compromised, which can involve increased levels of abuse to potential homicide risk (Gondolf, 2010). In ReNew's case, women's advocates called mothers in between sessions to assess safety and any other potential barriers to remain engaged in the program; including homelessness, legal questions, financial challenges and transport. Emily Cheesman, the senior women's advocate for ReNew, led a team of counsellors who monitored mothers' safety and provided them with a safe support person who they could contact for support outside of group sessions. The women's advocate role was crucial in both maintaining safety and women's engagement in ReNew. There were some occasions where, based on women's advocate's reports, we worked with young people and mothers outside of the group setting in order to effectively manage increases in violence use in between sessions. In these cases we were able to address the violence specifically and over a few weeks the violence reduced to a level where mothers felt safe to engage in program material again. The women's advocate role is a crucial aspect of working with APV that should be integrated in any APV intervention involving mothers and young people.

The final sub-group within the ReNew program are young person only groups, which focused on the impact of violence on the family, the impact of domestic violence on the young people and gender/relationship beliefs. In order to create an effective non-violence plan, it is important to develop a shared understanding of what constitutes violence within the mother/son dyad. We used a coercive control model, which incorporates verbal abuse, financial abuse, physical abuse, emotional abuse and other forms of violence a person uses to exert control over another person within a relationship (Stark, 2007). Routt and Anderson (2011) adapted DIAP's conceptualisation of power and control to a family abuse wheel, which focused specifically on how coercive control inverts power structures within a family where young people assume control of the mother/child dyad. Activities use coercive control as a foundation to explore how young people's use of violence impacts family members, explore motivations for violence use, discuss safe behaviours they can choose other than violence and generate a better understanding of what constitutes violence.

Joint group sessions, mothers' only sessions and young people only sessions all work together to complement each other to reduce violence use at home and increase attachment strength. At the core of APV is how young people conceive of relationships and normalise pro-violent beliefs where violence is used to solve problems within a relationship (Temple et al., 2013). In other words, young people who use violence see violence as a tool they can use within a relationship. Attachment activities with mothers, along with deconstructing coercive control and gender beliefs in young people, work symbiotically to challenge pro-violent relationship constructions. Young people and mothers experience safe and respectful interactions in session, which gives them a tangible model of how safe relationships operate. For some families, safe and respectful interactions in session are some of the first positive interactions they have had in a number of years and provide an alternative to how they see their attachment and how they see themselves. Most importantly, these sub-groups combine to provide an experience that reinforces that they both have the capacity to change.

4.3 Working with Young People Using Violence

There is a dearth of research and information on how to effectively engage young people who have witnessed domestic violence in an APV intervention program. The ideas explored in this section of the chapter rely on my experience working with young people in the ReNew program. One crucial aspect of working with young people who have witnessed IPV and are using violence towards their mothers is that they are victims of domestic violence as well. Young people often talked about how they were told that they "are just like their dad," which led to shame, anger and fear. Over time young people, and others within the family, see young people using violence as perpetrators, or perpetrators in waiting, which negatively impacts young people's willingness for change.

The central question in working with young people in an APV program is, how do we overcome the negative perceptions they have of themselves, and the shame associated with those perceptions, to create meaningful change? Initially, facilitators must develop a genuine therapeutic relationship with young people using violence in order to humanise young people and move away from only viewing young people through a perpetrator lens. Similar to other children who have experienced interpersonal trauma, young people who have witnessed domestic violence, such as those in the ReNew program, need psychological safety and security in order to embark on change (Perry & Pollard, 1998). Such relationship building creates a sense of safety through relating to the young person via an attachment based, open and engaged demeanor (Hughes, 2017). When facilitators remain open and engaged young people become less defensive and more open to processing their experience and evaluating their use of violence.

One case example is a young person, Jeff, who came into the ReNew program after years of witnessing IPV and using violence at home towards his mother. He witnessed severe acts of physical violence including strangulation, hearing his father call his mother a "bitch" and "useless," as well as hearing death threats if they ever left. Once he and his mother left the relationship he assumed the power role in the relationship and used verbal abuse, threats of physical violence, destroying property and threats to use a weapon to control the relationship with his mother. This dynamic of using coercive control and instrumental violence within the mother/son dyad is a common relational structure in APV (Harbin & Madden, 1979; Cottrell & Monk, 2004; Simmons et al., 2018). At the time of the initial interview for the ReNew program, Jeff's mother said that Jeff's use of violence at home was escalating and the program was her last hope for their relationship.

Jeff agreed to try the ReNew program for three sessions, but was insistent he would leave the group after the third session and not return. During the first three sessions, the group played some get to know you games, worked with mothers on creating goals for the program, created a group non-violence plan and played attachment based games with bubbles and balloons. Jeff spent hours interacting with his mother in a safe way, laughing and having fun with her, as well as making connections with other young people and mothers in the group. Also, during this time Leia and I discovered that Jeff enjoyed acting in school performances and had a recent performance. Along with work on IPV, emotional regulation and remaining non-violent, Jeff spoke to us and other mothers in the group about his experiences acting and what he enjoyed about performing on stage. After every session, Jeff tell Leia and I that he enjoyed the session and he was not returning to the group, at which point we thanked him for coming and said we would see him next week. Jeff finished the entire 20 sessions and he and his mother spent Friday nights during group cooking dinner together and playing video games. For his mother, this was the first time she felt that it was possible to have a safe and emotionally meaningful relationship with her son, while Jeff felt that he was capable of change and a positive relationship with his mum was a real possibility. Being open and engaged in the young person's life outside of ReNew reinforced that we viewed him as a young person first and foremost and the violence did not define who he was, but was something we could all work together to change over time. Remaining open and forging a genuine relationship with Jeff built on respect and care, enabled him to participate in the group long enough to engage in the material and create sustainable change within his life.

4.4 What We Learned Working with Young People in ReNew

Even though young people who engaged in the ReNew program initially appeared to lack empathy for their actions, they all expressed a deep desire to have a healthy relationship with their mothers. Leia and I would often reflect to the young people that the fact they were willingly engaging in a program that challenged them on their use of violence sent a strong message to their mothers that they valued their relationship with them. Furthermore, mothers often commented on how proud they were that their sons were owning up to their violence and working towards rebuilding the relationship. However, timing is important. Activities meant to enrich sons' sense of empathy, challenge pro-violence beliefs and increase safety staged too early in the therapeutic process actually elicited defensiveness and created increased rigidity in young people.

Leia and I learned that one difficult challenge facing facilitators is balancing mother's safety with relationship building activities with young people using violence. Young people entering the program were engaged in severe levels of physical violence, use of weapons, threats to kill their mothers/siblings, destruction of property and leaving home for days at a time. Furthermore, mothers came to initial interview sessions expressing that the ReNew program is their last hope for the relationship, sometimes locking themselves in their room for safety and living at home terrified of their son's use of violence. High levels of risk for mothers' safety overlapping with heightened arousal and elevated levels of despair for mothers combined to create an environment of hyper-vigilance amongst facilitators, which sometimes manifested itself in a reliance on program content to the detriment of relationship building amongst young people.

One example of placing elevated importance on content over a trauma informed approach is creating young people's individual non-violence plans during the first session. During this activity young people reviewed the Family Abuse Wheel from Step Up (Routt & Anderson, 2011) which broke down coercive control behaviours and involved writing out a non-violence plan consisting of specific violent behaviours young people used and how they were not going to engage in those behaviours during the course of the program. Young people became defensive during this session and minimised the impact of their use of violence. Some stated that they would not change their behaviour, that they wanted to "hurt" their mothers and espoused that they "did not care" what impact their violence had on the family. Instead of being open to change and maintaining safety, young people often became more rigid and agreeing on behaviour goals became challenging and potentially counterproductive.

The focus on behaviour based interventions above trauma informed therapeutic interventions early in the program reinforced seeing young people as perpetrators of violence, as opposed to viewing young people as victims of interpersonal trauma who were also using violence at home. In essence, we viewed young people through a behavioural lens, which inadvertently reinforced shame at the detriment of relationship. Hughes (2017) espouses that therapists working with young people who have experienced trauma remain open to promote a safe relationship, which reduces defensiveness. In essence, the relationship itself is a therapeutic intervention crucial in trauma work. Open and caring relationships buffer young people who have experienced interpersonal trauma against elevated stress responses, promoting healing and healthy development (Perry & Dobson, 2010). In order to challenge young people's beliefs and use of violence, we needed to create emotional safety within the session through relationships.

As facilitators in ReNew, we needed to reconcile the conflict between the need for immediate safety for mothers and maintaining trauma informed approach of open relationship building with young people using violence. We replaced the first session on individual non-violence plans with a group non-violence contract, in which the group agreed not to engage in verbal, emotional and physical abuse both during and outside of session for the duration of ReNew. This group contract gave the group a level of safety we could enforce and monitor without creating defensiveness and reinforcing shame within young people. Alongside the behaviour based group non-violence contract, the first two group sessions employed relationship/attachment based games between mothers and sons, as well as with the entire group, and short ten minute activities designed to create open, engaged and caring relationships with both mothers and facilitators. We then moved the individual non-violence plan for young people from session one to session eight, which was far more constructive and young people were able to achieve their non-violence goals more effectively. The overarching lesson from this experience is that one cannot sacrifice relationship building over behavioural based content when working with APV. In ReNew, this sacrifice counter intuitively increased mothers' safety risks as young people became more rigid in their pro-violence beliefs and more defensive about their use of violence. In reality, a general group non-violence plan coupled with trauma informed relationship building reduced violence more effectively by virtue of young people feeling valued and emotionally safe enough to honestly engage in their specific non-violence plans in later sessions.

Challenging gender beliefs and violence use were key aspects in promoting a healthier construction of intimate relationships for young people in ReNew. Through working with young people using violence, we observed that young people's violence towards their mothers was not driven by anger or other internal motivations, but by their belief system. Mothers reported that their son's physical violence drastically reduced as soon as they engaged in the program; however, their use of verbal abuse and abuse towards siblings remained consistent until the final few sessions of ReNew where their violence use overall reduced precipitously. Mothers attributed the initial reduction in severe physical violence to attending a program on APV and knowing that the facilitators would ask him how he was progressing on the group non-violence plan. In other words, the thought of being held accountable was enough to elicit some initial change. However, mothers reported that their son's violence use would spike halfway through the program and when one form of violence would decrease another form of violence would escalate. For example, a young person's use of physical violence would greatly reduce, but his level of violence towards his siblings would become more frequent. Research suggests that young people use violence within their intimate partner relationships, and relationships with their mothers, due to a belief system structured around normalising violence use to solve problems and get one's needs met (Temple et al., 2013; Werner & Nixon, 2005; Oransky & Fisher, 2009). This belief system accounts for why young people test the family system with increased violence halfway through the program, adapting their violence use during the early sessions of the program in order to remain in control of the relationship. We learned that solely focusing on violent behaviours is undercut by the young person's ability to use other forms of violence within the relationship. Activities challenging young people's beliefs about violence in relationships and gender norms begin to alter how they construct relationships.

Most importantly, the most effective way to alter how young people using violence conceive of relationships is strengthening their attachment with their mothers. Domestic violence undermines mother's attachments with their children and provides children with a model of how relationships operate and influence young people's use of violence towards their mothers and towards intimate partners in future relationships (Levendosky et al., 2011; Lee et al., 2014). Conversely, families that described strong attachment behaviours within the mother/child dyad also report emotional closeness, adherence to boundaries and effective problem solving (Chanmugam, 2014). These findings suggest that working with young people using violence in isolation will not achieve the attachment strength necessary to promote sustained violence reduction. From an attachment perspective, an increase in emotional closeness between mothers and sons challenge sons' pro-violence beliefs within relationships, which will not only have a positive impact on their current relationships with their mothers, but will also promote healthy intimate partner relationships in the future. In ReNew, we found our work with mothers and sons as a team not only reduced forms of violence young people were specifically addressing, but violence we did not cover specifically in group also reduced and mothers reported young people initiating positive interactions with their siblings for the first time. This research, along with our observations working with young people, illustrates the power of safe and strong attachments on violence reduction. A 15 year old son in the ReNew summed this finding up concisely when he pointed at his mother and said "There used to be a lot of fighting, but now it's us against them."

Working with young people engaged in APV is a complex undertaking with numerous factors jostling for priority within the facilitator's mind. Safety, trauma informed practice, attachment building and relationship building are all factors one must synthesise into a cohesive APV intervention program in order to appropriately and effectively work with mothers and sons. If a facilitator sacrifices one of these factors to focus more time on others, there can be unforeseen consequences on young people and families. Trauma, attachment, behavioural interventions, challenging beliefs and safety all complement each other and build symphonically as the program progresses. Facilitators may think there is insufficient time for relationship and rapport building games with the group in order to appropriately work thought the content, but paradoxically, a safe relationship with young people and mothers is needed to effectively work thorough the content. We found that working with young people engaged in APV is centrally about a genuine care and desire to walk with them on their journey, as opposed to an evaluation of their use of violence.

4.5 Hope for the Future

ReNew was both the most challenging and rewarding work in my ten year career in working in domestic violence. Mothers and sons who engaged, and completed, the ReNew program displayed positive attachment behaviours within the 20 sessions that I did not see in families I worked with for years in individual therapy. One activity that embodies the hope we found in working with these mothers and young people is the Mother's Day activity we facilitated with each of the four ReNew groups.

We decided to facilitate a special Mother's Day session during our mothers' only group in order to celebrate and reinforce their commitment to improving their relationships with their sons. Work with young people in ReNew culminates in an activity in one of the final sessions where young people make amends for a violent incident that happened in the past. Young people find this reparation activity extremely challenging; therefore, Leia and I facilitated some similar structured activities leading into the final two sessions. One of these early activities was writing a Mother's Day card about what they appreciate about their mothers, delivered to mothers at the mothers' only group during their Mother's Day session. Young people were able to write about how they appreciated their mother's strength, her sacrifices in protecting him from violence in the past, her unconditional love for him and her sense of humour. These were all personality traits young people and mothers had talked about during previous joint sessions, which enabled young people to engage in the Mother's Day card activity without frustration or distress.

During the Mother's Day session we found that a large number of mothers had never had a Mother's Day celebration before that mothers' group session. Many stated that their partner would never allow Mother's Day to be celebrated and when they left that relationship their sons continued to not observe the day. We talked about the grief and loss involved in not having the dream family they wished for and how IPV impacted their ability to form strong emotional relationships with their children. After this discussion, and some celebratory chocolate and cake, we gave each mother her Mother's Day card from her son and reflected how much dedication both she and her son had to rebuilding the relationship after violence. Mothers cried and reflected on how proud, and astonished they were that their sons were willingly participating in a six month group focused on their use of violence. They commented on how their sons were also victims of violence and were endeavoring to become violence free. For these mothers their sons were no longer perpetrators who were "just like their dads," but were also victims of violence who were capable of change.

This change in mindset from a young person using violence as a perpetrator incapable of change, to a son who is capable of having an emotional relationship with his mother was life changing for these families. For example, a 16 year old young person, named Justin, came into the original intake interview with his mother, Kirsty, and they sat at opposite ends of the counselling room. Justin would mutter vulgarities and insults under his breath when his mother spoke and Kirsty talked about how ReNew was Justin's last chance and how she believes that he cannot change. They both attended ReNew and during the early sessions were not able to agree on a positive memory where they spent a safe time together without violence, which led to Kirsty sobbing during the session and saying that their family was beyond help. They continued to engage in the program and Justin's use of violence at home greatly reduced. Kirsty attended the Mother's Day group and cried as she shared that the group was the first Mother's Day she ever had and talked about instances of severe physical abuse, strangulation and death threats from her ex-partner. After reading the card she said that Justin is a "good kid" and he is trying his best. In the next session, both Justin and Kirsty were sitting next to each other on the couch. When Leia and I asked Kirsty what has changed in her family since the program started five months ago, Kirsty leaned closer to us and said "He lets me hug him now!" and embraced Justin around his waist, while he looked at us and smiled. We asked Justin what was different for him and he said that he never knew how much Kirsty protected him from his dad and that she was doing her best for him. Kirsty and Justin now saw each other in a different light. For Justin, Kirsty is someone who sacrificed in order to protect him and his siblings. For Kirsty, Justin is her son who is also a victim of violence, as opposed to a perpetrator incapable of empathy. Hugging each other on the couch not only conveyed the message that Justin is worth loving and is capable of change, but it also says to Kirsty that she can be a capable mother whose son loves her. Intersubjective messages of love and maternal capacity are the catalyst for changes within the family, which will lead to reductions in APV and reductions in violence use within Justin's future relationships.[1]

4.6 Moving Forward

APV where there is a history of IPV is a phenomenon that hinders a family's functioning and cannot be treated by law enforcement responses alone (Armstrong et al., 2018; Douglas & Walsh, 2018). My professional experience working with young people using violence towards their mothers taught me a great deal about how to keep young people engaged in a therapeutic program, while simultaneously addressing their violence. I believe that is it crucial for support professionals to move from a behaviour based model of intervention to an attachment/trauma informed model. Even though young people's violent behaviour and use of coercive control jeopardise a mother's safety, the violence itself is perpetuated and maintained by an elaborate construction of relationships where violence is a problem solving tool (Izaguirre & Calvete, 2017). Moving forward, APV interventions must incorporate attachment based activities with mothers and sons in order to challenge these relational constructions. Moreover, a strictly behavioural approach without a trauma informed relational facilitation may lead to defensiveness amongst young people, which renders APV interventions ineffective. If young people feel that they are being judged or evaluated, they may leave after the first session and not return. A facilitator cannot influence change in a young person engaging in APV if that young person does not attend the intervention program. Young people, and mothers, need to internalise that they are not defined by their trauma experience and that they are human beings first who deserve care and respect. We told young people that we were interested in helping them achieve the relationship with their mum that they wanted, but did not know how to reach. We, as professionals, must care for the young person while holding them accountable for the violence, as opposed to defining the young person as the violence.

Note

1. Currently, the ReNew pilot is complete and the program described in this chapter is no longer active. The Brisbane Domestic Violence Service and Talera currently facilitate a program called ReNew, but it does not resemble the structure outlined in this chapter. I am currently involved in the Side by Side program in Logan, Queensland with YFS (Youth and Family Services), which is a mother/son group program, which is 15–17 weeks long and is similar to ReNew.

References

Armstrong, G., Muftic, L., & Bouffard, L. (2018). Factors influencing law enforcement responses to child to parent violence. *Journal of Interpersonal Violence,* 1–19.

Buel, S. (2004). Addressing family violence within juvenile courts. *Journal of Aggression, Maltreatment and Trauma., 8*(3), 273–307.

Chanmugam, A. (2014). Got one another's backs: Mother-teen relationships in families escaping intimate partner violence. *Journal of Human Behavior in the Social Environment, 24*(7), 811–827.

Cottrell, B., & Monk, P. (2004). Adolescent-to-parent abuse: A qualitative overview of common themes. *Journal of Family Issues, 25*(8), 1072–1095.

Douglas, H., & Walsh, T. (2018). Adolescent family violence: What is the role of legal responses? *Sydney Law Review, 40*(499), 499–526.

Edenborough, M., Jackson, D., Mannix, J., & Wilkes, L. M. (2008). Living in the red zone: Experience of child-to-mother violence. *Child & Family Social Work, 13*(4), 464–473.

Evans, S., Davies, C., & DiLillo, D. (2008). Exposure to domestic violence: A meta-analysis of child and adolescent outcomes. *Aggression and Violent Behavior, 13*(2), 131–140.

Fish, E., McKenzie, M., & MacDonald, H. (2009). *Bad mothers and invisible fathers: Parenting in the context of domestic violence*. Domestic Violence Resource Centre.

Gallagher, E. (2016). Empowering parents: The *Who's in Charge?* program. In A. Holt (Ed.), *Working with adolescent violence and abuse towards parents* (pp. 34–46). Routledge.

Gondolf, E. (2010). The contributions of Ellen Pence to battering programming. *Violence Against Women, 16*(9), 992–1006.

Harbin, H., & Madden, D. (1979). Battered parents: A new syndrome. *American Journal of Psychiatry, 136*(10), 1288–1291.

Holt, A. (2011). The terrorist in my home: Teenagers' violence towards parents—Constructions of parent experiences in public online message boards. *Child & Family Social Work, 16*(4), 454–463.

Hughes, D. (2017). Dyadic developmental psychotherapy (DDP): An attachment focused family treatment for developmental trauma. *Australian & New Zealand Journal of Family Therapy, 38*(4), 595–605.

Humphreys, C., Mullender, A., Thiara, R., & Skamballis, A. (2006). 'Talking to my mum': Developing communication between mothers and children in the aftermath of domestic violence. *Journal of Social Work, 6*(1), 53–63.

Humphreys, C., Thiara, R., & Skamballis, A. (2011). Readiness to change: Mother-child relationship and domestic violence intervention. *British Journal of Social Work, 41*(1), 166–184.

Izaguirre, A., & Calvete, E. (2017). Exposure to family violence as a predictor of dating violence and child-to-parent aggression in Spanish adolescents. *Youth & Society, 49*(3), 393–412.

Jackson, D. (2003). Broadening constructions of family violence: Mothers' perspectives of aggression from their children. *Child and Family Social Work, 8*(4), 321–329.

Lee, M., Reese-Webber, M., & Khan, J. (2014). Exposure to family violence and attachment styles as predictors of dating violence perpetration among men and women: A mediational model. *Journal of Interpersonal Violence, 29*(1), 20–43.

Levendosky, A., Bogat, A., & Huth-Bocks, A. (2011). The influence of domestic violence on the development of the attachment relationship between mother and young child. *Psychoanalytic Psychology, 28*(4), 512–527.

Oransky, M., & Fisher, C. (2009). The development and validation of the meanings of adolescent masculinity scale. *Psychology of Men and Masculinity, 10*(1), 57–72.

Pence, E., & Paymar, M. (1993). *Education groups for men who batter: The Duluth model*. Springer.

Perry, B., & Dobson, C. (2010). The role of healthy relational interactions in buffering the impact of childhood trauma. In E. Gil (Ed.), *Working with children to heal interpersonal trauma: The power of play* (pp. 26–43). Guilford Press.

Perry, B., & Pollard, R. (1998). Homeostasis, stress, trauma and adaptation: A neurodevelopmental view of childhood trauma. *Child and Adolescent Psychiatric Clinics of North America, 7*(1), 33–51.

Routt, G., & Anderson, L. (2011). Adolescent violence towards parents. *Journal of Aggression, Maltreatment and Trauma, 20*(1), 1–19.

Simmons, M., McEwan, T., & Purcell, R. (2018). "But all kids yell at their parents, don't they?": Social norms about child-to-parent abuse in Australia. *Journal of Family Issues, 40*(11), 1486–1508.

Stark, E. (2007). *Coercive control: How men entrap women in personal life*. Oxford University Press.

Sternberg, K., Lamb, M., Guterman, E., Abbott, C., & Dawud-Noursi, S. (2005). Adolescents' perceptions of attachments to their mothers and fathers in families with histories of domestic violence: A longitudinal perspective. *Child Abuse & Neglect, 29*(8), 853–869.

Temple, J., Shorey, R., Tortolero, S., Wolfe, D., & Stuart, G. (2013). Importance of gender and attitudes about violence in the relationship between exposure to interparental violence and the perpetration of teen dating violence. *Child Abuse & Neglect, 37*(5), 343–352.

Werner, N., & Nixon, C. (2005). Normative beliefs and relational aggression: An investigation of the cognitive bases of adolescent aggressive behavior. *Journal of Youth and Adolescence, 34*(3), 229–243.

David Burck is a senior child counsellor and Side by Side (an adolescent violence program) co–author/co–facilitator at YFS (Youth and Family Services) in QLD. He has twelve years experience working with children who have witnessed domestic violence, children in out of home care and adolescents using violence in the home. He was also the co–facilitator/co–author of the ReNew program, which was a group program that worked with mothers who experienced domestic violence and sons who witnessed domestic violence and used violence against their mothers. Dave has a Masters of Counseling from the University of QLD and is currently working on his PhD, researching adolescent–to–mother violence at the University of QLD. He has published an article in the journal Advances in Social Work and Welfare Education entitled Silenced Mothers: Exploring Definitions of Adolescent–to–Parent Violence and Implications for Practice, which was awarded the editor's choice.

Chapter 5
Mothers and Step-Mothers Engaging with Law in Their Response to Adolescent Family Violence

Heather Douglas

Abstract Drawing on interviews with mothers and step-mothers who have experienced adolescent family violence (AFV) by their children or step-children, this chapter considers how the interviewees explain and respond to this form of violence. Explanations include that a current or previous partner, usually the children's father, has co-opted the adolescent to abuse her, that the adolescent is jealous of her because she is a new partner of the adolescent's father, and the adolescent's difficulties of adjusting to a new cultural context. Some identified drug use and mental health issues experienced by the child. This chapter considers when and how the interviewees use and interact with the law in response to AFV. It considers the interviewees' experiences of engaging with a range of legal responses including police and criminal justice, child protection services, civil protections orders and family law. In several cases, interviewees report that justice professionals have misunderstood the link between AFV and intimate partner violence and consequently the interviewees' experience of intimate partner violence has been exacerbated. The article shows the need for justice professionals to have an improved understanding of AFV, its diverse contexts and the risks of legal engagement.

5.1 Introduction

In this chapter I draw on an interview study involving eight mothers and step-mothers who had experienced the use of violence by their child or stepchild to explore their engagements with the legal system. Their stories show how their experiences of violence, and engagement with legal processes in response to it, changed over a three year period. Women expressed a range of reasons for the abuse including that a current or previous partner, usually the children's father, had co-opted the adolescent to abuse her, that the adolescent is jealous of her because she is a new partner of the adolescent's father, and the adolescent's difficulties of adjusting to a new cultural context. One woman identified drug use and other struggles internal to the child as an

H. Douglas (✉)
Law School, University of Melbourne, Melbourne, Australia
e-mail: douglash@unimelb.edu.au

K. Fitz-Gibbon et al. (eds.), *Young People Using Family Violence*,
https://doi.org/10.1007/978-981-16-1331-9_5

explanation for the abuse. This chapter considers when and how the interviewees use and interact with the law in response to AFV. It considers the interviewees' experience of engaging with a range of legal responses including police and criminal justice, child protection services, civil protection orders and family law. In several cases, interviewees report that justice professionals have misunderstood the link between AFV and intimate partner violence and consequently the interviewees' experience of intimate partner violence has been exacerbated. This chapter highlights the need for justice professionals to have an improved understanding of AFV, its diverse contexts and the reasons for, and risks of, legal engagement.

5.2 Background

Howard (2011, p. 2) defines AFV as 'an abuse of power perpetrated by adolescents against their parents and other family members, including siblings. It occurs when an adolescent attempts to physically or psychologically dominate, coerce and control others in their family'. In this chapter adolescent is defined as a person aged between 12 and 18 years of age. This is primarily because the women in the Brisbane Study, outlined in the next section, still talked about their 18 year olds as children. Definitions of adolescent vary between studies with some including children as young as ten and as old as 21 (McKenna & O'Connor, 2012; Haw, 2010; Elliott et al., 2018, p. 2). Both adolescent boys and girls have been reported to be violent towards a family member, although studies report perpetrators are more commonly male (Condry & Miles 2014, p. 261; Holt, 2016a, 2016b, p. 3; Howard, 2015). Studies have also identified gender differences in the way adolescent violence is perpetrated, suggesting that adolescent girls are more likely to be verbally abusive than boys (Williams et al., 2017; Haw, 2010, p. 7). Generally a range of behaviours is associated with AFV including physical and psychological abuse, financial abuse, property damage and intimidation (Haw, 2010, p. 7).

There are many similarities between AFV and intimate partner violence (IPV). Both involve the use of tactics of power and control (Daly & Nancarrow, 2009, p. 153; Howard, 2015). Victims may be reluctant to report the violence to police or to other service providers, resulting in the victim experiencing isolation (Howard & Abbott, 2013; Routt & Anderson, 2011, p. 10). Victims generally want the violence to stop rather than to separate from their abuser or have their child removed (Haw, 2010). However there are also obvious differences between IPV and AFV including that violent intimate partners are usually able to live independently while many adolescents are not (Downey, 1997, p. 77; Daly & Nancarrow, 2009, p. 153). Furthermore adult perpetrators of IPV usually have the capacity to take responsibility for their violence while some adolescents may struggle to understand their behaviour (Domestic Violence Resource Centre, 2010). Daly and Nancarrow (2009, p. 169) identify another difference, at least in the context of a son's violence against his mother, which they describe as the 'recursive trap'. They explain that this refers to the fact that the responsibility of the violence is diffused with mothers feeling partly to blame for it and sons developing a victim status that allows the adolescent to minimise and excuse his own behaviour.

5.3 The Legal Landscape

There are a number of potential legal interventions available that could be harnessed to respond to AFV. Criminal justice interventions, child protection, civil protection orders and family law interventions may be relevant and useful in the context of AFV (Douglas & Walsh, 2018). This chapter focusses on law in Queensland, Australia as this is where the interview study that is the focus of this chapter took place. However legal options are similar across the English speaking world.

The age of criminal responsibility varies. In Queensland children aged under the age of ten years are not criminally responsible while children aged ten years to 14 years may be held criminally responsible if it can be proved that at the time of doing the criminal act they had the capacity to know they should not do the act (s29(2) *Criminal Code 1899* (Qld)). If police are contacted they may decide to divert the adolescent into a restorative justice process like youth justice conferencing, caution the adolescent or take no action (Douglas & Walsh, 2018, p. 506). While it is possible for adolescent children to be charged with criminal offences, research has demonstrated that criminal justice interventions are taken in a minority of incidents involving AFV (Moulds et al., 2016, p. 550).

Similar approaches to child protection intervention exist throughout Australia (AIHW, 2019). Child protection legislation allows the state to intervene to keep children aged zero to 17 years old safe (AIHW, 2019, p. vi). According to the Australian Institute of Health and Welfare younger children are considered most vulnerable and notably, in the context of AFV, the median age of children in state care is eight years with children aged 15–17 years least likely to have received child protection services (AIHW, 2019, p. 16).

Similar to child protection intervention, each Australian state and territory provides for civil protection orders to protect a victim from domestic violence (Taylor et al., 2015) and each has a slightly different approach. Unlike other Australian states (Thomas et al., 2019), in Queensland a child can only be named as an aggrieved person or a respondent in a protection order if he or she has an intimate partner relationship with the other party or they are in an informal care relationship with the other party (section 22 *Domestic and Family Violence Protection Act (2012)* Qld). Notably data provided by the Queensland Department of Justice and Attorney General identifies that between June 2016 and June 2017, there were n229 applications for protection orders involving adolescent respondents, most of whom were 17 years old (n154, 67%) and in a couple, spousal or intimate personal relationship with the aggrieved (n202, 88%).[1] However, a Queensland mother or step mother cannot apply for a protection order against a respondent who is her child or step-child until the child reaches the age of 18 years (see schedule 5, *Domestic and Family Violence Protection Act (2012)* Qld). Section 8 of the *Domestic and Family Violence Protection Act 2012* (Qld) defines domestic and family violence broadly to include coercive and controlling behaviour so once the child turns 18 the mother or step-mother, or the adolescent, can apply for a protection order in a wide range of circumstances.

In Australia the *Family Law Act* 1975 (*Cth*) (FLA) applies throughout the country and provides for court determinations about property distribution and the residence and contact arrangements for children after their parents have separated. Under section 4AB of the FLA the definition of family violence includes coercive and controlling behaviour and the FLA applies to children up to the age of 17 years. While this legislation provides the court with a range of powers including the possibility of ordering children to attend counselling, there is broad recognition that as children become more mature, the court is less likely to make directions about them (Parkinson & Cashmore, 2008). This means that the family courts often decide not to make any directions or orders about adolescent children.

5.4 Brisbane Study

5.4.1 Methodology

How survivors of violence experience legal interventions continues to be an important consideration in creating and fine-tuning those responses (Kelly & Westmarland, 2015, p. 117). In this section I draw on interviews conducted as part of a larger qualitative study undertaken with 65 women in Brisbane, Australia who experienced IPV and engaged with the legal system. Women were interviewed on three occasions over approximately three years (Douglas, 2021). In the broader study six women were from an Aboriginal or Torres Strait Islander (ATSI) background and 24 women were from culturally and linguistically diverse (CALD) backgrounds. The women were initially approached by their IPV support workers or lawyers from a range of organisations in Brisbane, Australia who discussed the proposed study with them. At the time of recruitment, the women were all over 18 years old, had in the past twelve months experienced a violent relationship with an intimate partner and engaged with the legal system to respond to the violence. Support workers or lawyers arranged interviews if the woman was interested in participating. A narrative interviewing style was used to encourage the participants to tell their stories and describe their experiences at their own pace (Flick, 2007). Interviews were recorded and transcribed with the participants' consent.[2] The women were interviewed on three occasions over three years. While the focus of the interviews was on women's relationships with a violent intimate partner and their engagements with the legal system, eight of the women volunteered information about their engagements with the legal system as a response to issues of AFV involving their child or step-child. The experiences of these eight women are the focus of the discussion in this chapter. Pseudonyms

Table 5.1 Type of abuse experienced

Type of abuse experienced	Name of woman and background
Legal systems abuse	Shelley, Vera (CALD); Dalila (CALD)
Physical abuse	Vera (CALD), Jarrah (ATSI), Janet
Emotional abuse and threats	Shelley, Fiona, Jarrah (ATSI), Trisha (CALD); Dalila (CALD)
Property damage/theft	Fiona, Trisha (CALD), Jarrah (ATSI), Janet
Financial abuse	Janet
Stalking and monitoring	Trisha (CALD), Perlah (CALD)

are used throughout this chapter and some details have been left out to protect the anonymity of the interviewees.

As the women's stories set out below show, they experienced a variety of overlapping forms AFV (Table 5.1). Abuse included physical, emotional and financial abuse, stalking and monitoring, property damage and theft and legal systems abuse (AIJA, 2020, [3.1]).

The women identified a range of explanations about why their child or step-child was abusive to them. Their reasons included parental co-option by the father or encouragement from the father to carry out abuse, jealousy of step-children towards the woman, cultural differences between their home country and Australia and the child's mental health or drug abuse issues (see Table 5.2). Sometimes these explanations overlapped or women identified more than one explanation for the violence.

Women in the study identified a range of legal systems they engaged with as a result of AFV including police, the criminal, family and child protection systems, civil protection orders and in one case, private contracts (see Table 5.3). Most commonly women had interactions with police (n6 women) and child protection services (n3 women) and seven women had engaged with at least two aspects of the legal system, with Shelley engaged with four aspects of the legal system as a result of AFV. Only Perlah did not engage with the law in response to the AFV she experienced.

Table 5.2 Explanations for adolescent family violence

Woman's explanation for adolescent family violence	Name of woman and background
Parental co-option	Shelley; Fiona, Vera (CALD)
Jealousy	Trisha (CALD), Perlah (CALD), Jarrah (ATSI)
Cultural difference	Dalila (CALD), Trisha (CALD)
Mental health/drug abuse	Janet, Jarrah (ATSI)

Table 5.3 Engagement with legal systems in response to adolescent family violence

Woman's engagement with legal systems in response to adolescent family violence	Name of woman and background
Police	Shelley, Fiona, Jarrah (ATSI), Trisha (CALD), Dalila (CALD), Janet
Criminal law system	Shelley, Fiona, Janet, Vera (CALD)
Family law system	Shelley, Trisha (CALD)
Child protection system	Shelley, Jarrah (ATSI), Dalila (CALD)
Protection order system	Dalila (CALD)
Private contracts/victim assist	Vera (CALD)

While there was attrition from the broader study, all of the eight study women who experienced AFV were interviewed on three separate occasions over three years. The following sections are arranged thematically by women's main explanations for the abuse. Each section outlines women's experience over the period of the interviews, charting both their experience of AFV and their engagement with the legal system as a result.

5.4.2 *Parental Co-option*

5.4.2.1 Shelley

Interview 1: Shelley and her husband Pete lived together for more than 15 years before separating several years ago. They have three school aged children together, two are teenagers. Shelley had a parenting plan registered with the Family Court and the children lived with her and had contact with their father. Shelley says she became increasingly fearful of her two older children especially her 15 year old son:

> I was having conversations with … counsellors and my own doctor of how to navigate that space … my older two … they'd become Pete's weapons. I had mini-hims … he's infiltrated my home. 24/7 he would call them on their mobiles and I would see a change in their behaviour. I knew exactly when they'd had a phone call.

Things came to a head when Pete physically assaulted Shelley during a child handover. The police attended, there was mediation and then a family court report (AIJA, 2019, [10.4]) was prepared. The family court report recommended the children continue to live with Shelley but see their father regularly. Six months ago, after a handover, Shelley's teenage son got back in the car 'and proceeded to talk about how I could be killed and how I could be buried…. he goes "oh, a car accident would probably be a good way."' Once home Shelley felt upset and sent Pete a text about it. Her teenage son grabbed the phone and Shelley tried to take it back from him. At this point she says her daughter yelled 'that's assault'. The two older children then called the police who attended and took statements from Shelley and the children. The next day Shelley was charged with assault: 'I'm DNA tested, fingerprinted and treated like a criminal. I'm out on bail. Not allowed to ring my children because I'm on bail and they're the supposed witnesses.' The family court, after hearing from child protection authorities, has reversed the contact arrangements so that Shelley is only allowed to have supervised telephone contact with the children.

Interview 2: Shelley's assault charge was withdrawn as there was no evidence to support it. This took several months to resolve. Child protection services then found allegations of Shelley being violent to the children unsubstantiated. Eight months later the family court determined that the children should live with Shelley and have contact with their father. She says: 'In the end of the day I think we took too long to get to where we were, though. If [the judge] had done more, earlier, if that makes sense … but kids in a toxic environment for 12 months…' The two older children currently refuse to see her.

Interview 3: Shelley now has significant legal debt. She rarely sees her two teenage children. She believes that Pete continues to manipulate them against her. She says 'any chance that Pete gets, if you leave a crack in the door he will try to control or put you down'. She thinks the family court should have ordered counselling for the older children to ensure it took place.

5.4.2.2 Fiona

Interview 1: Fiona lived with her abusive partner, Tony, being bashed, strangled and emotionally abused for over twenty years but held off separating until the children were old enough to make their own decisions. They have two teenage sons who live with Tony. Fiona has a protection order and has commenced property proceedings in the family court. She says the house was to be sold and neither Fiona nor Tony were allowed to be in the house. While the house was empty everything, including the stove and the toilet, were stolen. A fresh drink container was found under the house and the police 'DNA tested, they finger printed, my son's DNA has been found so that's where I go now.' When asked: 'Are you happy to have your son charged?' Fiona's said: 'too darn right I am…. I may have to send my son to jail.' She says her son wrote a statement to police 'for all this gross, disgusting, wrong stuff …'. She believes her son worked with Tony to remove her security system that was provided by a local support service. In explaining her son's behaviour Fiona says: 'I believe that his father puts pressure on him. [My son's] very immature. [Tony] puts pressure on him to do stuff …'.

Interview 2: Fiona says things are a bit better with her sons. They currently have employment. She doesn't know what is happening with the stealing charges. She is still experiencing stalking from her ex-partner but the children are not causing any issues. She now sees her sons sometimes. In relation to her son who she believes stole from her she says: 'we haven't broached anything that happened, we just left it… I'll never trust him.' There was no change at interview 3.

5.4.2.3 Vera

Interview 1: Vera came to Australia as a tourist. After meeting and marrying her Australian partner, Nigel, she transitioned to a spouse visa (Segrave & Burnett-Wake, 2017) and later to permanent residence and citizenship. Nigel was financially and emotionally abusive and socially isolating towards Vera. Nigel had a gun and threatened to kill Vera. Last year Vera left. When I meet Vera she is living separately from Nigel. Their two teenage daughters, Sally and Mary, live with Nigel. The girls are too old for a family court custody order and decided to stay with Nigel. Vera says: 'I'm really worried because my girls is a prisoner. Nigel brainwash my girls.' Recently, Vera delivered a cooked meal to her daughters. Nigel became angry. Vera is seeking a property settlement and Vera believes his anger was a response to being served with a family law property application. She says Nigel hit and strangled her and she felt dizzy. With the help of their daughter Sally, Nigel pushed Vera into a bathroom and tried to lock her in. Nigel then instructed their daughter, Mary, to call the police. Vera tried to escape but Nigel strangled Vera again, making her 'see stars'. The police attended, removed Vera to the watch house overnight and applied for protection orders for both Nigel and Vera (mutual protection orders).

Interview 2: There are now mutual protection orders in place. Nigel has had their daughter Sally listed as a protected person on the order. Under the orders Vera must 'be of good behaviour and not commit domestic violence' to Sally and Nigel (a standard condition of protection orders in Queensland). Vera is concerned that Sally will lie to the police and Vera will be charged. While Nigel was ultimately charged with assault, at the hearing their daughter Sally testified that Nigel was acting in self-defence and Nigel was acquitted.

Interview 3: Mutual protection orders are still in place. Sally and Mary sometimes visit their mother. Vera is worried about them and wants to get cameras installed so that they cannot make false allegations against her. Vera has kept her current address a secret from Nigel. She asks if she should get a lawyer to draw up a promise for her girls to sign that they won't pass information about her address to their father.

5.4.2.4 Discussion: Parental Co-option

Shelley, Vera and Fiona identified the main reason that their adolescent child abused them was because they were co-opted or pressured by their father, the woman's abusive ex-partner. Their experiences identify a range of abusive behaviours. Both Shelley and Vera identified that their children had been pressured to lie to police at the behest of their father. These lies contributed to a spiralling series of events that had longer term consequences for the women, in both cases they were investigated and arrested, and in Shelley's case charged, by police for assaults that were ultimately withdrawn due to lack of evidence. Shelley was also investigated by child protection authorities. In these cases the law was used as a tool by the woman's abusive ex-partner to continue the pattern of abuse established during the relationship. Similarly, Fiona believed her ex-partner Tony had co-opted their son to remove all the property from the home, a shared asset from the marriage, while Fiona and Tony were court-ordered not to enter it. For Fiona, the family law was inadequately applied to the protection of her interests and her adolescent son should have been excluded from the property. Similarly Shelley thought the family court judge should have 'done more earlier'.

In all three cases the women's relationships with their adolescent children were deeply damaged as a result of the legal systems abuse. Shelley has little contact with her older children. Both Vera and Fiona reported a deep and lasting lack of trust for their offending child. Vera, for example, no longer trusted her daughter to maintain her secret address and wanted her to sign a contract to ensure her secret was preserved.

5.4.3 Jealousy

5.4.3.1 Trisha

Interview 1: Trisha was born overseas and met her Australian partner online. Trisha moved to Australia on a spousal visa and married Australian–born Jarrod. Jarrod has two teenage daughters, Imogen and Sarah, from a previous relationship who also live with them. Imogen is 16 years old. She says insulting racist things to Trisha, has broken Trisha's laptop and pushed Trisha down the stairs. Trisha called the police and the police took Imogen to the police station and then brought her home after a couple of hours. Recently, Imogen became very angry with Trisha when Trisha became pregnant. Trisha says that Imogen gave Jarrod an ultimatum that either Trisha left or Imogen would leave. After this Trisha and Jarrod slept in their car for a few days while Trisha decided what to do. They returned to the family home and Trisha gave birth to her son but things did not improve. Trisha experienced serious violence from Jarrod and again Imogen broke her computer. This device helped Trisha keep in contact with her family overseas. The police were called and Trisha moved into safe accommodation with her son.

Interview 2: Trisha is living in shared accommodation with her son. She has permanent residency and receives social security. She shares care of the child with Jarrod. There was a family court report (AIJA, 2020, [10.4]) produced and Trisha is concerned that the family report writer did not talk to Imogen or Sarah before finalising the report. She is worried the girls will harm her son on contact visits.

Interview 3: Trisha and Jarrod share care of their child. Trisha says she is being followed by Imogen. She has confronted Imogen and asked her to stop. Trisha says '[she] is stalking me.... I don't know why they don't stay away from me. I feel like, you should be happy now, I'm not living with you anymore, I'm not living with your dad anymore.' She doesn't want to involve police and does not know where to turn.

5.4.3.2 Perlah

Perlah described a similar experience to Trisha. Like Trisha she moved from overseas to marry her Australian-born partner. Perlah lived with her husband and his teenage daughter. Perlah experienced significant physical and emotional abuse from her husband and emotional abuse from his daughter. She eventually separated and obtained a protection order. After separating his daughter put insulting and rude posts about Perlah on Facebook. Perlah says the posts are embarrassing and she has shut down her Facebook account as a result. She is upset that she had to do this because this was one of the ways she communicated with her family overseas.

5.4.3.3 Jarrah

Interview 1: Jarrah reported that she had separated from her violent partner and was rebuilding her life with a new partner, Sam, and their young children. Things are going well.

Interview 2: Jarrah reported that Sam's 12 year old son Edward had come to live with them because his mother could not cope. Jarrah explained that Edward was starting fires, killing animals and hitting the young children and also abusing Jarrah 'verbally, physically, mentally' Jarrah said: 'he's fine with his father. It's me he's being abusive against and he's hoping that I might pack up and leave and take the kids with me. That way he's got his father to himself.'

Interview 3: Jarrah reported that Edward was no longer living with them. He had started throwing things at Jarrah and attacking her and had tried to strangle one of the younger children. Jarrah said she had called the police but they refused to get involved because he was too young. She called child protection services but they told her there were parents able to care for him. Eventually, as they were unable to get any support, they sent Edward back to live with his mother, who they already knew has difficulty coping with Edward's behaviour but they felt they had no choice.

5.4.3.4 Discussion: Jealousy

Trisha, Perlah and Jarrah reported that the main reason for the adolescent's abuse was their jealousy. In all three case studies the child was a step-child to the woman.

The women all believed that the child's violence was directed at encouraging them to leave. In Trisha's case the child specifically made an ultimatum that if Trisha did not leave the child would. Trisha and Perlah separated from their partners as a result of their partner's violence coupled with the abuse they experienced from their step-child. Notably both Trisha and Perlah experienced technology–facilitated abuse, for Trisha a broken laptop and for Perlah Facebook stalking leading Perlah to disconnect. The abuse disrupted their ability to communicate with their families overseas exacerbating their social isolation (Douglas et al., 2019). Both Trisha and Perlah continued to experience abuse after separation but did not take any legal action to respond to it.

Trisha and Jarrah had called the police to respond to the AFV but had an unsatisfactory response. Jarrah's experience of trying to contact child protection for support was also unsatisfactory. Trisha speculated that the family courts could have done more in her case, for example in preparing the family court report (AIJA, 2019, [10.4]) the consultant could have also talked to the adolescent children to ensure that safe arrangements were made for Trisha's child. Notably, both Trisha's and Perlah's experience was made more complex by the fact that they spoke English as a second language (Hale, 2011) and being recently arrived in Australia they had limited understanding about their legal rights (Judicial Council on Cultural Diversity, 2016, p. 7). Similar issues faced Dalila whose experience is discussed below.

5.4.4 Cultural Differences

5.4.4.1 Dalila

Interview 1: Dalila lived with her family in a refugee camp overseas for some years before the family was resettled in Australia. Dalila continues to live with her partner despite experiencing serious physical violence from time to time. She spoke about cultural conflict between herself, her children and state institutions. The police and child protection authorities have attended at her home on several occasions but have not taken any action. Sometimes Dalila's 17 year old son, Arthur, calls the police. She says:

> …it's my son Arthur, because he used to smoke inside the room, then I said you're not allowed to do that because it's a government house, he need to smoke outside. Then he started yelling. You know children in Australia they never listen to the parent.

Dalila says her son is violent towards her, but Arthur tells police that Dalila is violent to him. Many of the tensions are about her children's failure to come home in the evenings. Dalila says: 'In my country, the children can't come and go at night time. But here if they [go for two days] outside… if you said "why you come late?" then they shout and call police straight away.'

Interview 2: Her 16 year old daughter reported to the police that Dalila hit her. Dalila was charged with assault and had to go to court several times before her daughter retracted her statement and the matter was dismissed:

> Then after that I went three times to the court. Then I went they said, oh no evidence for you we need more evidence. Go back home. Then they make another one. Oh, we just need more evidence. Three times. Four times and then they just said this court is dismissed. Because no more evidence. See. Because she went back to the police. Said "I'm a liar. My mum didn't do something like that".

Interview 3: By the third interview Arthur has had his 18th birthday. The police were called to the house often by both Dalila and Arthur. The police obtained mutual protection orders and both Dalila and Arthur are now required to be of good behaviour to each other. A few weeks after the protection order was made Dalila was charged with breach of the protection order but she denies breaching it. She did not share what the breach entailed but said that eventually her son went to the police and explained that the breach incident never occurred. Dalila was very unhappy about the experience:

> That's why we are parent now we cry in the heart ... What can we do? We don't have power? Our children now come badly ... The government need to arrest me for nothing, when I'm right ... the government give more right for the children... Right now our children have freedom here... [but the children] took freedom in the wrong way.

5.4.4.2 Discussion: Cultural Differences

Past research has identified the increased vulnerability of refugee women to abuse as a result of past trauma and the challenges of resettlement in a new culture (Rees & Pease, 2006). Dalila and her children had experienced protracted stays in refugee camps and significant cultural change. Dalila experienced a sense of lack of power in responding to AFV and felt that legal systems, especially police and courts, supported her children rather than her. Dalila suggests that her children have taken hold of the freedoms available to them in Australia and used them in the 'wrong way.' Her children have also quickly developed understanding and facility with the legal system and, at least from Dalila's perspective, have used it in a way that has negatively impacted on her.

5.4.5 Mental Health/Drug Abuse

5.4.5.1 Janet

Interview 1: Janet has recently separated from a violent partner and has obtained a protection order against him. Janet lives with her 17 year old son Ryan (from a different relationship). Ryan uses various illicit drugs and this has caused tensions between Janet and Ryan. At the moment things are calm and Janet believes Ryan is currently only using cannabis.

Interview 2: Janet's son Ryan is now 18 years old and has been using the drug ice. He has smashed the walls in the house. Janet says she is scared of him: 'I was sitting on my chair. I didn't go near my son. I didn't like him smashing the walls.' Janet's sister called the police and when they arrived Janet told them she couldn't take it anymore. The police applied for a protection order and a one year order was granted. Janet explains Ryan 'is not to live at my house unless consented by me by text or email. If I ask him to leave the house he is to pack his stuff immediately and move and he's not allowed 100 m near my house unless consented by me. He has to do a behavioural course.' Janet says he needs to be taught a lesson. Ryan has also been charged with assaulting a police officer. Ryan still lives with Janet but he has been stealing her money, he knows her PIN and takes her money all the time.

Interview 3: Since the last interview, Ryan has been in hospital with drug induced psychosis: 'he's hearing voices…he won't hand me the car keys… I rang the cops'. They didn't want to help: 'I rang the afterhours number [no one] wants to help me, this kid shouldn't be on the …street. I said, he's a danger to me and everyone else. He wants to kill me at the moment.' Ryan was placed under an emergency mental health examination order at the hospital. After he settled down he came back to live with Janet. Last week the police raided the house where Janet and Ryan were living and found drug paraphernalia. Janet took responsibility for it:

> Because Ryan was having a bad time, I couldn't let the kid take the rap. [Ryan's friend] took the rap for half the other shit and then I'm just like, oh…I just - with two years off ten years clean record, I got the lowest minimum. I got $150 if I misbehave to pay fine and four months good behaviour.

Janet knew that Ryan had been selling drugs in the basement but does not feel she can stop it. Recently police raided the house again and Ryan was charged. He is now on probation and one of his conditions is that he lives with Janet.

5.4.5.2 Discussion: Mental Health/Drug Abuse

Janet and Ryan have a complex relationship. Janet explains most of Ryan's violence as being a result of his drug use. As Ryan grew older and his drug use became more problematic, Janet was increasingly willing to engage with the criminal justice system. At interview 2 her sister calls the police, at interview 3 Janet calls the police herself. At interview 2 Janet says that Ryan needs to be taught a lesson and the punitive criminal law system can do this. By interview 2, Ryan is 18 years old so Janet has access to the protection order system and the police assist her to obtain an order. By interview 3 Ryan has spiralled into drug-induced psychosis and Janet takes responsibility for a drug charge because Ryan is 'having a bad time.' Despite the violence Janet has experienced from Ryan, he is court-ordered to live with her under a probation order. She has received no support to help her cope.

5.5 What Can We Learn from the Women's Experiences?

The women's stories highlight the complexity of AFV both in how and why it is perpetrated and in the way legal responses are harnessed to respond to it. Their stories illustrate how circumstances change over time, often adding to their complexity.

Four of the eight study women were from a CALD background. Although this is a small sample, the CALD women's experiences highlight that they may be particularly susceptible to AFV. While the jealousy of step-children and issues associated with limited English-language facility and cultural transition were highlighted, so too was CALD women's vulnerability to isolation (Rees & Pease, 2006). CALD women's experience of AFV is worthy of further research.

Women did report some positive experiences of engaging with the legal system. For example police assisted Trisha to move to safety. However, overall, the women were not well-served by legal responses, reflecting the findings of previous research (Douglas & Walsh, 2018; Fitz-Gibbon et al., 2018). In some instances the legal system seemed to be harnessed to abuse them.

Three of the women were involved with the family law system (Shelley, Fiona, Trisha). All three women identified limitations with the approach of the family court. Based on what turned out to be false allegations, Shelley's children were ordered to live with their father while she was investigated. The investigation took over a year resulting in her being estranged from her older children. Due to the ages of the two older children no orders were made for them to attend counselling. Similarly, due to their older age, Fiona's sons were not included on the family court property orders that contained a condition that neither Fiona not her ex-partner could attend the house. Her sons were free to go to the house and Fiona believes one stripped the house of its contents. Trisha was disappointed that the family court report did not include interviews with her step-daughters, one of whom was abusive during and after the relationship had ended. Trisha was concerned about her sons contact visits in the presence of the step-daughter. Notably all three women saw greater scope for the family law system to provide support.

Both Dalila and Vera had mutual protection orders obtained by police. In Dahlia's case her adolescent son was the other party, in Vera's case her ex-partner was the other party but her adolescent daughter was a protected person on the order. Neither felt protected by the orders. Indeed Dahlia had been charged with a breach of the protection order and Vera was concerned she would be charged. Both Dahlia and Vera felt that their children were able to manipulate the legal system to the woman's detriment.

Earlier studies have identified that victims of AFV who are the parents or carers of the perpetrator may be reluctant to engage police fearing insufficient support or betrayal or loss of trust with the child (Fitz-Gibbon et al., 2018). Some women in this study were reluctant to engage police or if they did call them, they were provided with insufficient support or inconsistent support (Trisha, Fiona, Jarrah, Dalila). In this study two of the women turned to the criminal law system once their sons turned

18 years old. Ultimately Janet thought her 18 year old son needed to be 'taught a lesson' and Fiona was prepared to 'send him to jail'.

What is most novel in this small study is some of the women experienced legal systems abuse (Douglas, 2018) in the context of AFV. For example Shelley, Vera and Dalila reported that their adolescent children made false reports to police and child protection agencies and gave false evidence in court. Shelley, Dalila, Vera and Janet directly experienced how criminal justice responses may miscarry, criminalising them and, in effect, extending their experience of IPV and coercive control via the criminal justice system. Some studies have identified this phenomenon in the context of adult IPV (Coker & Macquoid, 2015). Notably while most studies consider how victims of AFV might engage usefully with legal responses, Shelley, Vera and Dalila highlight the problem of adolescent perpetrators harnessing the legal response unwittingly, knowingly or sometimes in conjunction with the woman's abusive ex-partner, as part of the abuse. Their stories deepen our understanding of AFV and of the potential, and risks, of engaging with law as a response.

Notes

1. This information was provided by the Queensland Department of Justice and Attorney General, 25 July 2017.
2. The study was approved by the University of Queensland, Human Ethics Committee.

References

AIHW: Australian Institute of Health and Welfare. (2019). *Child protection Australia 2017–18*. Australian Government.

AIJA: Australasian Institute of Judicial Administration. (2020). *National domestic and family violence bench book*. Retrieved from March 15, 2021 https://www.dfvbenchbook.aija.org.au/

Coker, D., & Macquoid, A. (2015). Why opposing hyper-incarceration should be central to the work of the anti domestic violence movement. *University of Miami Race and Social Justice Law Review, 5*, 585–618.

Condry, R., & Miles, C. (2014). Adolescent to parent violence: Framing and mapping a hidden problem. *Criminology & Criminal Justice, 14*(3), 257–275. https://doi.org/10.1177/1748895813500155

Daly, K., & Nancarrow, H. (2009). Restorative justice and youth violence towards parents. In J. Ptacek (Ed.), *Restorative justice and violence against women* (pp. 150–176). Oxford University Press.

Domestic Violence Resource Centre Victoria. (2010). *A coordinated response to adolescent violence in the home*. Domestic Violence Resource Centre.

Douglas, H. (2018). Legal systems abuse and coercive control. *Criminology and Criminal Justice, 18*(1), 84–99. https://doi.org/10.1177/1748895817728380

Douglas, H., & Walsh, T. (2018). Adolescent family violence: What is the role for legal responses? *Sydney Law Review, 40*(4), 499–526.

Douglas, H., Harris, B., & Dragiewicz, M. (2019). Technology-facilitated domestic and family violence: Women's experiences. *British Journal of Criminology, 59*(3), 551–570. https://doi.org/10.1093/bjc/azy068

Douglas, H. (2021). *Women, intimate partner violence, and the law*. Oxford University Press.
Downey, L. (1997). Adolescent violence: A systematic and feminist perspective. *Australian and New Zealand Journal of Family Therapy, 18*(2), 70–79.
Elliott, K., McGowan, J., Benier, K., Maher, J., & Fitz-Gibbon, K. (2018). *Investigating adolescent family violence: Background, research and directions*. Monash University, Monash Gender and Family Violence Research Program.
Fitz-Gibbon, K., Elliot, K., & Maher, J. (2018). *Investigating adolescent family violence in Victoria: Understanding experiences and practitioner perspectives*. Monash University, Monash Gender and Family Violence Research Program.
Flick, U. (2007). *Designing qualitative research*. Sage.
Hale, S. (2011). *Breaking through the language barrier: Empowering refugee and immigrant women to combat domestic and family violence through cultural and language training report*. University of Western Sydney.
Haw, A. (2010). *Parenting over violence: Understanding and empowering mothers affected by adolescent violence in the home*. The Patricia Giles Centre.
Holt, A. (2016a). Introduction. In A. Holt (Ed.), *Working with adolescent violence and abuse towards parents: Approaches and contexts for intervention* (pp. 1–12). Routledge.
Holt, A. (2016b). Adolescent-to-parent abuse as a form of "domestic violence": A conceptual review. *Trauma, Violence, & Abuse, 17*(5), 490–499. https://doi.org/10.1177/1524838015584372
Howard, J. (2011). *Adolescent violence in the home: The missing link in family violence prevention and response* (Stakeholder Paper No. 11). University of New South Wales: Australian Domestic and Family Violence Clearinghouse.
Howard, J. (2015). *Adolescent violence in the home: How is it different to adult family violence?* Australian Institute of Family Studies.
Howard, J., & Abbott, L. (2013). *The last resort: Pathways to justice*. Peninsula Health in Partnership with Victoria Legal Aid and City of Greater Dandenong Youth Services.
Judicial Council on Cultural Diversity. (2016). *The path to justice: Migrant and refugee women's experience of the courts—A report for the Judicial Council on Cultural Diversity*. Judicial Council on Cultural Diversity.
Kelly, L., & Westmarland, N. (2015). Naming and defining 'domestic violence': Lessons from research with violent men. *Feminist Review, 112*, 113–127 (2015). https://doi.org/10.1057/fr.2015.52
McKenna, M., & O'Connor, R. (2012). *Walking on eggshells…Child and adolescent violence in the family*. Flinders University, Relationships Australia, Southern Junction Community Services.
Moulds, L., Day, A., Mildred, H., Miller, P., & Casey, S. (2016). Adolescent violence towards parents: The known and unknowns. *Australian and New Zealand Journal of Family Therapy, 37*(4), 547–557.
Parkinson, P., & Cashmore, J. (2008). *The voice of the child in family law disputes*. Oxford University Press.
Rees, S., & Pease, B. (2006). *Refugee settlement, safety and wellbeing: Exploring domestic and family violence in refugee communities*. VicHealth.
Routt, G., & Anderson, L. (2011). Adolescent violence towards parents. *Journal of Aggression, Maltreatment and Trauma 20*(1), 1–11 (2011). https://doi.org/10.1080/10926771.2011.537595
Segrave, M., & Burnett-Wake, C. (2017). Addressing family violence through visa sponsor checks: A step in the right direction? *Current Issues in Criminal Justice, 29*(2), 155–165.

Taylor, A., Ibrahim, N., Wakefield, S., & Finn, K. (2015). *Domestic and family violence protection orders in Australia: An investigation of information sharing and enforcement*. ANROWS.

Thomas, K., Fitz-Gibbon, K., & Maher, J. (2019). The use of protection orders in response to adolescent family violence: Mapping divergent Australian approaches and the merits of this criminal justice intervention. *Forthcoming: Current Issues in Criminal Justice.*

Williams, M., Tuffin, K., & Niland, P. (2017). 'It's like he just goes off, BOOM!': Mothers and grandmothers make sense of child-to-parent violence. *Child and Family Social Work, 22*(2), 597–606.

Legislation

Criminal Code 1899 (Qld).

Domestic and Family Violence Protection Act 2012 (Qld).

Family Law Act 1975 (Cth).

Heather Douglas is a Professor of Law in the Melbourne Law School at the University of Melbourne. Recent research focuses on women's experience of legal engagement as part of their response to domestic and family violence. Currently, she is exploring the legal response to non-fatal strangulation. She is the project lead on Australia's National Domestic and Family Violence Bench Book and the author of many books and articles on domestic and family violence. Her most recent book is *Women, Intimate Partner Violence and the Law* (2021, Oxford University Press). Heather was appointed a Fellow of the Australian Academy of Law in 2013 and a Fellow of the Academy of Social Sciences in Australia in 2017.

Chapter 6
Missing the Mark: The Problem of Applying a 'One Size Fits All' Standard Legal Response to Adolescent Family Violence Perpetration

Elena Campbell

Abstract For many years 'child to parent violence' or 'adolescent violence in the home' (AVITH) was seen as separate to broader family violence policy. More recently justice systems have begun to impose the same legal response to adolescents using violence in their home as would be applied in the context of adult perpetration. While the experience of adolescent perpetration—both by victim-survivors and perpetrators—can be highly gendered, lessons from the 'PIPA project' (Positive Interventions for Perpetrators of Adolescent violence in the home) suggest that this issue is significantly complex. The research suggested that the blunt instruments of the justice system may cause more problems than they solve—turning victim-survivors away from help; putting children at risk of criminalisation, including those with disability; and diverting attention from what, in many cases, is the real source of violence. Accordingly, this chapter challenges the value of imposing a 'one size fits all' approach, critiquing the predominant legal response used in Victoria, Australia, and proposing options which can more appropriately address the experience of adolescents who may perpetrate—but also experience—harm.

6.1 Introduction and Background

This paper offers a critical discussion of the use of family violence intervention orders[1] (FVIOs) as the default legal response to adolescent violence in the home (AVITH) in Victoria. This discussion occurs in the context of a dynamic reform environment and a highly proactive systemic response to family violence overall, with recognition by the Victorian Royal Commission into Family Violence (RCFV) that the legal and wider systemic response to AVITH required more policy and research attention (State of Victoria, 2016a, 2016b). This recognition by the RCFV

[1] This is the term for civil family violence protection orders in Victoria and is the standard initial legal response.

E. Campbell (✉)
Centre for Innovative Justice, RMIT University, Melbourne, Australia
e-mail: elenaeve.campbell@rmit.edu.au

K. Fitz-Gibbon et al. (eds.), *Young People Using Family Violence*,
https://doi.org/10.1007/978-981-16-1331-9_6

informed the development of a multi-jurisdictional study, the 'PIPA project' (Positive Interventions for Perpetrators of Adolescent violence in the home), (Campbell et al., 2020), conducted across three Australian states (Victoria, Tasmania and Western Australia) which critically examined and compared legal responses to AVITH in jurisdictions at different points in policy and legislative development. This paper draws on the PIPA project's findings in relation to the Victorian legal response to AVITH and, in particular, its use of the same FVIOs which are used to respond to adult intimate partner violence as the predominant legal response to AVITH.

The PIPA project used a mixed methods approach, combining two primary research strands, the first being qualitative data collection via focus groups and interviews across the three jurisdictions with 157 practitioners from a wide range of service types who encountered young people and families in the context of AVITH. Across the three jurisdictions, this included police, court and legal practitioners, practitioners working in specialist AVITH and family violence services, as well as practitioners working in more universal or therapeutic service provision. In the Victorian component of the research, 82 practitioners participated in the focus groups, with some practitioners having worked across a number of different contexts in relation to AVITH. For this reason, participants were not identified by the service type in the reporting of the research except where specifically relevant, such as where they were from a legal or police background and commenting on a specific area of their practice. The second strand of data collection combined reviews of 385 legal and court case files from legal assistance and court contexts in the participating jurisdictions. Data collection was supported by a template designed to elicit the narrative behind the adolescent's experience and the impact of legal system intervention.[2] As legal and court files record some data, such as demographic data, in variable and inconsistent ways, each file was primarily qualitatively analysed, although some descriptive quantitative data were captured where it was conclusive. Varying sample sizes and strategies were ultimately data driven, given the capacity of practitioners to identify and access them and to fit the research team's capacity and project timeline. The findings reported in this paper are derived from a thematic analysis of Victorian files included in the research, with randomly selected samples from the Children's Court of Victoria (100), Victoria Legal Aid (100) and Youthlaw (25). As adolescents were the subject of some files across multiple legal and court contexts, double counts and cases which were classified as marginal[3] were excluded, with the merged sample of Victorian files ultimately totalling 139.

---

[2]Importantly, they were also designed to ensure that re-identification of information was not possible, with considerations in relation to legal information supported by Deeds of Confidentiality with the relevant organisations, in addition to approvals from relevant human research ethical review bodies.

[3]Cases were classified as 'marginal' where the facts of the case more appropriately fitted into other contexts of violence, while those classified as 'potential AVITH' remained in the sample for analysis.

6.2 Victorian Legislative and Policy Environment

While the PIPA project examined the legal and service response in three Australian jurisdictions, as noted above, this paper focuses primarily on the current (but evolving) response in the Victorian jurisdiction. This is because the use of family violence by adolescents has been identified in the definition of family violence in relevant Victorian legislation for over a decade (*Family Violence Protection Act* 2008) and has, accordingly, attracted the predominant and undifferentiated legal response to family violence over that time. For the purposes of the comparison in the wider PIPA project, this contrasts with the Tasmanian context, where legislation only includes intimate partner violence perpetrated by those aged 16 and above within its definition of family violence. It also contrasts to a lesser extent with Western Australia, which only expanded its definition of family violence to include perpetration in contexts beyond intimate partner violence in 2017.

This paper also focuses on Victoria because this state has undergone a period of unprecedented reform as a result of the RCFV and the accompanying government commitment to implement each of the RCFV's 227 recommendations. As such, the Victorian context offers a glimpse of a jurisdiction in flux, as well as one which has long been responding to AVITH as a clearly articulated concern.

To this end, since the expansion of the Victorian definition of family violence, Victoria Police data reveals a consistent pattern of identified AVITH. This includes around 10% of respondents to family violence incidents reported to police being young people aged 19 years or younger (State of Victoria, 2016b, p. 150) and seven per cent being children aged 17 years or younger (Crime Statistics Agency, 2018a).[4] Further, children 17 years or younger have represented around four per cent of respondents in family violence intervention order (FVIO) applications across the Children's and Magistrates' Court of Victoria (State of Victoria, 2016b, p. 151; Crime Statistics Agency, 2018b). This was the data relied on by the RCFV in its identification of AVITH as an issue of significant concern and in its conceptualisation of AVITH as being firmly within the remit of mainstream family violence policy (State of Victoria, 2016a, p. 149).

While the RCFV framed AVITH within mainstream family violence policy, it acknowledged that adolescents using family violence were highly vulnerable, and often reliant on those experiencing their violence for safety and care (State of Victoria, 2016a, p. 158). The RCFV also recognised that the goal of intervention should be safety for all concerned and repair, rather than termination, of relationships where possible (State of Victoria, 2016b). As such, the RCFV recommended the expansion of AVITH specific community-based behaviour change interventions, a number of which had been piloted in the Victorian context prior to that time (State of Victoria, 2016b).

[4]This is the PIPA researchers' calculations based on the figures that are published by the Crime Statistic Agency data sheet seven (Crime Statistics Agency, 2018a) from 1 July 2013 to 30 June 2018.

The RCFV also recommended the introduction of specific supports for victim-survivors and perpetrators of AVITH in Children's Court environments; the expanded use of diversionary and restorative options; as well as the introduction of specific crisis accommodation linked with therapeutic interventions (State of Victoria, 2016b).[5] Further, it recommended the inclusion of adolescent perpetration in its revised risk assessment and management framework for family violence, known as the Multi-Agency Risk Assessment and Management Framework, or 'MARAM' (State of Victoria, 2016a, p. 167).[6]

The RCFV further recognised that Victoria Police do not have the power to issue immediate police orders against adolescent respondents (known as Family Violence Safety Notices, or FSVNs, in Victoria) and recommended that this remain the case, despite their prevalent use in relation to adult respondents, and instead recommended that police intervention be accompanied by a therapeutic focus (State of Victoria, 2016a, p. 171).[7] The RCFV did not have the opportunity to explore the fact that, while the Victoria Police Code of Practice (the Code) recognises the vulnerability of adolescent respondents (Victoria Police, 2017), the Code does not go on to articulate whether or how Victoria Police should respond differently as a result of this vulnerability.

The RCFV did not explore existing tensions in relation to adolescent perpetration in terms of the imperative in the Code for police to apply for a FVIO on behalf of the victim-survivor 'wherever the safety, welfare or property of a family member appears to be endangered by another family member' (Victoria Police, 2017), leaving attending police with little discretion. Rather, the proactive Victorian response would appear to propel police to apply swiftly to a court for a FVIO where they attend a family violence incident where this has been reported either by a family member or another party, such as a neighbour, and identify an adolescent as a perpetrator, particularly in the absence of a FVSN.

The Code lists, as compulsory police action, 'making perpetrators accountable, by pursuing criminal and/or civil options where there is sufficient evidence to do so, regardless of whether an arrest has been made and/or where the [affected family member] is reluctant' (Victoria Police, 2017, p. 19). In the majority of cases applications for FVIOs are brought on behalf of family members by Victoria Police, with the Code stating that police must on no account advise family members to seek their own order (Victoria Police, 2017).[8] This translates into a consistent rate of around

[5]Important to note, the state wide expansion of specific adolescent focused behaviour change interventions and the provision of specific crisis accommodation had not been implemented at the time of writing, although existing community based interventions had received additional funding.

[6]A key principle of the MARAM includes that family violence used by adolescents is a distinct form of family violence which requires a different response. The MARAM's victim-survivor focused practice guidance, released in early 2020, also includes guidance on AVITH.

[7]This contrasts with WA, where police are able to issue immediate police orders against adolescents, including orders excluding adolescent respondents from the home. See Division 3A, *Restraining Orders Act* 1997 (WA).

[8]Again, this contrasts with WA, where the PIPA researchers heard and observed on case files that police will rarely apply for protection orders on behalf of family members and where police

70% of all FVIO applications being brought by Victoria Police (Crime Statistics Agency, 2018c).

Against the backdrop of the tension between the proactive police response and the acknowledged vulnerability of adolescent respondents, the RCFV did not have the opportunity to critique in any detail the value of imposing the standard family violence in Victoria, being a FVIO and prosecution of potential breaches, in the context of adolescent perpetration. Notably, the RCFV did interrogate the fact that the *Family Violence Protection Act* (2008) does not require any consideration of whether the person subject to a FVIO is able to understand its conditions. This contrasts with requirements in Victoria in relation to the imposition of protection orders outside family violence contexts (*Personal Safety Intervention Orders Act* (2010, ss 61(2)(a) and (b); ss 35(2)(a) and (b))). It also contrasts with the rebuttable presumption in criminal law across all Australian jurisdictions that a child aged between 10 and 14 will not have the capacity to form the requisite intent to offend (Australian Institute of Criminology, 2005).

This legislative and policy setting, combined with the broad legislative definition of family violence in Victoria, sees adolescent perpetrators of family violence captured within the standard initial legal response to family violence in Victoria. The question to which this chapter now turns is whether this is a useful approach, as examined through the findings of the PIPA project in relation to the Victorian data.

6.3 Findings from the PIPA project

6.3.1 Relevance of Data Sources

The PIPA research team embarked on the project with the aim of contributing to the evidence base regarding the prevalence and demographics around AVITH perpetration, as well as knowledge around the impacts of the legal response on adolescents and their families. Similarly, the PIPA research team expected to see a particular conceptualisation of AVITH—a primarily gendered behaviour which replicated conventional patterns of coercive control found in adult perpetration and which is referred to in various definitions of AVITH in relevant literature (Routt & Anderson, 2011; Condry & Miles, 2014; Holt, 2016; Fitz-Gibbon et al., 2018).

orders are used to remove the person using family violence in the intervening period and to give the victim-survivor the opportunity to seek a protection order on their own (Ombudsman Western Australia, 2015; *Restraining Orders Act* 1997, s 30A). By contrast, in Tasmania, where use of family violence by adolescents was not captured by family violence legislation at the time of writing, the PIPA research revealed that adolescents were nevertheless experiencing a response for their use of family violence and being excluded from their homes as a result via the use of generic (i.e. not family violence specific) civil restraint orders. In these scenarios, case files revealed that police will encourage victim-survivors to apply to a court for a restraint order in person, with this also sometimes being the *precipitating* event for police involvement in terms of criminal charges.

Instead, the PIPA team found a complexity and variation which complicated, rather than clarified, our understanding in relation to the scale of AVITH in Victoria. It also complicated our understanding in relation to the kinds of adolescents and families who were experiencing AVITH and the patterns which it followed. This complexity and variation intersected in multiple ways, making any inclination to describe 'typologies' of AVITH futile, as other studies in this area have similarly concluded (Condry & Miles, 2014; Miles & Condry, 2016).[9]

Further, the PIPA research confirmed the importance of understanding data sources—in terms of articulating or conceptualising a problem; the nature of data actually recorded; as well as in terms of developing an appropriate response (Holt, 2016; Simmons et al., 2018). This made it important to acknowledge that a large proportion of the data on which the PIPA research was based derived from legal case files (with the Victorian files relating to FVIO matters and related criminal matters) and therefore told us about the types of behaviour and circumstances which were attracting a legal response, rather than about the prevalence or phenomenon of AVITH itself.

Despite this, the research team noted that, across the overall project findings, research participants from legal settings and from wider community service provision settings reported similar patterns in relation to their client base. The primary differentiation was found in descriptions from practitioners working in specialist AVITH contexts, who tended to describe patterns of behaviour by adolescents which were more likely to echo coercive control than the patterns described by practitioners from other settings, who tended to describe contexts of intergenerational or complex trauma.

Most relevant to the focus of this paper, the variation we found on the case files and heard about from Victorian practitioners strongly suggested that those adolescents attracting a standard Victorian family violence legal response were not just adolescents at the 'pointy end' of AVITH perpetration, as a number (4) of participating practitioners labelled the more serious physical violence they saw in their client base, but simply those who had come to the attention of the legal and service system for a wide range of behaviour. Accordingly, one of the findings from the PIPA research is that police and court data may only be telling us about those adolescents *attracting a standard Victorian legal response* in the context of being identified as a perpetrator of family violence, rather than how many adolescents are actually using AVITH. This suggested that the statistics on which the RCFV and policy makers have relied may not have reflected the true nature or scale of the issue and that more detailed and nuanced data collection is required as a result.

[9]"Typologies" of adult family violence perpetration are disputed and are not appropriate for application to adolescent family violence (see Boxall et al., 2015). See also Daly and Wade (2016), who describe challenges in categorising the character of reported incidents of adolescent to parent violence used in South Australian court files they reviewed.

6.3.2 Variation in Circumstances

In particular, while the research did reveal some Victorian cases which appeared to involve the anticipated patterns of behaviour referred to above, these files also included features which complicated this analysis, such as disability and pre-existing trauma. For this reason, the PIPA team opted not to attempt a typology of different forms of AVITH. Similarly, the Victorian files also featured matters in which the behaviour, the risk of future family violence and the potential fear of the affected family members as described on the file did not appear to meet the legislative definition of family violence. This included, for example, one matter which was described in case notes by police as involving a one-off incident between teenage siblings in which they could identify no past or ongoing risk, nor fear of future behaviour on the part of the named affected family member (AFM). Despite this, police had applied for an FVIO, presumably as a result of the risk-averse imperative in the Code.

To this end, Victorian police participating in the research repeatedly referred to concerns about, as one participant described it, 'being damned if we do and damned if we don't', in terms of how they responded to police callouts. Legal practitioners (3) and practitioners from community service providers (4) specifically echoed this in their own observations. Another police participant referred to a fear of 'having to explain this to the Coroner's Court', with this concern often driving their decision making in the field. While legal practitioners across the Victorian focus groups expressed sympathy for this position, all (19) simultaneously voiced frustration that individual police did not always appear to understand the legislative definition of family violence and were consequently bringing FVIO applications which should never come to court. Where courts took a similarly risk-averse approach, this meant that some adolescents appeared to be attracting a standard legal family violence response—and being made subject to an interim FVIO with the attendant risks of criminalisation upon breach—in circumstances which lawyers, and even police, argued were not necessarily warranted.

Further to this, the case files revealed matters (29) in which adolescents had been made subject to FVIOs where concerns were expressed by parents that the driving factor behind the adolescent's behaviour was suspected mental health or alcohol and other drug (AOD) issues. This included where the case file narrative indicated a history of the adolescent having experienced family violence themselves, as is discussed further in Sect. 6.3.5, and where the subject of a dispute between a parent and adolescent then appeared to be the adolescent's use of AOD.

This finding is certainly not included to suggest that mental health or AOD issues are driving or causal factors of family violence. Rather, what it suggested to the PIPA team—supported by practitioner feedback in focus groups—was that (suspected) AOD or mental health concerns may be the symptoms of prior family violence *victimisation*, but with a standard family violence legal response then imposed upon the adolescent labelled as a *perpetrator* instead. This family violence response was then harnessed to refer adolescents to applicable mental health or AOD services. Files indicated that this either included police responding to a reported family violence incident and then taking the adolescent to a hospital emergency department for mental health treatment (3) or a Magistrate ordering participation in a mental health or AOD service as a condition of an FVIO (4). Referral pathways to mental health or AOD services were more likely to be pursued once matters tipped over into the criminal sphere via a breach of the FVIO; or where there was a concurrent criminal matter which could be used as a lever. This suggested that families had not been linked to services or supports prior to the intervention of the standard family violence legal response—with that response being used as the only mechanism available to facilitate access or engagement.

6.3.3 Age

In addition to the variation of circumstances in which adolescents were experiencing a standard family violence response when identified as AVITH perpetrators, the research indicated that *very young* adolescents were also experiencing this response. While the research team's expectation was that the majority of adolescents on case files and described by practitioners would be older adolescents, a significant minority of adolescents (47% of girls (16)) and (25% of boys (26)) featured in the Victorian data set were aged 10–14 years.

To this end, all Victorian legal practitioners participating in the research (19) criticised the absence of any requirement in the standard family violence legal response to consider whether a respondent to an FVIO had the capacity to understand or comply with the order. Two practitioners specifically described having raised this with the court and/or with police and being met with a disinterested response, while one Victorian case file indicated that the young respondent's age had been raised by a lawyer with the presiding Magistrate as relevant to the client's comprehension of the FVIO, with the Magistrate then indicating that age or capacity to understand an order would not be relevant unless the respondent attracted a criminal response upon any future breach.

All Victorian legal practitioners participating in the research similarly described or otherwise commented on the challenge of explaining to their young client what an FVIO meant and, in some cases, the fact that the order did not allow them to return home. Several (4) practitioners from other service contexts similarly described the challenge of explaining this to their client's parent, who had simply wanted the violence to stop (and had consented to their child being removed for a short time as a form of respite), but who now wanted them home where the parent knew that the adolescent was safe.

This concern was made all the more acute in the absence of specific crisis accommodation or when adolescents were likely to be excluded from any crisis accommodation that *was* available in the event that they used violence against staff or other residents. Further, the lack of any requirement in the *Family Violence Protection Act* 2008 that risk be a consideration when a court ordered that a young person be excluded from the home (beyond identification of whether the person with whom they were to reside had a criminal record) meant that adolescents were being placed in other locations without consideration of either their own or other people's safety.

For example, 31% of adolescents in the Victorian Children's Court sample[10] were excluded from their home by an interim or final FVIO, with 21% placed with their grandmother, who may then face the risk of violence herself; 12% with a separated father, who may well have been the original perpetrator of family violence; and eight per cent were placed with a girlfriend, who may then experience intimate partner violence as well.[11] While placement with family would be assumed in most cases to be preferable to out of home care, the file review nonetheless indicated that there had not been any consideration by the court of any risk to the relevant family members posed by a potential continuation of violence from the adolescent, or risk posed to the adolescent by the family member instead. This included a lack of any consideration reflected on the file about supports which may be required to ensure that the placement was functional or safe. Further, five participating practitioners echoed suggestions in existing studies that exclusion from the home could also exacerbate risk to the original victim-survivor (usually a mother), with the fragile trust in the relationship damaged by the system's intervention (Howard & Abbott, 2013). While some studies suggest that some parents find intervention or protection orders useful, particularly for the purposes of short term respite (Gallagher, 2004), the PIPA study suggests that these orders are likely to be experienced as overly punitive or unhelpful where the question of risk is not examined; and where families are not provided with support to repair relationships and recover over the longer term.

Overall, this suggested to the PIPA research team that the standard legal response to family violence in Victoria may simply be delaying, dispersing or displacing risk, rather than properly addressing it. Crucially, parents may be unlikely to call police or seek further assistance from the family violence system where they are concerned about their 13 or 14 years old (or older adolescent) being excluded from the home or risking criminal charges if they returned home.

6.3.4 Disability

Signalling similar concerns in terms of the capacity of adolescents (of any age) to understand or comply with the standard legal response to family violence was the extent to which disability—and, in particular, neurodevelopmental disorder or diversity—featured in the PIPA research. In particular, while 47.4% of the Victorian files featured adolescents who were identified as having some sort of disability,

[10]This was the Victorian sample which contained the most reliable detail about this particular issue.

[11]The location of the placements in the remainder of the Victorian sample examined was either inconclusive or not recorded at all on the file.

24% specifically featured adolescents who were identified as having a cognitive impairment or, most specifically, Autism Spectrum Disorder (ASD).[12]

Victorian focus group participants (43) similarly identified that a significant cohort of their client base were adolescents who had ASD or another form of neurodevelopmental condition which impacted their capacity to regulate their emotions or behaviour, as well as their capacity to understand or comply with the conditions of a FVIO. Further, the case file review indicated that attending police may recognise the adolescent's disability or lack of capacity upon attendance, with one file note, in particular, recording that the adolescent 'did not know right from wrong because of their disability'. Despite this recognition, police had proceeded with an application for an interim FVIO and the court had granted it. This appeared to be because of the system's focus on averting risk and on ensuring that an interim FVIO was in place as a first step.

All but one Victorian police participant (16) described their frustrations about the lack of discretion which they felt was afforded to them by the Code. Two described examples in which they had used discretion—including where the adolescent and family was already known to them. What was clear was that the standard family violence legal response was frequently being used to impose an interim FVIO (and sometimes a final FVIO) on adolescents who, not only by virtue of their age, but by virtue of their cognitive or neurodevelopmental capacity, had little to no chance of understanding what had occurred or what they were required to do.

The PIPA research team heard from a cross-section of Victorian focus group participants (21) that parents with adolescents who were using violence at home, but who had an ASD or other variation of cognitive capacity, were particularly unlikely to seek the assistance of the standard family violence response. This was in part because these parents knew that their child could not understand or comply with an FVIO and, equally, could not understand or cope with being excluded from the home, even temporarily. This parental anxiety was even more acute given that mandatory reporting requirements carried the potential of child protection intervention—intervention which was unlikely to address the violence of an adolescent, but was more likely to result in the removal of younger siblings instead. Here it is worth noting that the absence of a framework in relation to AVITH on the part of child protection authorities was a significant finding not only in the Victorian component of the PIPA research but across all three jurisdictions examined.

6.3.5 Trauma and Ongoing Family Violence

In addition to disability, the impact of trauma on adolescents using AVITH (or identified as such) was an overarching and dominant theme from the PIPA research. Certainly, prior experience of family violence and abuse amongst perpetrators of

[12]In accordance with contemporary usage, ASD includes Asperger's Syndrome. *Diagnostic and Statistical Manual of Mental Disorders (DSM-5)* (American Psychiatric Association, 2013).

AVITH is well recognised in existing literature (Campo, 2015; Cochran et al., 2011; Holt, 2013; Kwong et al., 2003). This has been described in terms of 'social learning', whereby young perpetrators replicate or 'replay' the violence and controlling behaviour which they have seen exhibited by adults in their lives, including by adopting the role of these adults once they are out of the adolescent's life (Kwong et al., 2003; Fergusson et al., 2006; Margolin & Baucom, 2014).

The link between trauma and perpetration of AVITH was the most commonly discussed theme across the focus groups, with the majority of Victorian participants (74) either overtly nominating it as an issue or concurring that it was a predominant theme which they saw in their practice. Accounts by practitioners included adolescents and children using quite severe violence against their sole parent mother or siblings after they had escaped their abusive father; as well as adolescents being 'coached from the sidelines' by a separated father to undermine or even commit family violence against their mother (Douglas & Walsh, 2018). Practitioners also described sole parents (usually mothers) attempting to compensate for their former partner's neglectful parenting in ways which were then exploited by their distressed children, or struggling amidst their own trauma to assert authority or impose boundaries. Four practitioners specifically nominated as an issue children being returned home from visits with their abusive father 'escalated' and distressed—and therefore more likely to lash out at their mothers, rather than at the original perpetrator, who remained firmly out of view (Routt & Anderson, 2011; Daly & Wade, 2016).

In addition to this 'social learning', a strong theme from the research was the impact of early childhood and ongoing trauma on children's neurological and behavioural development. Rather than simply replicating violence, practitioners across the Victorian focus groups (38) reported that their clients were just as likely to have developmental delays as a result of trauma. This in turn impacted on their capacity to learn; to regulate behaviour or emotions; and to understand or comply with standard family violence legal responses. Strong evidence to this effect led to the PIPA research team's conclusion that recognition of developmental trauma disorder (van der Kolk et al., 2009; Bremness & Polzin, 2014) was something with which the standard Victorian legal response to family violence needed to grapple, just as it needed to come to terms with neurodevelopmental disorder and diversity in adolescents, as discussed in the previous section.

The PIPA researchers heard that a lack of capacity to regulate emotions and behaviour, as well as to understand or comply with legal orders, was not limited to adolescents in this context. Practitioners (23) from different service types volunteered that parents and wider family members could similarly struggle to regulate their own behaviour and, as a result, to impose boundaries or model appropriate responses to conflict. This was particularly in scenarios where parents were also struggling with mental health or AOD issues, as well as their own experiences of trauma, whether from adult relationships or their families of origin.

Accordingly, the same cross-section of practitioners described standard family violence legal responses being used as what four participants across different focus groups specifically labelled as 'quasi-parenting tools'. This was described as particularly being the case in contexts where families were accustomed to—and therefore relatively unperturbed by—legal system intervention, with multiple family members often having 'orders' against each other in multiple directions, without these orders necessarily having any meaningful or constructive effect.

In contexts of 'co-dysregulation', as one practitioner described it, this meant that adolescents were the recipient of the standard Victorian family violence legal response in circumstances where they were not necessarily the only, or even the *predominant*, perpetrator. Rather, the research indicated that these adolescents were being identified as the target of a response designed to operate in terms of a 'victim/perpetrator' binary, rather than in terms of intergenerational trauma *and* perpetration or the complexity this combination brings.

In this regard, 11 Victorian practitioners across different service types and focus groups specifically referred to their concern that adolescents often did not feel able to voice their experiences, or to feel believed by authorities when they did. Further, the civil context in which so many matters were being heard via FVIOs (at least initially) meant that, as two Victorian legal practitioners noted, lawyers were less likely to seek instructions about their young clients' former experiences of violence, abuse or neglect. This was because civil protection order regimes are concerned with preventing future violence, rather than imposing consequences for past perpetration or offending. Accordingly, legal practitioners were less likely to seek instructions regarding factors which might mitigate sentence, such as prior experience of family violence or other forms of trauma. This in turn impacted on the extent to which these prior experiences were recorded or were otherwise apparent on case files.

Seven legal practitioners reported and five case file reviews indicated that adolescents did sometimes disclose their prior experience of trauma and family violence to lawyers, but then instructed these practitioners that they did not want this discussed in open court for fear of repercussions from their parents. This placed legal practitioners in a difficult bind as a result of their client confidentiality obligations. Combined, the scenarios described above—either of practitioners being less likely to ask about prior experience of family violence because of the civil FVIO context, or of practitioners being unable to present evidence of this experience in court when it was disclosed by their young clients—meant that adolescents were bearing the brunt of the standard Victorian family violence legal response because their experiences were less likely to be disclosed to the court.

Further, participant observations and case file reviews pointed to a small but concerning trend for FVIOs to be used as a deliberate tool by a minority of parents to perpetuate ongoing family violence against their adolescent children. In one case described to the research team, this was in the context of a mother's acute mental health issues and broader disadvantage. Across the Victorian practitioners (19) and case files (5), however, the research indicated that this trend was occurring predominantly in the context of well-resourced families, with both parents generally presenting as AFMs. As noted above, legal practitioners (7) told the PIPA research team that, where they suspected that their young client was being subject to ongoing abuse, they would attempt to have their client referred for assessment by the Children's Court Clinic. This enabled risk assessments and disclosures about experience of violence to be disclosed confidentially to the court.[13]

Far from denigrating the majority of families who come into contact with the legal system or stigmatising parent victim-survivors of AVITH, this research finding suggests that adolescents who are identified by police as perpetrators of family violence may sometimes not only have experiences of prior victimisation, but be victim-survivors of ongoing family violence at the time they are brought to court. Equally it suggests that wider family violence may be present in households which would otherwise be considered by the legal system to be protective and well-functioning—violence which had otherwise gone undetected by the system because of the specific socio-economic factors in the relevant families' lives, with them less likely to interact with service or legal system mechanisms as a result.

As this misuse of the system by a particular cohort of parents was not likely to be brought to the court's attention, the extent to which it was apparent even within the limits of legal case files examined suggested to the PIPA researchers that this may be an issue of wider concern.

Certainly, the abuse of standard family violence responses is increasingly recognised (and enacted) in the context of adult intimate partner violence, whereby adult perpetrators will attempt to 'get in first' or lodge strategic applications against the victim-survivor of their abuse as a form of further control and to deny a victim-survivor access to her children (Douglas, 2018; Mansour, 2014; Reeves, 2018). These findings from the PIPA project, however, suggest that the imposition of the standard family violence legal response in Victoria may also be colluding inadvertently in the perpetration of family violence by adults *against* adolescents and children—hardly the purpose for which this response was designed.

6.4 Options for Reform

While the PIPA project identified failures of the standard Victorian family violence legal response to address the complexity of AVITH, this did not lead the PIPA researchers to conclude that an entirely separate, or entirely non-legal, response was necessarily required. Examples across the research—both more broadly and specific to Victoria—indicated that police and legal intervention could be useful and constructive where it was delivered with requisite nuance and discretion; and where it linked families with, rather than drove families from, necessary supports.

For example, police and other practitioners offered examples in which families had sought police intervention because of very real fears for their safety—including the safety of other children in the family—which other chapters in this wider edited

[13]It should be noted here that the RCFV recommended that the availability of the Children's Court Clinic be expanded beyond criminal and child protection matters to be available to child respondents (State of Victoria, 2016a, p. 173).

collection describe. Certainly, as is the case in relation to family violence more broadly, the majority of police attendances in relation to AVITH are instigated by family members calling for assistance because they want the violence to stop, rather than because they want their child in contact with the justice system (Howard & Abbott, 2013). Where police are relied upon as the only system intervention which equates with immediate safety, this puts these first responders in the difficult situation of not knowing how to respond after the most immediate risk has abated, especially when referral or respite pathways are absent.

Similarly, the imposition of a FVIO or equivalent was described as potentially useful where contact with a court enabled adolescents and their families to be linked with appropriate services or interventions which could help to assess, manage and ultimately reduce risk and increase safety. For example, practitioners in one focus group worked in connection with a particular court which had established referral pathways to specific AVITH-focused interventions. These referral pathways were supported by and endorsed by attending police as well as the practitioners from other services participating in the specific focus group.

Further, where contact with a court enabled a family to be linked in with court-based support practitioners who could conduct risk assessments and then provide outreach support following court attendance, this was also considered to have significant potential benefit.[14] Where the standard family violence legal response enabled adolescent offenders to be linked with multidisciplinary therapeutic responses and case management, (via the state wide legislative scheme which is now in place through the Children's Court Youth Diversion scheme), this was reported to have significant benefits for the clients with whom Victorian practitioners worked, albeit in the context of the criminal justice response where an adolescent had breached an FVIO or where the matter had attracted other criminal charges.

In fact, full implementation of all of the relevant RCFV recommendations specific to AVITH—including the state wide expansion of adolescent focused behaviour change interventions and the provision of crisis accommodation linked to therapeutic treatment, as well as the inclusion of adolescent perpetration in the MARAM framework—was seen by Victorian practitioners to hold potential, particularly as the existing system was so location-dependent in terms of access to services or support.

What was clear from the PIPA research, however, was that these reforms would not be sufficient to mitigate potential harm caused by the current standard family violence legal response which, when directed towards AVITH, was often missing the mark. This conclusion led the PIPA research team to make a range of recommendations which could, if implemented, potentially improve the way in which the Victorian family violence legal response is experienced by adolescents and their families, in turn increasing the likelihood that families would seek the assistance of the family violence system.

---

[14]The introduction of Applicant and Respondent Practitioners in the Melbourne Registry of the Victorian Children's Court has been in operation since September 2018 in accordance with Recommendation 126 of the RCFV. The use of these roles is currently being evaluated by the Department of Justice and Community Safety.

6.4.1 Considering Capacity of Adolescent Respondents

Central to the PIPA project's conclusions in relation to the Victorian context, civil protection order mechanisms need to consider the capacity of adolescent respondents to understand and comply with these orders. This means that standard family violence legal responses should contain sufficient nuance to be able to take account of a respondent/perpetrator's age; their cognitive ability; and any developmental delay or impairment which has resulted from a child's prior experience of trauma. In addition, the PIPA research found that these responses should also be able to take account of the capacity of families to support the adolescent in compliance with an order, where co-occurring issues such as mental health or AOD concerns, or prior experience of trauma amongst parents, may work against a child's ability to remain, or to keep their family, safe.

Understanding an adolescent's capacity also had significant implications for 'one-size-fits-all' policing responses which do not allow for discretion in terms of whether a police member will apply for an FVIO regardless of their assessment of an adolescent's ability to understand or comply with it.

The requirement to consider capacity also has relevance for access to legal representation for adolescent respondents in the context of civil protection order applications. Although legal representation is available for adolescent respondents to FVIO applications in the Victorian context, where adolescents are not linked to legal representation and are therefore unable to provide instructions, this has implications for a court's ability to assess their capacity to understand the intervention which is being imposed.

6.4.2 Whole-of-Family Risk Assessments and Support

The PIPA research suggested that assessments of the risk posed by and towards all members in a family should be considered to ensure that a standard family violence legal response did not inadvertently collude in, or perpetuate, abuse *against* children and adolescents. This includes the extent to which an adolescent has been identified as the predominant perpetrator in a context of multi-directional and intergenerational violence and chaos; as well as in scenarios in which the standard family violence legal response is being deliberately misused by a small cohort of well-resourced adults.

The PIPA researchers found that legal advice and assistance was essential in order to facilitate disclosures. However, the project's recommendations also identify the need for specialist family violence risk assessment at the point of legal system contact so that police and courts can be informed of relevant considerations—including the extent to which the imposition of a protection order itself may *increase* risk in the short or longer term. This focus on risk across a family as a whole is consistent with the holistic and comprehensive approach to risk assessment and management developed in Victoria in accordance with RCFV recommendations (State of Victoria, 2016a, p 167).

6.4.3 Understanding How to Work with Adolescents

Essential to facilitating disclosures and identifying risk is the capacity to build trust and engagement with young people. In particular, one of the findings of the PIPA research was that the compliance based approach of the standard family violence legal response in Victoria was not equipped to work with adolescents who, because of their prior experiences of trauma or lack of service support, often had no good reason to trust an adult, or the service system overall. To this end, the benefits of outreach based service provision, as well as proactive, relationship based policing were reported by research participants and observed on some case files.

The time and incremental steps often involved in developing these relationships of trust, however, were not supported by legal responses or service interventions which operated on the basis of 'compliance' models and attendance at regular appointments. Accordingly, the PIPA project recommended an increased emphasis on outreach and longer term engagements across interventions with adolescents, including those which could be facilitated at the point of legal system interaction.

Related to the first two areas of reform signalled above, discretionary and risk-focused policing responses should also be able to work with adolescents and their families in ways which develop ongoing relationships and trust. Where police have established relationships with families experiencing family violence or wider legal system intervention, police may then be better placed to use their knowledge appropriately in terms of responding to adolescent capacity, as well as making appropriate and accurate assessments of ongoing risk.

6.4.4 Workforce Development

The need to develop discretionary and risk-focused policing responses is just one strand of the workforce development that the PIPA research concluded was required to improve the application of family violence responses to AVITH. This workforce development presents a challenge across all workforce sectors in current family violence responses. For example, the PIPA researchers heard that specialist family violence workforces outside AVITH specific contexts had trouble responding to AVITH because they were accustomed to working within firm 'victim/perpetrator' dichotomies, rather than within contexts in which victim-survivors may also be *perpetrating* violence. Practitioners reported that Victorian family violence workforces needed to shift towards seeing children as victim-survivors in their own right, in addition to recognising their strong connection to their mother's experience and trauma.

Further to this, the PIPA research found that statutory child protection responses should develop a framework for responding to AVITH which does not involve removal of younger siblings as the only option available. Families may be deterred from contacting police or engaging with family violence or other services which had mandatory reporting obligations, for fear of child removal. This was a particular concern in the context of Aboriginal and Torres Strait Islander communities, with practitioners from Victorian Aboriginal Community Controlled Organisations (3) indicating that Aboriginal families were highly unlikely to report adolescent use of violence for this reason. A further implication of the PIPA research is that standard family violence legal responses are unlikely to be appropriate in responding to violence perpetrated by adolescents with cognitive impairments, but that this was the response that families were receiving where no other service supports had been available at all. To this extent, the PIPA research noted that AVITH is just the tip of the iceberg in terms of the urgency of recognising the intersection of disability with legal system interaction (Bower et al., 2018).

6.4.5 Responding to AVITH is Responding 'Ten Years Too Late'

Perhaps of most concern in the PIPA project's findings is that the standard family violence legal response in Victoria may in many cases be failing to protect children experiencing family and other forms of interpersonal violence. Practitioners reported that the absence of adequate and sufficiently early intervention in the lives of children exposed to trauma had meant that a number of participants (9) across the focus groups, including in the other participating jurisdictions, volunteered that any intervention in relation to AVITH was intervention which was occurring 'ten years too late'.

Certainly, a failure to intervene effectively in the perpetration of AVITH by adolescents may come at a cost to the system down the track—both in terms of potential perpetration in adulthood, as well as broader justice system involvement. Research participants indicated, however, that the failure to intervene adequately in adult perpetration of family violence against children was coming at significant cost to the existing family violence system already. This included that children remained largely invisible to the system as victim-survivors as the RCFV described (State of Victoria, 2016a, pp. 129–130), only to become highly visible as perpetrators in adolescence.

This does not mean that adolescents perpetrating violence in their homes and against their families should not experience intervention or be held to account. Rather, the PIPA findings indicate that adolescents should not be assumed to be the predominant or sole perpetrator where an original adult perpetrator (or perpetrators) may well have been missed by the system and continue to remain out of view. The PIPA findings similarly indicate that the standard family violence legal response needs to come to terms with the impacts of trauma, as well as the variation in respondent capacity to understand or comply with a one-size-fits-all response.

+ Trauma is not always VIOLENCE

6.5 Conclusion

As this wider edited collection demonstrates, perpetration of family violence by adolescents is a serious concern and one which should be the subject of greater focus across family and domestic violence responses more broadly. This includes recognition of the very real fear and risk faced by many families, often in isolation. Overall, however, the PIPA project's findings suggest that it is not a useful approach simply to replicate standard family violence legal responses and impose these upon adolescents.

Rather, any meaningful attempt to respond effectively to adolescent perpetration must ensure that the mechanisms at a system's disposal—both legal and service based—have the nuance and flexibility necessary to respond to complexity and variation. Further, responses must be able to assess for and respond appropriately to risk—including risk which may be present across a whole family and which may be impacting upon an adolescent's behaviour.

In addition, family violence responses require the capacity to recognise and understand where behaviour may be being driven by other factors impacting on an adolescent's capacity to regulate behaviour or emotions, as well as to understand or comply with the legal system's expectations. As such, standard family violence legal responses must be cognisant of the palpable need for services and support amongst families who may be struggling with the impacts of trauma and disability in isolation.

Perhaps most importantly, standard family violence legal responses must make greater efforts to intervene in and acknowledge the harms of exposure to family violence in the lives of children and young people at a much earlier point. As the PIPA project findings indicate, current responses may not only be deterring families from seeking further help. Where the impacts of original or intergenerational perpetration have been missed or ignored, they may also be coming ten years too late.

Acknowledgements The author also wishes to acknowledge the conscientious work and analysis of PIPA project coordinator, Jessica Richter.

References

Australian Institute of Criminology. (2005). *The age of criminal responsibility* (Crime facts info no. 106). AIC.

Bower, C., Watkins, R. E., Mutch, R. C., Marriott, R., Freeman, J., Kippin, N. R., Safe, B., Pestell, C., Cheung, C. S. C., Shield, H., Tarratt, L., Springall, A., Taylor, J., Walker, N., Argiro, E., Leitão, S., Hamilton, S., Condon, C., Passmore, H. M., & Giglia, R. (2018). Fetal alcohol spectrum disorder and youth justice: A prevalence study among young people sentenced to detention in Western Australia. *BMJ Open, 8*(2), 1–10 (2018). https://doi.org/10.1136/bmjopen-2017-019605

Bremness, A., & Polzin, W. (2014). Commentary: Developmental trauma disorder—A missed opportunity in DSM V. *Journal of the Canadian Academy of Child and Adolescent Psychiatry, 23*(2), 142–145.

Boxall, H., Rosevaar L. & Payne, J. (2015). Domestic violence typologies: What value to practice? Trends & Issues in crime & criminal justice No. 494. Retrieved from https://aic.gov.au/publications/tandi/tandi494

Campbell, E., Richter, J., Howard, J., & Cockburn, H. (2020). *The PIPA project: Positive interventions for perpetrators of adolescent violence in the home (AVITH)* (Research report, 04/2020). ANROWS.

Campo, M. (2015). *Children's exposure to domestic and family violence: Key issues and responses* (CFCA paper no. 36). Australian Institute of Family Studies.

Cochran, J. K., Sellers, C. S., Wiesbrock, V. S., & Palacios, W. R. (2011). Repetitive intimate partner victimization: An exploratory application of social learning theory. *Deviant Behaviour, 32*(8), 790–817 (2011). https://doi.org/10.1080/01639625.2010.538342

Condry, R., & Miles, C. (2014). Adolescent to parent violence: Framing and mapping a hidden problem. *Criminology & Criminal Justice, 14*(3), 257–275 (2014). https://doi.org/10.1177/1748895813500155

Crime Statistics Agency (CSA). (2018a). *Victoria Police family violence data dashboards.* Retrieved December 20, 2018 from https://www.crimestatistics.vic.gov.au/family-violence-data-portal/family-violence-data-dashboard/victoria-police

Crime Statistics Agency (CSA). (2018b). *Children's Court of Victoria family violence data dashboards.* Retrieved December 20, 2018 from https://www.crimestatistics.vic.gov.au/family-violence-data-portal/family-violence-data-dashboard/childrens-court

Crime Statistics Agency (CSA). (2018c). *Magistrates' Court of Victoria family violence data dashboards.* Retrieved July 9, 2019 from https://www.crimestatistics.vic.gov.au/family-violence-data-portal/family-violence-data-dashboard/magistrates-court

Daly, K., & Wade, D. (2016). Gender and adolescent-to-parent violence: A systematic analysis of typical and atypical cases. In A. Holt (Ed.), *Working with adolescent violence towards parents: Approaches and contexts for intervention* (pp. 148–168). Routledge.

Diagnostic and Statistical Manual of Mental Disorders (DSM-5). (2013). American Psychiatric Association.

Douglas, H. (2018). Legal systems abuse and coercive control. *Criminology & Criminal Justice, 18*(1), 84–99.

Douglas, H., & Walsh, T. (2018). Adolescent family violence: What is the role for legal response? *Sydney Law Review, 40*(4), 499. https://www.austlii.edu.au/au/journals/SydLawRw/2018/20.html

Fergusson, D. M., Boden, J. M., & Horwood, L. J. (2006). Examining the intergenerational transmission of violence in a New Zealand birth cohort. *Child Abuse & Neglect, 30*(2), 89–108 (2006). https://doi.org/10.1016/j.chiabu.2005.10.006

Fitz-Gibbon, K., Elliot, K., & Maher, J. (2018). *Investigating adolescent family violence in Victoria: Understanding experiences and practitioner perspectives.* Monash Gender and Family Violence Program, Monash University.

Gallagher, E. (2004). Youth who victimise their parents. *Australian and New Zealand Journal of Family Therapy, 25*(2), 94–105 (2004). https://doi.org/10.1002/j.1467-8438.2004.tb00591.x

Holt, A. (2013). *Adolescent-to-parent-abuse: Current understandings in research, policy and practice*. Policy Press. https://doi.org/10.2307/j.ctt1t6p748
Holt, A. (2016). *Working with adolescent violence towards parents: Approaches and contexts for intervention*. Routledge, Taylor & Francis Group.
Howard, J., & Abbott, L. (2013). *The last resort: Pathways to justice*. Digital Reprographics.
Kwong, M. J., Bartholomew, K., Henderson, A. J. Z., & Trinke, S. J. (2003). The intergenerational transmission of relationship violence. *Journal of Family Psychology, 17*(3), 288–301 (2003). https://doi.org/10.1037/0893-3200.17.3.288
Mansour, J. (2014). *Women defendants to AVOs: What is their experience of the justice system?* Women's Legal Services NSW. https://www.wlsnsw.org.au/wp-content/uploads/womendefAVOsreport.pdf
Margolin, G., & Baucom, B. R. (2014). Adolescents' aggression to parents: Longitudinal links with parents' physical aggression. *Journal of Adolescent Health, 55*(5), 645–651. https://doi.org/10.1016/j.jadohealth.2014.05.008
Miles, C., & Condry, R. (2016). Adolescent to parent violence: The police response to parents reporting violence from their children. *Policing and Society, 26*(7), 804–823. https://doi.org/10.1080/10439463.2014.989158
Reeves, E. (2018). *Systems abuse: Research brief*. Monash Gender and Family Violence Prevention Centre. https://arts.monash.edu/__data/assets/pdf_file/0005/1529852/rb-systems-abuse.pdf
Routt, G., & Anderson, L. (2011). Adolescent violence towards parents. *Journal of Aggression, Maltreatment &Trauma, 20*(1), 1–19. https://doi.org/10.1080/10926771.2011.537595
Simmons, M., McEwan, T., Purcell, R., & Ogloff, J. R. P. (2018). Sixty years of child-to-parent abuse research: What we know and where to go. *Aggression and Violent Behavior, 38*, 31–52. https://doi.org/10.1016/j.avb.2017.11.001
State of Victoria. (2016a). *Royal commission into family violence: Report and recommendations*, Vol II, Parl Paper No 132 (2014–2016).
State of Victoria. (2016b). *Royal commission into family violence: Report and recommendations*, Vol IV, Parl Paper No 132 (2014–16).
van der Kolk, B., Pynoos, R., Cicchetti, D., Cloitre, M., D'Andrea, W., Ford, J., & Teicher, M. (2009). *Proposal to include a developmental trauma disorder diagnosis for children and adolescents in DSM-V*. Official Submission from the National Child Traumatic Stress Network Developmental Trauma Disorder Taskforce to the American Psychiatric Association. Retrieved December 20, 2018 from https://www.traumacenter.org/announcements/DTD_papers_Oct_09.pdf
Victoria Police. (2017). *Code of practice for the investigation of family violence* (3rd ed.). Retrieved December 20, 2018 from https://content.police.vic.gov.au/sites/default/files/2019-01/Code-of-Practice-for-the-Investigation-of-Family-Violence-Edition-3-V3-FINAL.pdf?_ga=2.86617435.27411390.1556498288-1868960958.1556498288

Elena Campbell has worked in legal and social policy for twenty years and was formerly a lawyer, political staffer and speechwriter. With particular experience in equal opportunity and gendered violence reform, Elena has also worked as a consultant for a range of organisations, including the Australian Human Rights Commission. Now Associate Director at the Centre for Innovative Justice, RMIT University, Elena leads a research program directed at reforming the system's response to family violence. This includes research into perpetrator interventions; work supporting the implementation of Royal Commission recommendations; and research into the response to young people using violence in the home.

Chapter 7
Understanding Child-to-Parent Homicide in the Canadian Context

Myrna Dawson and Emily Hill

Abstract Family and domestic violence research has largely examined women and children as victims although recent research has also begun to focus on women as perpetrators. Still lacking, however, are examinations of children as perpetrators of domestic and family violence. Fewer still are studies that contribute to our understanding of children as perpetrators of lethal domestic and family violence, particularly against close relatives or parents, referred to as parricide. Research in the Canadian context is largely absent, but scholarly literature draws attention to the themes of mental illness, child abuse and other forms of family violence as common precursors in other countries. Drawing from a unique Canadian dataset that spans more than three decades, this paper examines 135 cases of parricide to identify victim, perpetrator and incident characteristics, including precursors and motives as well as criminal justice outcomes. Parricides are compared using key distinguishing characteristics (e.g. sex of perpetrator/victim, relationship type) to determine variations in surrounding context and factors. Implications for intervention and prevention and priorities for future research will be discussed.

7.1 Introduction

Family and domestic violence research has largely examined women and children as victims although recent research has also begun to focus on women as perpetrators. Still lacking, however, are examinations of children as perpetrators of domestic and family violence. Fewer still are studies that contribute to our understanding of children as perpetrators of lethal domestic and family violence, particularly against close relatives or parents, referred to as parricide. Research in the Canadian context is largely absent, but scholarly literature draws attention to the themes of mental illness, child abuse and other forms of family violence as common precursors in other countries. Drawing from a unique Canadian dataset that spans more than four

M. Dawson (✉) · E. Hill
Centre for the Study of Social and Legal Responses to Violence, University of Guelph, Guelph, Canada
e-mail: mdawson@uoguelph.ca

K. Fitz-Gibbon et al. (eds.), *Young People Using Family Violence*,
https://doi.org/10.1007/978-981-16-1331-9_7

decades, this paper examines 135 cases that involved the killing of parents by children to identify victim, perpetrator and incident characteristics, including precursors and motives surrounding these killings. Whether and how Canadian parricides differ from those documented in other countries will be discussed as well as implications for intervention and prevention and priorities for future research.

7.2 Literature Review

Parricide is an understudied phenomenon (Hillbrand et al., 1999). In part, this dearth of research and attention may be attributed to the rarity of such cases or to public perceptions of parents as unworthy victims (Miles & Condry, 2015). When such killings have been studied, samples typically comprise small-scale case studies and/or clinical samples (Bourget et al., 2007; Ewing, 2000; Heide, 1993b; Heide & Petee, 2007a; Holcomb, 2000; Marleau et al., 2003; Novović et al., 2013; Walsh et al., 2008). This section provides an overview of current research and knowledge about parricide, revealing the complex nature of this violence, its lack of recognition, and the need for regional-specific data when informing effective interventions.

While the term 'parricide' was once used to describe the killing of older family members, it has come to be more narrowly defined as the killing of one's parent(s) (Ewing, 2000; Heide, 2013d; Holt & Shon, 2018), including matricide—the killing of one's mother—and/or patricide—the killing of one's father (Heide, 2013d). Other subtypes exist, including multiple parricide or double parricide—where two parents are murdered—or extended parricide—where other relatives are killed during the parricidal incident (Fegadel & Heide, 2015, 2017). These acts may occur as a single attack or stem from a cumulative history of abuse against one's parent (Holt, 2017).

This chapter adopts a broad definition of parent to include biological, step-, and adopted parents, though the focus of research has been primarily biological relationships. In addition, some publications include both parricide and attempted parricide acts in their analyses (e.g. Boots & Heide, 2006; Fegadel & Heide, 2015; Liettu et al., 2009, 2012; Shon & Barton-Bellessa, 2012), instead of only cases where a death has occurred. There is evidence that attempted parricides and completed parricides are similar in characteristics (Marleau et al., 2003). Regardless, these definitional inconsistencies are worthy of note as they may impact research results and suggested interventions.

Research estimates that between one and four percent of reported homicides in Western countries, such as England, the United States, and Canada fit the parricide classification (Boots & Heide, 2006, p. 419; Fedorowycz, 2001, p. 19; Holt, 2017, p. 572). In Canada, specifically, 3.8% of homicides between 1990 and 1999 involved the killing of parents (Fedorowycz, 2001, p. 11). However, prevalence varies depending on context. In her review of the literature, Holt (2017, p. 570) notes the heightened prevalence of parricide in South Korea where parricide accounts for five percent of the total homicides and most often involves elderly victims (Jung et al.,

2014). This example illustrates the importance of investing in research in different regions and not making overly broad generalizations on parricide findings.

The rarity of parricide should not take away from the importance of this issue. Compared to other forms of homicide, adolescent involvement in parricide is high (Heide, 1995b). In addition, while U.S. data indicate that certain forms of parricide have been declining in numbers in recent years (Heide, 2013a, 2014; Heide & Petee, 2007a; Walsh et al., 2008), parricide has been simultaneously growing as a proportion of total family homicides (Holt, 2017).

7.2.1 Perpetrator and Victim Profiles

7.2.1.1 Perpetrator Characteristics

The vast majority of parricide perpetrators are adults (Bourget et al., 2007; Buyuk et al., 2011; Heide, 1993a, 2013a, 2013b, 2014; Heide & Petee, 2007a; Holt, 2017; Holt & Shon, 2018). This contrasts available media representations of a significantly higher number of adolescent-perpetrated parricide compared to reality (Boots & Heide, 2006; Heide & Boots, 2007). When adolescents do kill, data suggest that young men typically perpetrate in later adolescence whereas young women offend earlier, in mid-adolescence (Walsh et al., 2008). Very few cases exist involving children 10 years of age or younger (Heide, 1993a).

U.S. data reveal that the average age of parricide perpetrators is between 23 and 30 years, depending on the parent type (Heide, 1993a, pp. 533–536). Children who kill fathers or stepfathers are typically younger than those who kill mothers or stepmothers (Heide, 1993a; Liettu et al., 2009). Further, children who kill stepparents are typically younger than those who kill a biological parent counterpart (Heide, 1993a, 2013a, 2014). Fegadel and Heide (2015) in their study of multiple parricide found that those who kill by themselves are typically older than those who kill with accomplices, though these results were limited by a small sample size. These findings demonstrate that while parricide is typically a crime of young adults, relationship and offense characteristics may impact perpetrator age.

The literature finds consensus in reporting parricide perpetrators of all ages as most often Caucasian (Fegadel & Heide, 2015, 2017; Heide, 1993a, 2013d, 2014; Heide & Petee, 2007a; Holt, 2017; Liem & Reichelmann, 2014; Viñas-Racionero et al., 2017; Walsh et al., 2008). In their national study of 5781 parricides over a 24-year period, Heide and Petee (2007a, p. 1389) found 70% of perpetrators to be Caucasian. However, within parricide figures a disproportionate number of Black perpetrators are also reported (Heide, 1993a; Heide & Petee, 2007a; Walsh et al., 2008).

Parricides are also overwhelmingly perpetrated by sons (Bourget et al., 2007; Buyuk et al., 2011; Fegadel & Heide, 2015, 2017; Heide, 1993a, 1995b, 2013a, 2013b, 2014; Heide & Petee, 2007a; Holcomb, 2000; Holt, 2017; Kilday, 2016;

Marleau et al., 2003; Shon & Roberts, 2010; Shon & Williams, 2013; Viñas-Racionero et al., 2017; Walsh et al., 2008). According to Statistics Canada figures, 90% of Canadian parricide perpetrators between 1961 and 1989 were men (Marleau et al., 2003, p. 269). Similarly, Hillbrand et al. (1999, p. 180) reviewed all available parricide research and found that across the literature male adolescent perpetrators outnumbered female adolescent perpetrators with a ratio of 15:1.

7.2.1.2 Victim Characteristics

When examining the characteristics of parricide victims, parents killed are typically middle-aged, in their later 40s or 50s (Fegadel & Heide, 2015, pp. 729–731, 2017, p. 14; Heide, 1993a, pp. 533–535). However, some studies have found that the mean age of parricide victims extends into their early 60s (Bourget et al., 2007, p. 307; Holt, 2017, p. 573). The age of the victim varies based on their relationship to their children. Heide (1993a, pp. 533–535) found that fathers, mothers, stepfathers, and stepmothers killed in parricidal incidents were, on average, 54, 58, 46, and 50, respectively. Thus, stepparents are typically younger than their biological parent counterparts and male parents are typically younger than their female parent counterparts (Heide, 1993a, 2013a, 2014). When young perpetrators are the sole unit of study, the age of victims naturally decreases with biological parents on average being 46 years old and stepparents 42 years of age at the time of their death (Walsh et al., 2008, p. 213).

As with perpetrators, victimized parents are most often Caucasian (Fegadel & Heide, 2015; Heide, 1993a, 2013a, 2014; Heide & Petee, 2007a; Holt, 2017; Walsh et al., 2008); however, female parents are more likely to be Caucasian than male parents (Heide, 1993a; Heide & Petee, 2007a). Once again, Black victims are over-represented when compared to population statistics and should be given consideration in safety and intervention planning (Holt, 2017).

Research findings on the typical gender of parricide victims are not consistent. Some studies assert that victims of parricide are equally likely to be mothers as they are fathers (Fegadel & Heide, 2015; Holt, 2017). In contrast, other studies claim that a majority of parricide victims are male (Bourget et al., 2007; Buyuk et al., 2011; Hillbrand et al., 1999; Marleau et al., 2003; Shon & Roberts, 2010; Walsh et al., 2008). The gender of the victim may differ depending on the characteristics of the perpetrator and homicide. Research on parricidal killers with psychotic disorders reveal that mothers are equally at risk of dying by parricide as are fathers (Marleau et al., 2003). Marleau et al. (2006, p. 324) discovered in their study that fathers were targeted more by adolescent perpetrators, but the gender segregation evened out when perpetrators entered adulthood. Daughters may be more drawn to kill their biological mothers than their fathers (Shon & Williams, 2013; Walsh et al., 2008). Whether parricides are equally distributed between male and female victims or dominated by patricide, what is clear is that fathers are at a much greater risk for lethal violence as compared to non-lethal violence against parents which appears to be a mother-targeted form of abuse (Walsh & Krienert, 2009). Overall, it can be said that parricide appears to be a crime perpetrated by adult, Caucasian sons against their middle-aged, Caucasian parents.

7.2.2 *Parricide Typologies and Risk Factors*

In her book on adolescent parricide, Heide (1995b) drew from the literature to propose a typology of the parricidal killer, providing great insight into three factors essential to understanding parental risk. This typology included: (1) the abused child, (2) the mentally ill child, and (3) the antisocial child (Heide, 1995b). In studies on cases reported in the media, it appears that over two-thirds fit into at least one of these typologies (Boots & Heide, 2006; Heide & Boots, 2007). Reflecting on her prior work, Heide (2013d) described how the typology has remained relevant over 20 years since its conception, evidenced by its applicability to cases and its use in clinical and research settings. Heide (2013d, 2017) then expanded the typology to include a fourth category: the enraged child.

Heide's (1995b, 2013d) typology has dominated the parricide literature, justifying its prominence in this chapter's review. Furthermore, family violence, mental illness, and antisocial behaviors are all individual and relational factors, perhaps indicating that extreme violence against parents is an issue arising from close, personal interactions. Supporting this contention, Diem and Pizarro (2010, p. 528) find that only 10% of parricide variation is sourced to social structure factors. Following a review of the typology of risk factors, additional risk markers that have presented within the literature will be discussed.

7.2.2.1 Child Abuse

The abused child typology suggests that some children kill to protect themselves or other family members from grave danger or because they see no other way to end the abuse (Heide, 2017). This typology category is not evenly applied across all parricidal killers. In her more recent publication, Heide (2013d) clarified that the abused child was more applicable to adolescent perpetrators. This has been reiterated throughout the literature. These children may feel hopeless and isolated before the parricide and relieved afterwards (Heide, 1995c; Myers & Vo, 2012).

Findings confirm that adolescent parricide perpetrators often experience abuse throughout childhood (Buyuk et al., 2011; Evans et al., 2005; Heide, 1994; Holcomb, 2000; Myers & Vo, 2012; Post, 1982). Child abuse in parricide cases has been differentiated from other abuse scenarios as particularly frequent and severe (Myers & Vo, 2012) with abuse commonly escalating throughout adolescence (Post, 1982). Some research indicates that over 85% of these youth experience extreme abuse, albeit based on small sample sizes (Heide, 1994, p. 154; Myers & Vo, 2012, p. 719). Witnessing family violence is also common among parricide perpetrators (Heide, 2003; Marleau et al., 2003, 2006). In some circumstances there may even be a 'family conspiracy' (Sargent, 1962) in which another family member urges the child to kill (Ewing, 2000).

The abused child typology has received mixed support. A study on multiple parricides failed to find abuse as a major theme in cases reported in the media (Fegadel & Heide, 2015). Similarly, a Canadian study found that none of the adolescent perpetrators in their sample experienced sexual abuse, but one quarter were subjected to repeated violence within the home (Marleau et al., 2006, p. 324). Accepting the likelihood of abuse as a risk factor in some cases is a valid assumption, but not that all cases of parricide involve abused children. Shon and Williams (2013) explain that sometimes parents, rather than children, are the victims of prolonged abuse before the lethal incident. Further investigation may help to clarify the prevalence of abuse in these cases and the trajectory from abused child to parent killer.

7.2.2.2 Mental Illness

Severe mental illness has emerged as a primary explanation for adult-perpetrated parricide (Bourget et al., 2007; Heide, 2013d; Marleau et al., 2006), and in particular, matricide (Bourget et al., 2007; Heide, 2017; Holcomb, 2000; Liettu et al., 2009).[1] In contrast, adolescent perpetrators are often portrayed as "normal" children, not presenting with difficulties aside from their experiences of potential violence in the home (Buyuk et al., 2011; Ewing, 2000; Holcomb, 2000; Marleau et al., 2006). It is possible that these findings are skewed from a failure to properly assess adolescent killers (Heide & McCurdy, 2010) or from assumptions that such killings are more understandable given the widespread belief that youth who kill live in abusive homes (Holt, 2017).

Proponents of this typological category argue that mentally ill children kill directly because of their illness and are often out of touch with reality, experiencing hallucinations or delusions that encourage them to use violence (Heide, 2017). Schizophrenia is a common diagnosis among this population (Bourget et al., 2007; Heide, 2017; Marleau et al., 2003). All adult perpetrators in a Canadian study, representing 40% of the total sample in the province examined, experienced severe mental illness and, at trial, were found not criminally responsible on account of mental disorder (Marleau et al., 2006, p. 324). In England and Wales, police most commonly record parricidal incidents as "irrational acts" perpetrated by delusional individuals (Holt, 2017). This label is more often used in adult-perpetrated parricides and matricides—more than six times than in general homicide (Holt, 2017, p. 576). Similarly, successful use of mental state as a defense at trial for these perpetrators is nine times that of the general homicide population in that province (Holt, 2017, p. 579).

In cases where mental illness is a major impetus in the death(s), symptoms may be evident in the weeks or months before the incident (Shon & Roberts, 2010). Presenting symptoms are often combined with additional life stresses, substance

[1] This is likely due to the fact that mothers are more likely to be the caregivers for mentally ill children.

use, and a failure to take prescribed medication (Marleau et al., 2003, 2006; Shon & Roberts, 2010). Both family and personal history of mental illness may contribute to parricide and reveal an important consideration for assessment (Marleau et al., 2003).

7.2.2.3 Antisocial Behaviour

Research examining the antisocial child demonstrates that they kill for selfish gain, undeterred by others' pain, seeking things like money or freedom which they perceive is being prevented by the parent (Heide, 2013d). Often these killers present with histories of deviant behavior and have been diagnosed with conduct or antisocial personality disorders (Heide, 2017). These parricides appear to be carefully planned and premeditated (Shon & Williams, 2013). Research finds anti-social motivations and personality disorders more common in cases where multiple perpetrators commit multiple parricide (Fegadel & Heide, 2015) as well as in cases where fathers are killed (Liettu et al., 2009). In one Canadian study, 75% of adolescent perpetrators were diagnosed as having at least one personality disorder or related traits (Marleau et al., 2006, p. 323). Other research has shown that antisocial killing is uncommon among younger parricide perpetrators (Myers & Vo, 2012).

The antisocial child categorization, perhaps more than any other, shows that Heide's (1995) typological categories are not mutually exclusive (Ewing, 2000). Children may kill for seemingly antisocial, selfish reasons when, in reality, their demeanor is a survival mechanism or biological adaptation born out of childhood abuse and mistreatment (Ewing, 2000; Heide, 1995b; Heide & McCurdy, 2010). This typology also demonstrates the importance of developmental considerations in the study of parricide. It is not uncommon for antisocial perpetrators to have developed these behaviors early in life, but have them culminate into a lethal act later in their life course (Shon & Barton-Bellessa, 2012).

7.2.2.4 Rage

The enraged child kills in an unplanned outburst of anger which may be linked to deep-seated resentment and is sometimes exacerbated by substance use (Heide, 2017); however, few studies have explicitly examined this typological group of parricide killers. Many studies have recognized arguments and disagreements between parents as antecedents to parricide (Heide, 1993a; Heide & Petee, 2007a; Holt & Shon, 2018; Shon & Roberts, 2010; Shon & Williams, 2013; Viñas-Racionero et al., 2017). Fights may trigger a response where individuals kill to protect their identity, sense of self, and social boundaries (Shon, 2012). This illustrates that parricide may involve uncontrolled anger, shifting family dynamics, and tensions across the generations (Holt & Shon, 2018).

7.2.2.5 Other Emerging Risk Factors

As claimed in the enraged typology, substance use may be a possible risk factor for parricide (Marleau et al., 2003; Shon & Barton-Bellessa, 2012). For example, in a study in England and Wales, 35% of parricide perpetrators were under the influence of alcohol at the time of the killing (Holt, 2017, p. 575). Similarly, in a Canadian study, it was found that the majority of perpetrators engaged in heavy substance use in the month prior to the parricide (Marleau et al., 2006, p. 324). In contrast, a Turkish study of adolescent parricide perpetrators found no substance use among perpetrators (Buyuk et al., 2011). To date, though, research in this area is limited and findings remained mixed.

Firearms are also an emerging risk factor (Heide, 1993b; Liettu et al., 2012; Walsh et al., 2008) given their use by parricidal killers in the U.S. and other regions where gun control policies are more relaxed (Boots & Heide, 2006; Buyuk et al., 2011; Fegadel & Heide, 2015, 2017; Heide, 2014; Heide & Petee, 2007b; Post, 1982; Walsh et al., 2008). One explanation for firearm use is the physical strength hypothesis which states that, when the perpetrator is overpowered by the victim, they are likely to use tactics which increase their ability to kill (Heide, 1993b). This hypothesis is supported by research which finds fathers are more likely to be killed with firearms and adolescent perpetrators were more likely to use firearms than adult perpetrators (Heide, 1993b; Heide & Petee, 2007b; Liettu et al., 2012). However, this hypothesis has not held true across all studies (e.g. Buyuk et al., 2011; Holt, 2017; Walsh et al., 2008). For example, research from England and Wales—where stricter gun control laws exist—revealed much lower use of firearms to commit these crimes (7%) (Holt, 2017, p. 577). Similarly, firearms did not appear to be the weapon of choice for Canadian perpetrators (Bourget et al., 2007; Marleau et al., 2003, 2006). Clearly, context is relevant for assessing risk.

The type of relationship that exists between the perpetrator and the victim may also increase risk. Research finds biological parents at a greater risk than stepparents (Heide, 2013a, 2013d, 2014; Shon & Williams, 2013; Walsh & Krienert, 2009; Walsh et al., 2008), but this can vary across certain situations. For example, a larger percentage of adolescents are involved in the killing of stepparents, demonstrating that this may be a high risk time for these families (Heide, 1993a). Further, differing parent types may impact motivations; for example, Kirschner (1992) explains that adopted children may experience unique motivations for parricide, including identity confusion and feelings of rejection.

One factor that remains unclear is previous criminal or delinquent behavior. Some evidence supports the assertion that parricide perpetrators have a history of offending (Marleau et al., 2006; Shon & Barton-Bellessa, 2012). However, other research has shown that perpetrators, and adolescent perpetrators in particular, typically have little criminal or delinquent history (Bourget et al., 2007; Buyuk et al., 2011; Myers & Vo, 2012). This may be due, in part, to shorter life course during which to become involved in delinquent or criminal behavior, but more research into this risk factor is required.

7.3 The Current Study

7.3.1 Data

The data for this study were drawn from the *Canadian Geography of Justice Initiative* which is an ongoing project that documents homicide in Canada. Data were collected from coroner's records, police, prosecutor, court, and/or media files. For this chapter, we focus on Canada's most populous province—Ontario—for which data collection has been ongoing the longest and, as such, is the most comprehensive. Focusing on the years 1985–2012, 5405 homicides were documented in Ontario. The victim-perpetrator relationship was identified in 82% of the cases (N = 4455). Of these, three percent or 135 cases involved children who killed one or both of their parents or stepparents.[2] These completed parricides are the focus of this chapter.

Below, we describe available victim, perpetrator and incident characteristics for the total sample of parricides. Next, focusing on one of the most common typologies for parricide perpetrators developed by Heide (2017), which draws primarily from U.S. cases, we examine its appropriateness for understanding parricide in the Canadian context. Specifically, where information allows, we classify each case and, consequently, describe the distribution of cases by typological category providing illustrative case examples. Finally, we explore differences in key characteristics, including typological distributions, across parricides using the following comparisons: (1) minor child and adult child perpetrators; (2) female and male parricide perpetrators; (3) single and multiple victim parricide cases; (4) matricide and patricide; and, finally, (5) biological and stepparents. With respect to the first comparison, each province and territory in Canada decides the age at which a child becomes an adult or what is referred to as the 'age of majority'. Six provinces currently define the age of majority as 18 years of age and the remaining jurisdictions designate 19 years of age. We adopt the higher range with '18 years or younger' capturing minor children in this study.[3] The remaining comparisons are self-explanatory. We conclude by summarizing how parricides in Canada—using Ontario as a case study—appear to differ from those documented in other research, primarily US-based studies. We discuss implications of these findings as well as priorities for future research.

[2]This is lower than the national average which was, on average, 5.8% from 2007 to 2016 (Beattie et al., 2018); however, it is consistent with earlier official figures of 3.8% between 1990 and 1999 (Fedorowycz, 2001, p. 11). These variations might be expected, then, given that we focus on only one province over a longer and slightly different time period than the more recent figures.

[3]For more information, see https://www.canada.ca/en/immigration-refugees-citizenship/services/study-canada/study-permit/prepare/minor-children.html#toc1.

7.3.2 Variables

Drawing from prior research, we examine the relationship between the perpetrator and victim (i.e. biological or stepparent) as well as gender, age, race/ethnicity of victims and perpetrators and prior criminal record for the perpetrator. We also examine situational factors: the number of victims killed, substance use by the victim and/or perpetrator, whether the killing was premeditated, the method of killing (including the role of firearms), and location of the killing. Next, considering Heide's (2017) parricide typology, we examine the role of child abuse, mental illness, anti-social behaviour, and rage as precursors or motivations for these killing across all perpetrators and, then, by the five comparisons that distinguish characteristics of the parricide as discussed above.

7.3.3 Results

Table 7.1 shows the distribution of perpetrator, victim, and incident characteristics for the total sample (N = 135).[4] First, consistent with prior research, most parricides in Ontario were perpetrated by children against their biological parent(s) (93%) with the remaining cases involving stepparents (7%). Parricides were overwhelmingly committed by sons (93%) compared to daughters (7%), also consistent with the research summarized above. In Ontario, there was a larger proportion of older perpetrators than other, primarily U.S., studies. Specifically, the average age of perpetrators in our sample was 31 years compared to average ages that were between 23 and 30 years of age in other research (Heide, 1993a, pp. 533–536). The age of Ontario perpetrators ranged from 14 to 68 years old with most being adult children (90%). We will return to a comparison of minor and adult parricide cases later in this chapter.

Information for perpetrator race/ethnicity and prior criminal record is missing in a high proportion of cases. Reported distributions are based on cases where information was available and, as such, findings should be considered tentative and exploratory. In the Ontario sample, where information was available (34% of the cases), well over half of the perpetrators were Caucasian/white (52%), and the next largest race/ethnic category was Black (28%), followed by Indigenous (9%). Where information was available (43% of the cases), more than one third of the perpetrators (36%) had a prior criminal record of which 16% had a prior record for violence. Another three percent had charges pending. 2016 Census data from Statistics Canada indicates that Indigenous peoples are approximately 5% of the Canadian population, while 22% of Canadians identified as people of colour. Those identifying as Black account for 3.5% of the Canadian population.

[4]Percentages and raw numbers provided in Table 7.1 because small numbers can sometimes misrepresent percentage differences. Some variables have a high proportion of missing information as noted.

Table 7.1 Perpetrator, victim and incident characteristics for parricides in Ontario, 1985–2012 (N = 135)[5]

Variable	Total sample
	100% (n = 135)
Perpetrator-victim relationship	
Biological parent	93 (126)
Perpetrator characteristics	
Male perpetrator	93 (125)
Age (mean)	31 years
Adult child	90 (122)
Caucasian[6]	52 (24)
Prior criminal record[7]	36 (21)
Victim characteristics	
Female victim	56 (75)
Age (mean) 31–56	59 years
Race/ethnicity[8]	57
Situational characteristics	
Two or more victims	19 (26)
Perpetrator substance use[9]	62 (24)
Victim substance use[10]	25 (16)
Killing premeditated[11]	40 (21)
Primary method: stabbing	40 (48)
Firearms used	19 (23)
Killing in home of victim[12]	92 (109)
Case outcome	
Suicide	10 (12)
Murder conviction[13]	31 (28)
Manslaughter conviction	18 (16)
NGRI/NCRMD[14]	49 (42)

[5] Both percentage and numbers are provided because small numbers can misrepresent proportions that have specific characteristics. Some variables have a high proportion of missing data. Valid percent reported.

[6] Information is based on cases for which information was available (34%).

[7] Information is based on cases for which information was available (43%).

[8] Information is based on cases for which information was available (34%).

[9] The figure refers to overall substances use by perpetrators.

[10] The figure refers to overall substances use by victims.

[11] Percent rather than valid percent used because of the high proportion of missing cases (69%).

[12] This includes homes shared by the victim and the perpetrator and homes of the victim only.

[13] Based on 91 cases for which information was available and excludes cases in which the perpetrator died by suicide.

[14] Prior to 1992 the verdict was 'not guilty by reason of insanity'. Currently, the verdict is 'not criminally responsible by reason of mental disorder'.

Turning to victim characteristics, research findings on the gender of parricide victims lack consensus as noted. Some studies assert that victims of parricide are equally likely to be mothers or fathers (Fegadel & Heide, 2015; Holt, 2017) whereas other studies claim that the majority of parricide victims are male (Bourget et al., 2007; Buyuk et al., 2011; Hillbrand et al., 1999; Marleau et al., 2003; Shon & Roberts, 2010; Walsh et al., 2008). In Ontario, contrary to both documented patterns, the proportion of female victims—mothers—is higher (56%) than male victims (44%). Victim ages ranged from 31 to 94 years old in our sample with an average age of 59 which is, again, slightly higher than U.S. research which showed that victims were typically middle-aged, defined as late 40s or 50s. As with perpetrators, victim age will vary depending on gender of the victim and perpetrator and their relationship—an issue we will come back to below.

Given that most of the relationships in this sample are biological parents and children, it is expected that, where information is known (34% of the cases), race/ethnic distributions would be similar for victims and perpetrators, impacted only by whether the cases involving stepparents were intra- or inter-racial. That proved to be the case with well over one half of the victims being Caucasian/white perpetrators (57%). The next largest group of victims were Black (30%).[15]

With respect to the incidents, while typically singe-victim cases, Table 7.1 shows that one in five cases involved multiple victims (19%) and, specifically, two victims (13%), three victims (3%) and four victims (3%). As noted above, while substance use has been identified as a possible risk factor for these crimes (Marleau et al., 2003; Shon & Barton-Bellessa, 2012), there is no consistency in findings. In our sample, this information was missing for victims in over one-half of the cases (53%) and, for perpetrators, in over 70% of the cases. When it was noted, however, overall substance use at the time of the killing was significantly more likely for perpetrators (62%) than victims (25%). Furthermore, alcohol was more commonly documented for both victims (21%) and perpetrators (39%) compared to other substances (3% and 13% respectively).

While it is often difficult to determine if a killing was pre-planned, information was available in almost 40% of the cases to assess the role of premeditation. Focusing on this group of parricides, there was 'some evidence of premeditation' in 40% of these cases and 'clear evidence of premeditation' in 25% of the cases. Where information was known (90%), the most common method children used to kill their parent(s) was stabbing (40%) followed by beatings (29%) and shootings (19%). The remaining methods involved strangulation, suffocation, drowning, poison, and/or neglect. As such, it appears that Canada falls in line with those countries where firearms were not commonly used by homicide perpetrators, including those who commit parricide. It has been argued that the lower proportion of shooting deaths might be attributed to stricter gun controls, at least compared to the US, which may be relevant in the Canadian context (Bourget et al., 2007; Marleau et al., 2003, 2006). Where information was known (88% of the cases), the largest group of parricides

[15]Information for prior criminal record of the victim was missing in almost 80% of the cases and, therefore, was not examined.

occurred in a home shared by the perpetrator and the victim (64%) followed by the home of the victim (28%). The remaining killings took place in businesses, park/outdoor location, institution, or on the street.

Finally, with respect to case outcomes, about one in every 10 perpetrators died by suicide following the parricide. Of those who did not, and were subject to criminal prosecution, almost one-half (49%) were found not criminally responsible by reason of mental defect. The majority of the remainder were found guilty of murder (31%), either first- (8%) or second-degree (23%), or manslaughter (18%).

In summary, then, consistent with prior research, Ontario parricides were most often perpetrated by adult, Caucasian sons against their late middle-aged, Caucasian, biological parents. In Ontario, however, mothers were more often killed by their children than fathers. Finally, the largely single-victim cases typically involved more proximate methods to kill (i.e. stabbings and beatings) and most often occurred in the home of the victim and/or the perpetrator. There were a variety of case outcomes, the largest group of which saw the perpetrator found not criminally responsible.

Below, we turn to an examination of precursors and motives for these killings by examining the utility of Heide's typology for understanding parricide perpetrators in a Canadian province.

7.3.3.1 A Typology of Parricides in the Canadian Context

To examine the underlying precursors and motivations behind the Ontario parricides, we examined in detail the case narratives as described by media and court document with the goal of classifying each case, where possible, into one of Heide's four perpetrator categories: severely abused, severely mentally ill, dangerously anti-social, and enraged. We were able to do so with some confidence based on available information in 57% of the cases (N = 77). These perpetrators are the focus of this analysis. In eight of these cases, more than one category was relevant and, therefore, we coded two or more typological categories where appropriate. As a secondary goal, we also examine whether the precursor or motive varied by five key characteristics of the killings. Because 43% of the cases were excluded due to lack of information, any patterns described below should be considered tentative only.

Table 7.2 shows that over one half of the perpetrators who could be categorized fell into the severely mentally ill group (52%). The next most common category was the enraged perpetrator which comprised 34%. Representing only a small proportion of perpetrators were the several abused offenders (8%) and the dangerously anti-social offenders (7%). We acknowledge that it is often difficult to make conclusions about precursors or motives based on media reports; however, these reports often include court coverage. Furthermore, given increasing reliance on digital forms of media that are more readily accessible, recent research shows that newspaper coverage was found to be as informative, and often more so, than official data for various characteristics (e.g. gender, age, race/ethnicity) when reported, and victim-perpetrator relationship (Heide & Boots, 2007; Parkin & Gruenewald, 2017). Below, despite the dominance of adult, biological, male children as perpetrators in cases of parricide,

Table 7.2 Distribution of typological category for parricide in Ontario, 1985–2012 (N = 77)

Typological category	Total sample
	100% (N = 77)
Severely abused perpetrator[16]	8% (6)
Severely mentally ill perpetrator[17]	52% (40)
Dangerously anti-social perpetrator[18]	7% (5)
Enraged perpetrator	34% (26)

we tease out any differences in these killings when perpetrated by minor children, stepchildren, and female perpetrators or across mother or fathers and multiple victims are involved. We provide short narratives for some cases to illustrate the context surrounding these killings in more depth.

7.3.3.2 Comparing Minor-Child and Adult-Child Perpetrators

As noted above, most parricide perpetrators are adult children (90%); thus, when comparing older and younger killers, there are few cases involving those aged 18 and younger (N = 13) with which to compare to the larger, adult children group. Of course, their mean ages will differ by definition with the average age for minor children being 16 years old and the average age for adult children at 33 years of age. Similarly, the mean ages of their victims will also differ by definition with the average age of victims killed by minor children at 46 years old compared to victims killed by adult children at 61 years old.

Some other tentative findings require more research to specifically examine these characteristics and/or drawing on larger samples. First, patterns in the total sample of Ontario cases demonstrated that minor children were more likely to pre-plan the parricide (31%) compared to adult children (14%).[19] Second, minor children were more likely to stab their parent (69%) than were adult children (36%). Finally, looking at the smaller group of cases (N = 77) for which we were able to assign a typological category for parricide, it was not surprising that we were able to classify only three cases involving minor children given it is often difficult to get information on cases involving young offenders.[20] However, in the three cases we were able to classify,

[16]This was a secondary motive in three cases; 12% (9).

[17]This was a secondary motive in three cases; 56% (43).

[18]This was a secondary motive in one case and a third motive in another case; 9% (7).

[19]We remind readers that smaller numbers will misrepresent some of these patterns. For example, 31% of the minor children category is four cases compared to 17 cases which comprises the 14% of the adult children sample. Regardless, there is some evidence that the former may be more premeditated than the latter which has some implications for prevention.

[20]The Youth Criminal Justice Act is the law that governs Canada's youth justice system and applies to youth that are at least 12 but under 18 years of age who are alleged to have committed criminal offences. As a general rule, the identity of a young person should be protected which typically requires that there is a ban on publication of identifying information and access to information

three of the four categories were represented with only 'enraged perpetrator' not being represented. Given the dominance of adult child perpetrators, their distributions were the same as the sample as a whole.

7.3.3.3 Comparing Biological Parents and Stepparents

As noted, only nine of the 135 parricide cases in this sample involved stepparents. And, while patterns did not vary significantly between these cases and those involving biological parents, some differences were evident. First, despite female victims being more common than male victims in the total sample, only two (22%) of the seven stepparent victims were female compared to 58% of the biological parents being mothers. In other words, in Ontario, fathers were more likely to be victims of stepchildren than mothers. The opposite is true for biological children. Second, prior research has noted that children who kill stepparents were typically younger than those who killed biological parent counterparts (Heide, 1993a, 2013a, 2014). Similarly, in Ontario, the average age of perpetrators who killed their stepparents was 25 years compared to 32 years for children who killed biological parents. Third, research found that stepparents were typically younger than their biological parent counterparts and this was consistent with Ontario findings as well with the average age of stepparents at 53 years old compared to 60 years of age for biological parents. Finally, when examining the typology of parricide among stepparent parricide, in contrast to the role of mental illness in the biological parent group, there were no perpetrators classified as mentally ill among stepchildren. The severely abused (N = 2) and the enraged perpetrator (N = 2) were the most common. The remaining five cases did not have enough information to categorize.

7.3.3.4 Comparing Female and Male Perpetrators

Little research has compared the difference between female and male parricide perpetrators perhaps because there are so few female-perpetrated parricide cases. For example, in the Ontario sample, males outnumbered female perpetrators by over 12:1. Given the small numbers in the female group, and missing information for some variables, where possible, we identify differences between the female- and male-perpetrated parricides.

Average age of perpetrators or victims did not differ across the gender of the perpetrator; however, female perpetrators were more likely to kill mothers (70%) compared to male perpetrators (54%). Female perpetrators only killed single victims whereas male perpetrators killed multiple victims in 21% of the cases. They were

---

is restricted. This would influence the media coverage as well as the availability of public court documents. For more information, see https://www.justice.gc.ca/eng/cj-jp/yj-jj/tools-outils/back-hist.html.

equally likely to stab (33%) and beat (33%) their victims compared to male perpetrators who were more likely to stab (40%) their victims. Of the five cases involving female perpetrators for which we could assign a typological category, two were severely mentally ill, and each of the other three female perpetrators represented each of the remaining three categories. Given the dominance of male perpetrators, their distributions were similar to the sample as a whole.

7.3.3.5 Comparing Single-Victim and Multiple-Victim Parricide

All multiple-victim parricides involved biological parents and children and, as already noted above, male perpetrators. Male victims—fathers—were more often killed (63%) in multiple victim cases than were female victims or mothers (38%), contrary to the distribution of victim gender in the total sample where mothers outnumbered fathers. While firearms-related parricides were lower than stabbings and beatings overall, when examining multiple-victim parricides, shootings (43%) were more common than stabbings and beatings (29% each).

7.3.3.6 Comparing Matricide and Patricide

Some parricide studies have shown that female parents killed by their child are more likely to be Caucasian than male victims of parricide (Heide, 1993a; Heide & Petee, 2007a) and, while information is missing in the majority of cases, where available, Ontario patterns were similar. Specifically, female victims of parricide were Caucasian/white in 52% of the cases compared to 35% of the cases for male victims.

Matricides were more likely to be single-victim cases compared to patricides. When information was available, perpetrators in patricides were more likely to have been using alcohol and/or drugs (79%) compared to perpetrators in matricides (45%). Similarly, male victims were more likely (44%) than female victims (13%) to be using substances. In short, male perpetrators who killed male victims were the most likely to be using substances at the time of the killings.

The most common perpetrator typology for matricide was severely mentally ill (60%) followed by enraged (33%) which was similar to patricides with severely mentally ill (41%) followed by enraged (34%). However, there was higher representation of severely abused (19%) among patricides compared to matricides which did not present as a typological category. Dangerously anti-social was equally represented across matricides and patricides among the cases where information was available.

7.4 Interventions and Suggested Actions

While there were many similarities in parricide cases in Ontario compared to prior research, two differences were documented. First, there was a larger proportion of older perpetrators and victims in the Ontario sample compared to other, primarily U.S., studies. Second, the proportion of female victims—mothers—was significantly higher than male victims in the Canadian sample. In addition, when comparing parricides that differed across key characteristics (e.g. gender of perpetrator and victim, biological vs. step-relationships), some interesting patterns emerged that warrant further research, including: (1) Stepfathers were more likely to be victims of stepchildren than stepmothers; (2) No stepchild perpetrators were classified as mentally ill; (3) Female perpetrators killed single victims only whereas male perpetrators killed multiple victims in 21% of the cases; (4) Male victims or fathers were more often killed (63%) in multiple victim cases than were female victims or mothers (5) While firearms-related parricides were lower than stabbings and beatings overall, when examining multiple-victim parricides, shootings (43%) were more common than stabbings and beatings (29% each). We discuss these in more detail below as we discuss future areas of focus and priorities for research and practice.

7.4.1 Areas of Focus for Intervention

The parricide literature, including this chapter, identifies a range of risk factors and considerations that should inform interventions for children at risk of perpetrating parricide. There is particular support in the literature for available and accessible services tailored to meet the needs of children who have experienced abuse and those living with mental illness (Bourget et al., 2007; Buyuk et al., 2011; Diem & Pizarro, 2010; Evans et al., 2005; Fegadel & Heide, 2015; Heide, 1995a, 2013c; Liettu et al., 2009; Marleau et al., 2003; Post, 1982). The latter appears to be particularly relevant in the Canadian context given the high proportion of perpetrators who had some type of mental illness. However, our research, and other studies (Holt, 2017) have shown that many incidents are not caused by mental illness alone; thus, it is important that perpetrators of parricide are not pathologized (Shon & Williams, 2013).

Further, interventions must serve both adult and adolescent populations given both are represented among parricide perpetrators (Fegadel & Heide, 2015) and perhaps a greater recognition that adult children are the most common perpetrators of parricide is needed. Strategies should be tailored to the type of perpetrator to best address their needs and challenges and, while age is one factor, other characteristics are also key such as type of relationship and gender combination of the perpetrator and the victims. There are additional opportunities for intervention post-parricide in the form of mental health treatment and assessment, skills training, substance abuse treatment, as well as integrative, family, or biologically-informed therapy (Heide, 2013c, 2017; Heide & Solomon, 2013; McCann & Solomon, 1995). There are indications that parricide perpetrators, and adolescent perpetrators in particular, are capable of successful rehabilitation and re-entry into society (Hillbrand et al., 1999; McCann & Solomon, 1995), suggesting that interventions and supports should not be solely targeted to pre-parricide prevention.

7.4.2 Risk Assessment

Parricide, at times, seems unpredictable (Bourget et al., 2007; Ewing, 2000), particularly with adolescent killers (Evans et al., 2005; Marleau et al., 2006). Yet many at-risk perpetrators are in contact with health professionals or the education system prior to their crime (Ewing, 2000; Marleau et al., 2003; Post, 1982; Walsh et al., 2008). These frontline services provide the opportunity to offer supports, assess risk, and safety plan (Ewing, 2000; Heide & Petee, 2007a; Marleau et al., 2003; Viñas-Racionero et al., 2017; Walsh et al., 2008; West & Feldsher, 2010). Therefore, attention could be targeted to developing a validated risk assessment tool because this type of specific resource is not yet available (Evans et al., 2005; Ewing, 2000). In addition to increased awareness of risk factors for these types of killings, there is evidence that at least some of the incidents are preceded by threats, disclosures of intent to kill, or victim disclosure of fear (Bourget et al., 2007; Ewing, 2000; Liettu et al., 2009; Marleau et al., 2003, 2006; Viñas-Racionero et al., 2017). Thus, homicidal ideation and related vocalizations must be taken seriously (Bourget et al., 2007; Evans et al., 2005; Ewing, 2000; Liettu et al., 2009; Marleau et al., 2003, 2006; Viñas-Racionero et al., 2017).

7.4.3 Policy

How policies can work to increase or decrease family stress and conflict is another important consideration (Holt, 2017). Child-to-parent abuse is often focused on individuals, failing to look at the broader socio-political climate that may impact violence (Holt, 2012). Ways to reduce the reluctance to report such abuse as well as the barriers to service that often accompany family violence and mental illness should be explored, opening up a dialogue on how families can secure supports (Heide, 2013c; Marleau et al., 2003; Mass et al., 1984; Post, 1982). Though not as relevant within the Canadian context, the large number of cases where parents die by firearms should encourage jurisdictions to rethink gun control policies (Heide, 1993b; Heide & Petee, 2007b; Liem & Reichelmann, 2014; Liettu et al., 2012; Walsh et al., 2008). Strategies that have been successful in putting domestic violence onto the policy agenda may also be worth exploration (Holt, 2017).

7.4.4 Future Research

Further research on parricide, across disciplines, is encouraged (Holt, 2012). A number of topics including criminal justice outcomes, support post-offense, and comparisons between subgroups of perpetrators and victims present opportunities for greater investigation (Diem & Pizarro, 2010; Heide, 2017; Marleau et al., 2003; Wasarhaley et al., 2013). Prior studies demonstrate that characteristics do distinguish adult- and adolescent-perpetrated parricide and, thus, research which disaggregates cases by age and examines their unique properties would be insightful (Heide, 1995b).

To date, parricide research has been conducted primarily in the U.S. (Holt, 2017; Kilday, 2016). While this research has merit, it is important to understand parricide and parent abuse in varying contexts with different social and political climates (Holt, 2012). Culture, history, time, and geography may have an immense impact on research findings (Diem & Pizarro, 2010; Kilday, 2016; Muravyeva, 2016; Shon & Williams, 2013; Walker, 2016). Few studies have included Canadian data in their analyses. Furthermore, to our knowledge there have not been any in-depth studies on parricide undertaken in Canada's most populous province, Ontario. This study fills this gap by analyzing 148 cases of parricide across four decades within that province. It also addresses calls for larger, non-clinical studies of parricide (Fegadel & Heide, 2017; Heide, 2013a; Myers & Vo, 2012; Walsh et al., 2008). This study contributes to the knowledge base on parricide, examine the applicability of previous findings within the Canadian context, and provides clues for best practices within the region and beyond.

References

Beattie, S., David, J.-D., & Roy, J. (2018). *Homicide in Canada, 2017*. Juristat Catalogue no. 85-002-X.

Boots, D. P., & Heide, K. M. (2006). Parricides in the media: A content analysis of available reports across cultures. *International Journal of Offender Therapy and Comparative Criminology, 50*(4), 418–445. https://doi.org/10.1177/0306624X05285103

Bourget, D., Gagné, P., & Labelle, M.-E. (2007). Parricide: A comparative study of matricide versus patricide. *Journal of the American Academy of Psychiatry and the Law, 35*(3), 306–312. https://citeseerx.ist.psu.edu/viewdoc/download?doi=10.1.1.549.5897&rep=rep1&type=pdf

Buyuk, Y., Kurnaz, G., Eke, S. M., Ankarali, H. C., & Oral, G. (2011). Medico-legal evaluation of adolescent parricide offenders: Thirty nine cases from Turkey. *Journal of Family Violence, 26*(1), 1–7. https://doi.org/10.1007/s10896-010-9336-2

Diem, C., & Pizarro, J. M. (2010). Social structure and family homicides. *Journal of Family Violence, 25*(5), 521–532. https://doi.org/10.1007/s10896-010-9313-9

Evans, T. M., McGovern-Kondik, M., & Peric, F. (2005). Juvenile parricide: A predictable offense? *Journal of Forensic Psychology Practice, 5*(2), 31–50. https://doi.org/10.1300/J158v05n02_02

Ewing, C. P. (2000). Parricide. In G.-F. Pinard & L. Pagani (Eds.), *Clinical assessment of dangerousness: Empirical contributions* (pp. 181–194). Cambridge University Press.

Fedorowycz, O. (2001). Homicide in Canada—2000. *Juristat, 21*. Catalogue no. 85-002-XPE.

Fegadel, A. R., & Heide, K. M. (2015). Double parricide: An in-depth look at two victim homicides involving parents as victims. *Behavioral Sciences and the Law, 33*(6), 723–729. https://doi.org/10.1002/bsl.2189

Fegadel, A. R., & Heide, K. M. (2017). Offspring-perpetrated familicide: Examining family homicides involving parents as victims. *International Journal of Offender Therapy and Comparative Criminology, 61*(1), 6–24. https://doi.org/10.1177/0306624X15589091

Heide, K. M. (1993a). Parents who get killed and the children who kill them. *Journal of Interpersonal Violence, 8*(4), 531–544. https://doi.org/10.1177/088626093008004008

Heide, K. M. (1993b). Weapons used by juveniles and adults to kill parents. *Behavioral Sciences and the Law, 11*(4), 397–405. https://doi.org/10.1002/bsl.2370110407

Heide, K. M. (1994). Evidence of child maltreatment among adolescent parricide offenders. *International Journal of Offender Therapy and Comparative Criminology, 38*(2), 151–162.

Heide, K. M. (1995a). Society's role. In *Why kids kill parents: Child abuse and adolescent homicide* (pp. 151–162). Sage. https://doi.org/10.4135/9781483327174.n11

Heide, K. M. (1995b). The phenomenon of parricide. In *Why kids kill parents: Child abuse and adolescent homicide* (pp. 3–18). Sage. https://doi.org/10.4135/9781483327174.n1

Heide, K. M. (1995c). Which youths kill. In *Why kids kill parents: Child abuse and adolescent homicide* (pp. 33–43). Sage. https://doi.org/10.4135/9781483327174.n3

Heide, K. M. (2003). Youth homicide: A review of the literature and a blueprint for action. *International Journal of Offender Therapy and Comparative Criminology, 47*(1), 6–36. https://doi.org/10.1177/0306624X02239272

Heide, K. M. (2013a). Matricide and stepmatricide victims and offenders: An empirical analysis of U.S. arrest data. *Behavioral Sciences and the Law, 31*(2), 203–214. https://doi.org/10.1002/bsl.2056

Heide, K. M. (2013b). Parricide: Basic facts and literature. In *Understanding parricide: When sons and daughters kill parents* (pp. 47–73). Oxford University Press. https://search.ebscohost.com.subzero.lib.uoguelph.ca/login.aspx?direct=true&db=nlebk&AN=604143&site=ehost-live&scope=site

Heide, K. M. (2013c). Risk assessment and prevention. In *Understanding parricide: When sons and daughters kill parents* (pp. 355–370). Oxford University Press. https://doi.org/10.1093/acprof:oso/9780195176667.001.0001

Heide, K. M. (2013d). The phenomenon of parricide. In *Understanding parricide: When sons and daughters kill parents* (pp. 3–26). Oxford University Press. https://doi.org/10.1093/acprof:oso/9780195176667.001.0001

Heide, K. M. (2014). Patricide and steppatricide victims and offenders: An empirical analysis of U.S. arrest data. *International Journal of Offender Therapy and Comparative Criminology, 58*(11), 1261–1278. https://doi.org/10.1177/0306624X13495168

Heide, K. M. (2017). Parricide encapsulated. In F. Brookman, E. R. Maguire, & M. Maguire (Eds.), *The handbook of homicide* (pp. 197–212). Wiley-Blackwell. https://doi.org/10.1002/9781118924501

Heide, K. M., & Boots, D. P. (2007). A comparative analysis of media reports of U.S. parricide cases with officially reported national crime data and the psychiatric and psychological literature. *International Journal of Offender Therapy and Comparative Criminology, 51*(6), 646–675. https://doi.org/10.1177/0306624X07302053

Heide, K. M., & McCurdy, J. (2010). Juvenile parricide offenders sentenced to death. *Victims and Offenders, 5*(1), 76–99. https://doi.org/10.1080/15564880903048545

Heide, K. M., & Petee, T. A. (2007a). Parricide: An empirical analysis of 24 years of U.S. data. *Journal of Interpersonal Violence, 22*(11), 1382–1399. https://doi.org/10.1177/0886260507305526

Heide, K. M., & Petee, T. A. (2007b). Weapons used by juveniles and adult offenders in U.S. parricide cases. *Journal of Interpersonal Violence, 22*(11), 1400–1414. https://doi.org/10.1177/0886260507305528

Heide, K. M., & Solomon, E. (2013). Treating severely abused parricide offenders. In *Understanding parricide: When sons and daughters kill parents* (pp. 317–330). Oxford University Press. https://doi.org/10.1093/acprof:oso/9780195176667.003.0014
Hillbrand, M., Alexandre, J. W., Young, J. L., & Spitz, R. T. (1999). Parricides: Characteristics of offenders and victims, legal factors, and treatment issues. *Aggression and Violent Behavior, 4*(2), 179–190. https://doi.org/10.1016/S1359-1789(97)00056-6
Holcomb, W. R. (2000). Matricide: Primal aggression in search of self-affirmation. *Psychiatry, 63*(3), 264–287. https://doi.org/10.1080/00332747.2000.11024919
Holt, A. (2012). Researching parent abuse: A critical review of the methods. *Social Policy and Society, 11*(2), 289–298. https://doi.org/10.1017/S1474746411000625
Holt, A. (2017). Parricide in England and Wales (1977–2012): An exploration of offenders, victims, incidents and outcomes. *Criminology and Criminal Justice, 17*(5), 568–587. https://doi.org/10.1177/1748895816688332
Holt, A., & Shon, P. C. (2018). Exploring fatal and non-fatal violence against parents: Challenging the orthodoxy of abused adolescent perpetrators. *International Journal of Offender Therapy and Comparative Criminology, 62*(4), 915–934. https://doi.org/10.1177/0306624X16672444
Jung, S.-K., Lee, J.-R., Kim, J.-Y., Taq, G.-J., Oh, I.-J., & Myoung, E.-C. (2014). Analysis of parricide and filicide in Korea. *Korean Journal of Legal Medicine, 38*(2), 66–72. https://doi.org/10.7580/kjlm.2014.38.2.66
Kilday, A.-M. (2016). "Sugar and spice and all things nice?": Violence against parents in Scotland, 1700–1850. *Journal of Family History, 41*(3), 318–335. https://doi.org/10.1177/0363199016645053
Kirschner, D. (1992). Understanding adoptees who kill: Dissociation, patricide, and the psychodynamics of adoption. *International Journal of Offender Therapy and Comparative Criminology, 36*(4), 323–334. https://doi.org/10.1177/0306624X9203600406
Liem, M., & Reichelmann, A. (2014). Patterns of multiple family homicide. *Homicide Studies, 18*(1), 44–58. https://doi.org/10.1177/1088767913511460
Liettu, A., Säävälä, H., Hakko, H., Räsänen, P., & Joukamaa, M. (2009). Mental disorders of male parricidal offenders: A study of offenders in forensic psychiatric examination in Finland during 1973–2004. *Social Psychiatry and Psychiatric Epidemiology, 44*(2), 96–103. https://doi.org/10.1007/s00127-008-0419-9
Liettu, A., Säävälä, H., Hakko, H., Joukamaa, M., & Räsänen, P. (2012). Weapons used in serious violence against a parent: Retrospective comparative register study. *Scandinavian Journal of Public Health, 40*(6), 563–570. https://doi.org/10.1177/1403494812455731
Marleau, J. D., Millaud, F., & Auclair, N. (2003). A comparison of parricide and attempted parricide: A study of 39 psychotic adults. *International Journal of Law and Psychiatry, 26*, 269–279. https://doi.org/10.1016/S0160-2527(03)00037-2
Marleau, J. D., Auclair, N., & Millaud, F. (2006). Comparison of factors associated with parricide in adults and adolescents. *Journal of Family Violence, 21*(5), 321–325. https://doi.org/10.1007/s10896-006-9029-z
Mass, R. L., Prakash, R., Hollender, M. H., & Regan, W. M. (1984). Double parricide—matricide and patricide: A comparison with other schizophrenic murders. *Psychiatric Quarterly, 56*(4), 286–290. https://doi.org/10.1007/BF01064474
McCann, D., & Solomon, E. (1995). Intervention after the tragedy. In *Why kids kill parents: Child abuse and adolescent homicide* (pp. 139–150). Sage. https://doi.org/10.4135/9781483327174.n10
Miles, C., & Condry, R. (2015). Responding to adolescent to parent violence: Challenges for policy and practice. *British Journal of Criminology, 55*(6), 1076–1095. https://doi.org/10.1093/bjc/azv095
Muravyeva, M. (2016). Family authority, violence against parents, and parricide in Russia, 1600–1800. *Journal of Family History, 41*(3), 294–317. https://doi.org/10.1177/0363199016644587

Myers, W. C., & Vo, E. J. (2012). Adolescent parricide and psychopathy. *International Journal of Offender Therapy and Comparative Criminology, 56*(5), 715–729. https://doi.org/10.1177/0306624X11410587
Novović, Z., Mišić-Pavkov, G., Smederevac, S., Drakić, D., & Lukić, T. (2013). The role of schizoid personality, peritraumatic dissociation and behavioral activation system in a case of parricide. *Aggression and Violent Behavior, 18*(1), 113–117. https://doi.org/10.1016/j.avb.2012.11.004
Parkin, W.S., & J. Gruenewald. (2017). Open-source data and the study of homicide. *Journal of Interpersonal Violence 32*(18), 2693–2723.
Post, S. (1982). Adolescent parricide in abusive families. *Child Welfare, 61*(7), 445–455. https://search.ebscohost.com.subzero.lib.uoguelph.ca/login.aspx?direct=true&db=i3h&AN=25219438&site=ehost-live&scope=site
Sargent, D. (1962). Children who kill: A family conspiracy? *Social Work, 7*(1), 35–42. https://doi.org/10.1093/sw/7.1.35
Shon, P. C. H. (2012). Existential boundary crossings: An archival exploration of identity projects in nineteenth-century American parricides. *Human Studies, 35*(3), 445–457. https://doi.org/10.1007/s10746-012-9239-8
Shon, P. C. H., & Barton-Bellessa, S. M. (2012). Pre-offense characteristics of nineteenth-century American parricide offenders: An archival exploration. *Journal of Criminal Psychology, 2*(1), 51–66. https://doi.org/10.1108/20093821211210495
Shon, P. C. H., & Roberts, M. A. (2010). An archival exploration of homicide-suicide and mass murder in the context of 19th-century American parricides. *International Journal of Offender Therapy and Comparative Criminology, 54*(1), 43–60. https://doi.org/10.1177/0306624X08324472
Shon, P. C. H., & Williams, C. R. (2013). An archival exploration of 19th-century American adult female offender parricides. *OMEGA—Journal of Death and Dying, 67*(3), 247–268. https://doi.org/10.2190/OM.67.3.a
Viñas-Racionero, R., Schlesinger, L. B., Scalora, M. J., & Jarvis, J. P. (2017). Youthful familicidal offenders: Targeted victims, planned attacks. *Journal of Family Violence, 32*(5), 535–542. https://doi.org/10.1007/s10896-016-9836-9
Walker, G. (2016). Imagining the unimaginable: Parricide in early modern England and Wales, c.1600–c.1760. *Journal of Family History, 41*(3), 271–293. https://doi.org/10.1177/0363199016644706
Walsh, J. A., & Krienert, J. L. (2009). A decade of child-initiated family violence: Comparative analysis of child-parent violence and parricide examining offender, victim, and event characteristics in a national sample of reported incidents, 1995–2005. *Journal of Interpersonal Violence, 24*(9), 1450–1477. https://doi.org/10.1177/0886260508323661
Walsh, J. A., Krienert, J. L., & Crowder, D. (2008). Innocence lost: A gender-based study of parricide offender, victim, and incident characteristics in a national sample, 1976–2003. *Journal of Aggression, Maltreatment and Trauma, 16*(2), 202–227. https://doi.org/10.1080/10926770801921584
Wasarhaley, N. E., Golding, J. M., Lynch, K. R., & Keller, P. S. (2013). The impact of abuse allegations in perceiving parricide in the courtroom. *Psychology, Crime and Law, 19*(9), 783–799. https://doi.org/10.1080/1068316X.2012.684056
West, S. G., & Feldsher, M. (2010). Parricide: Characteristics of sons and daughters who kill their parents. *Current Psychiatry, 9*(11), 20–25. https://link.galegroup.com/apps/doc/A259009884/AONE?u=guel77241&sid=AONE&xid=4489027a

Myrna Dawson is a Professor of Sociology, Research Leadership Chair, and Director of the Centre for the Study of Social and Legal Responses to Violence (www.violenceresearch.ca), University of Guelph. She is Director of the Canadian Femicide Observatory for Justice and Accountability (www.femicideincanada.ca) and Co-Director of the Canadian Domestic Homicide Prevention Initiative with Vulnerable Populations (www.cdhpi.ca). She has spent the past 20 years researching social and legal responses to violence with emphasis on violence against women and children, including domestic and familial violence.

Emily Hill is a Research Associate with the Centre for the Study of Social and Legal Responses to Violence (CSSLRV). After graduating from the University of Guelph's Criminal Justice and Public Policy program as a President's Scholar and the J. W. Skinner Medalist, Emily is now pursuing a combined degree in Law and Social Work (JD/MSW) at the University of Toronto. Her education experiences, including as a CSSLRV Research Assistant, affirmed her passion for social justice and law. She is particularly interested in studying violence against women and the effects of early victimization on one's life trajectories.

Chapter 8
Children Who Kill Their Adoptive Parents: Case Characteristics and Illustrations

James T. Hubbell, Kathleen M. Heide, and Norair Khachatryan

Abstract The killing of parents, frequently referred to as parricide, often generates extensive news coverage because of its taboo nature. Research on parricide has focused almost exclusively on biological offspring who kill mothers and fathers with a few studies on stepparents. To date, however, virtually no research exists on adopted sons and daughters who kill their adoptive parents because this type of victim-offender relationship has not been coded in existing US homicide databases. This article briefly reviews the scant literature available on adoptees who kill their adoptive parents. Thereafter, a content analysis of news reports of 39 juvenile and adult adoptees in the United States who killed their adoptive parents is presented. Analyses include the characteristics of offenders and victims (e.g., age, race, gender), incidents (e.g., number of victims and offenders), and case-related variables (e.g., weapons used, other charges). Attention focuses on the processing of offenders from the initial charge through conviction and sentencing. The article concludes with a comparison of adoptees and biological offspring who commit parricide, observations that emerged from these news accounts, acknowledgment of the limitations of this study, and a discussion of directions for future research.

8.1 Introduction

Brandon Menard stunned the community of Northridge, California when he murdered his adoptive parents and adopted teenage sister in 2006. His father succumbed to a gunshot injury and 17 stab wounds. Brandon stabbed his mother four times, and his sister eight times. Police discovered his sister in the backyard with the phone she used to call 911. The only member of the family not killed was his adopted brother, Scott, who was not home at the time of the incident. Ultimately, Brandon

J. T. Hubbell
School of Criminal Justice, University at Albany, State University of New York, Albany, NY, USA

K. M. Heide (✉) · N. Khachatryan
Department of Criminology, University of South Florida, Tampa, FL, USA
e-mail: kheide@usf.edu

K. Fitz-Gibbon et al. (eds.), *Young People Using Family Violence*,
https://doi.org/10.1007/978-981-16-1331-9_8

pled guilty to three counts of first-degree murder and received three life sentences without parole ("Northridge man gets life in prison for murdering adoptive family," 2011; Sodders, 2006).

All who knew the family expressed shock over the violent deaths of the Menard family, whom they described as normal and kind. Any family disagreements seemed typical. Moreover, friends of Brandon claimed the Eagle Scout was even-tempered, studious, friendly, and funny. Why then would he brutally murder his family who by all accounts treated him with love and kindness? No motive has ever been given. Even after confessing to the crimes and pleading guilty, Brandon Menard has continued to remain silent on the matter much to the dismay of the surviving family members (Hopkins & Abrams, 2006; "Northridge man gets life in prison for murdering adoptive family," 2011).

Unfortunately, this case represents only one of many instances of adoptees killing their adoptive family members without any clear motive. Awareness of this phenomenon typically comes from journalistic accounts, leaving many questions unanswered (Carangelo, 2018, 2019).

To date, there is no criminological research that systematically explores the phenomenon of adopted children killing parents in the US (see Hubbell et al., 2019 for an international sample and Hubbell et al. in press for an exploration of attachment in adoptive parricide in the US). Parricides committed by adopted children have largely been ignored except for qualitative studies with small samples (see, Jaffé, 1997; Kirschner, 1992; Lewis et al., 2001). Furthermore, US national crime data sets (e.g., Supplemental Homicide Report; National Incident-Based Reporting System) do not have adoptive relationships as possible codes. Most studies on parricide have therefore been limited to biological and stepparent relations (Fegadel & Heide, 2015; Heide, 1993, 2013a, 2013b, 2014; Walsh et al., 2008). Thus, quantitative studies of parricidal adoptees are needed to bridge the gap in the literature.

The current study presents data regarding adoptees who killed their adoptive parents in the US. A content analysis was conducted using newspaper articles concerning 39 adopted parricide cases. Information pertinent to possible motives, offenders, accomplices, victims, homicide incident characteristics, and court proceedings was obtained to provide insight into this unique phenomenon.

8.2 Literature Review

A review of the literature emphasizing violence perpetrated by adoptees, clinical studies of adoptees who committed parricide, the influence of biological parents on mental health in adoptees, and attachment disorders suffered by adoptees is presented below. Fifteen studies focusing on comparing adoptees and non-adoptees or examining unique struggles faced by adopted children are included. Older articles typically had to be included for review due to the dearth of studies contrasting adoptees and non-adoptees. As such, the articles span from 1965 to 2013. Three of these studies used samples from Denmark (Kety et al., 1968; Mednick et al., 1984; Moffitt, 1987) and one used a sample from Canada (Langevin et al., 1983) while the remainder of studies included used US samples. As established by the review below, more research is needed to further elucidate the unique relationship between adoption and homicide.

8.2.1 *Violent Characteristics of Adoptees*

Five studies have examined how adopted and non-adopted children differ in terms of general behavioral problems and antisocial behaviors. These studies, which are reviewed below, included one that compared adoptees and non-adoptees at a psychiatric hospital, a meta-analysis reviewing the results of 66 research articles, and a national study of adoptees (Grotevant et al., 2006; Menlove, 1965; Wierzbicki, 1993). One additional study considered adoption as a risk factor in a comparison of killers, non-violent offenders, and the general public in a psychiatric institute; another reported the frequency of female serial killers being adopted (Keeney & Heide, 1994; Langevin et al., 1983).

In one of the earliest studies of adoptees, Menlove (1965) sampled 51 adopted children and compared them to non-adoptees in terms of aggression. The sample encompassed children who were admitted to a psychiatric hospital and were under 15 years old. Social history interviews and outpatient evaluations were used to obtain data on each participant. One-third (33%) of the adopted children had no siblings in their adoptive families while 43% had one sibling, 20% had two siblings, and 4% had three siblings. They averaged 10 years of age.

The author matched adoptees and non-adoptees based upon socioeconomic status, race, age, number of siblings, and evaluation period. Nine symptoms of aggression were used as dependent variables including sexual acting out, fire-setting, impulsiveness, temper tantrums, legal difficulties, sadism, hostility, hyperactivity, and negativism. These symptoms were rated based upon their presence or absence, with the exception of legal difficulties; this item was measured by a child being legally delinquent, showing strong indications of delinquency, displaying mild indications of delinquency, or having no legal difficulties. Adoptees were found to be significantly more likely to display signs of hyperactivity, hostility, and negativism.

Menlove then compared children who had been adopted before and after six months of age. These two groups were matched with members of the control group. Children adopted prior to six months exhibited significantly higher passive-aggressive traits than the control group. Children adopted after six months displayed significantly higher hyperactivity when compared to the control group. There were no significant differences between the two groups of adoptees on aggressive symptomatology. Menlove concluded that adoption status appeared to be responsible for the aggressive symptoms with more serious forms of aggression prevailing in those adopted after six months of age. The author did not consider traumatic experiences that occurred prior to adoption as possible contributing factors to aggression.

Wierzbicki (1993) examined 66 studies in a meta-analysis of psychological difficulties in adoptees. For inclusion, studies had to be in English, contain information on adoptees' biological parents and their psychological disorders, and have large enough samples to determine effect sizes. The results of the meta-analysis found adoptees and non-adoptees significantly differed in the clinical population. Adopted children were disproportionately represented in clinical populations. They also exhibited more externalizing behaviors, severe symptoms, and academic difficulties. Wierzbicki defined externalizing behaviors as general delinquency, peer conflict, aggression, hyperactivity, running away, and conflict disorder. He operationalized general severity as length of stay in mental health facilities and how well the individual adjusted to the clinical environment. Wierzbicki concluded that adoptees engaged in more delinquent acts and did not acclimate to clinical settings as well as non-adoptees.

Grotevant et al. (2006) employed data from the National Longitudinal Study of Adolescent Health in the US to investigate the development of antisocial behavior in 337 adopted and 10,339 non-adopted children. The authors controlled for variables related to early experiences, peers, and family. The adopted sample contained 47.8% males and 52.2% females who ranged in age from 18 to 26 years with an average age of 21.9 years. Over half of the adoptees (51.6%) were adopted before six months of age while 16.2% were adopted from seven months to two years, 12.7% were adopted from three to six years, and 19.4% were adopted after six years. The non-adopted group was comprised of 46.7% males and 53.3% females whose ages ranged from 18 to 28 years with an average of 21.7 years. The researchers defined aggressive antisocial behavior as violent behavior directed against other people or animals. Three-fourths of adoptees did not display aggressive behavior per this definition. Similarly, 81% of non-adopted young adults demonstrated no aggressive antisocial behavior. Unlike Menlove (1965), the adopted and non-adopted groups did not differ significantly in terms of aggression. However, the results of the study may have been affected by the use of self-report data.

Adoption status has also been noted as a potential influencing factor in homicide. Langevin et al. (1983) inspected demographic traits of 109 homicide offenders and 38 nonviolent offenders in Canada. A psychiatric institute collected data on the two groups, which were subsequently contrasted with non-criminals. Medical records and responses to the Parent Child Relations Questionnaire were also used to gather data. Only 15% of homicide offenders were adopted or fostered compared to 34% of nonviolent offenders ($F/\chi^2 = 6.81$). All non-criminal subjects were raised by their biological parents. Thus, the homicide offenders were significantly more likely than nonviolent offenders to have been raised by their biological parents. The authors did not provide further insight into why the frequencies of adoption significantly differed across the groups; however, the study is notable for mentioning adoption as a demographic trait.

Moreover, Keeney and Heide (1994) analyzed 14 female serial killers and their demographic information. At the time of arrest, the women were aged between 19 and 59 years with a mean age of 38 years. Data regarding the sample's race was limited to the 11 subjects with available data, which showed that they were all white. Only two of them were raised in traditional households, that is, with their biological parents; four were adopted or fostered by strangers, and another four were reared in non-traditional homes consisting of both relatives and nonrelatives. Analysis indicated that 43% of the victims were under some form of care by the female serial killers and 37% were family members; the remaining 20% of victims were strangers, acquaintances, or lovers. Although tests of statistical significance could not be conducted due to the small sample size, it is worth noting that almost 30% of the female serial killers were adopted. This result further indicates that adoption may have its own unique pathway to violence in individuals.

8.2.2 Clinical Studies of Adopted Children Who Killed Adoptive Parents

In a direct study of adoptees who killed, Lewis et al. (2001) studied six male adoptees, one of whom killed their adoptive parents, using information from official records, psychiatric evaluations, EEGs and standard neurological evaluations. Records indicated five of the adoptees suffered severe head injuries and possessed abnormally developed central nervous systems *in utero*. All participants exhibited symptoms of psychiatric disturbances before their crimes, and all had biological parents who demonstrated psychosis. Surprisingly, no subject mentioned their biological family to the researchers during the psychiatric evaluations, but remarks made by four of them suggested that they perceived themselves to have been abandoned by their adoptive parents. Evidence collected also indicated the adoptive parents of four of the participants abused them. Further, one adoptive mother claimed her son never received any injuries even though she admitted to physically abusing him. The remaining subject received bizarre punishments from his mentally ill adoptive parents. Despite the small sample size, the authors reported the offenders were similar to typical violent offenders. Thus, the study concluded that the homicidal acts of the adoptees were attributed to family histories of mental illness as well as abusive adoptive parents rather than the status of being adopted. In contrast, Jaffé (1997) concluded that adoption contributed to the murder of an adoptive father and the attempted murder of an adoptive mother by one adoptee in a detailed case study.

Previously, Kirschner (1992) analyzed seven cases in which he acted as an expert witness to determine why adoptees killed their adoptive parents. He reported that the majority of the adoptees had been in dissociative states during the murders. The families typically acted in ways that stigmatized the biological parents of the adoptees. For instance, parents would typically ignore questions from their children about the adoption and denied the possible negative impact of adoption. Additionally, adoptive parents sometimes assumed problematic behaviors in their children resulted from poor genetics. The adoptive parents would then reinforce this view by speaking poorly of the biological parents, contributing to adoptees fantasizing that they were abandoned by negative biological parents or that they were stolen by their adoptive parents. These family dynamics and how the adoptees interpreted them worked in tandem with one another to create extreme displays of rage akin to dissociation, having deadly results.

Later, Kirschner and Nagel (1996) further described the homicides as acts of catathymic violence, defined as explosions of rage that occur with no prior displays of aggressions. The authors cited seven adoptees as evidence for catathymic murder in which the adoptees killed their adoptive parents. These explosions of rage occur from growing perceptions of rejection and abandonment from being adopted. The authors stated these incidents are always due to underlying feelings of rejection that resurface. Although the study utilized only qualitative data to support this assertion, it is one of the only studies to examine the phenomenon of adoptees who commit parricide in detail and attempt to demystify the motivations for these crimes.

8.2.3 Adoptees and Their Biological Parents

Aside from the psychological reasons for violence in adoptees, studies examining the biological causes for psychopathology have also been conducted. For example, Kety et al. (1968) attempted to extricate the role of genetics in developing schizophrenia. Using only official record data, the authors analyzed 33 cases of schizophrenic adoptees and matched them with 33 adoptees who did not show signs of schizophrenia. Approximately 9% of biological relatives exhibited symptoms of schizophrenia in adoptees diagnosed with the disorder compared to only 1.9% of individuals related to the control group, a statistically significant difference. Conversely, fewer adoptive relatives displayed signs of schizophrenia in both groups. There were no statistically significant differences between the groups, and the instances of adoptive relatives with schizophrenia were randomly distributed. Thus, the development of schizophrenia in the adoptees primarily relied on genetic factors as opposed to environmental factors.

Similarly, Mednick et al. (1984) investigated a hypothesized link between criminal convictions in parents, both biological and adoptive, and convictions among 14,427 adoptees. The number of convictions received by the biological fathers significantly predicted the number of convictions received by male adoptees. The relationship was significantly stronger for biological mothers' convictions predicting the male adoptees' convictions. One-fifth of sons in the sample were convicted when the biological parents only were convicted, as opposed to only 14.7% of sons when only adoptive parents were convicted, and 13.5% of sons when neither set of parents had been previously convicted. Additionally, the average number of convictions in male adoptees increased in relation to the biological parents' number of convictions. Accordingly, the findings from this study suggested that criminality in adoptees was primarily rooted in genetics rather than the environment.

Moffitt (1987) similarly used the Danish Adoption Cohort Register to analyze the association between mental illness in biological parents and violent offending as well as recidivism in 6700 male adoptees. Adoptees who had at least one biological parent hospitalized for mental illness were significantly more likely to have been convicted than adoptees for whom neither biological parent had been hospitalized. This difference was not found for repeated recidivism. However, adoptees whose biological parents recidivated multiple times were twice more likely to recidivate, and adoptees whose biological parents had also been hospitalized were four times more likely to recidivate. Moffitt found no significant relationship between violent offending and parental mental illness or criminality. Additionally, there were no significant differences found based upon the adoptees' ages of adoption. Thus, the results supported the assertion that biological parents highly influence the criminal behavior of their offspring through genetic factors.

Kerr et al. (2013), however, found different results when comparing 346 adoptees from the Early Growth and Development Study with their biological mothers and adoptive mothers in terms of antisocial behavior and depression. Overall, the study supported both environmental and genetic causes of antisocial behavior and depressive symptoms. Depression and antisocial behavior in adoptive mothers as well as biological mothers predicted internalizing and externalizing behaviors in adoptees. The authors advised adoption may therefore play a key role in negating risks present in adoptees from their biological mothers.

8.2.4 Adoptees and Attachment

The heart of psychological research on adoptees examines the attachments adoptees are able to create with others despite disrupted attachments with their biological parents. Researchers frequently view this under the lens of reactive attachment disorder. Reactive attachment disorder (RAD) is described in the DSM-V with the following symptoms: the child fails to respond to emotional comfort from caregivers, displays idiopathic tantrums, rarely exhibits positive emotions, and has constrained peer interactions. The chief criterion for this diagnosis is that these symptoms are believed to result from deprived emotional care such as emotional neglect, recurrent changes in primary caregivers, or living in settings that lack the capacity for the formation of attachments to caregivers (American Psychiatric Association, 2013).

Hall and Geher (2003) used RAD as a key variable of interest in comparing 21 children with the diagnosis and 21 children without the diagnosis based on survey responses from the parents and children. Only 29% of children without RAD were being raised by adoptive or foster parents compared to 90% of children with RAD. Moreover, parents of children diagnosed with RAD reported significantly higher degrees of withdrawal, social problems, thought problems, attention deficits, somatic complaints, delinquent behavior, aggressive behavior, and anxiety/depression for their children. The children with RAD were also significantly lower in terms of empathy. Further supporting that RAD mainly impacts adoptees, children with RAD were placed with 4.90 caregivers on average since birth, while those without the disorder only averaged 1.43 caregivers.

In addition to RAD, attachment styles have also been used to characterize an individual's ability to form attachments to others. The four types of attachment styles are secure, insecure-avoidant, insecure-ambivalent, and insecure disorganized (Main & Solomon, 1990; van IJzendoorn et al., 1999). When children have secure attachments, they explore their environments when caregivers are near, become upset when caregivers exit, and return to them. On the other hand, children with insecure-avoidant attachments rarely explore new environments when their caregivers are near, do not notice when caregivers leave, and fail to notice when they return. Likewise, children who display the insecure-ambivalent attachment do not seem to care about the return of their caregivers after leaving; they do, however, exhibit emotional distress when their caregivers exit. Lastly, insecure-disorganized children behave in a combination of ways of the above attachment styles (Allen, 2011).

Utilizing these attachment styles to examine how adoption impacts children, Barone and Lionetti (2011) analyzed the attachment styles of 20 three to five-year-old adoptees from National Adoption Facilities; 25% of the sample participants were securely attached to their adoptive parents, while 35% demonstrated insecure-disorganized attachments, 30% displayed insecure-avoidant attachments, and 10% showed insecure-ambivalent attachments. The researchers contrasted these frequencies with 64 Italian preschoolers from the general population in a previous study. Subsequent analyses revealed the two groups significantly differed in that 63% of the preschoolers in the general population sample were securely attached to their parents. These findings further highlight the link between adoption status and insecure attachments.

As the literature exemplifies, the impacts of adoption still require elucidation. Although there is a consensus on difficulties with attachment in adoptees, studies have found mixed results as to adoption's impact on violent behavior and homicide. Additionally, clinical research on adoptees has only used a handful of participants, restricting the external validity. Clinical research also has not explored the incident or victim characteristics of the homicides.

The current study contributes to the literature by examining the victim, offender, and incident characteristics of adoptive parricides in the US. This study also enhances prior research through its larger sample size of 39 adoptees who committed parricide. Furthermore, the data collected span multiple decades, which allows the population of adopted parricide offenders to be better represented in analyses.

8.3 Methods

The current study employs content analysis, which allows for the analysis of desired variables through a process that consists of proposing a research question, developing an appropriate sampling strategy of text, and creating domains of interest (Pedhazur & Schmelkin, 1991). Robson (2002) explained that content analysis is useful for both low subjective inference (e.g., incident-level variables) and high subjective inference (e.g., possible motivations) data coding and subsequent analyses. As discussed below, the establishment of inter-rater reliability is paramount to demonstrating that the data can be coded independently.

8.3.1 Sample Generation

The primary inclusion criterion was that an adoptee killed or attempted to kill at least one adoptive parent. The inclusion of attempted homicides occurs frequently in homicide research as the offender's intent was to kill despite the actual outcome. External factors such as the response time of ambulances, offender's accuracy in shooting, wound location, and victim's health often are the differences between life and death, regardless of the offender's intent (Block, 1977; Heide et al., 2001). Multiple-offender homicide situations were included if the adoptee was one of the offenders. In addition, multiple-victim homicide incidents were included if at least one victim was an adoptive parent of an offender.

Data were gathered from newspaper articles covering adoptive parents who were victims of a completed or attempted homicide by an adopted child. Access World News, Lexis Nexis, and Google were searched to find cases similar to a previous content analysis of parricide by Boots and Heide (2006). The Boolean phrase "adopted" AND ("kill" OR "murder") AND ("parent" OR "mother" OR "father") was used to locate cases.

Four or more different newspaper articles were collected per each incident using the above three data sources as well as local newspapers. This number of newspaper accounts was needed to verify information, resolve inconsistencies, and shed greater light on the incidents. Articles for each case came from at least two of the data sources. Because of the infrequency of parricide committed by adoptees, cases spanned from 1975 to December 2018 in the US to have a sufficient sample size.

The offenders were required to have been adopted by non-relatives who were unknown to them and have had no biological relatives as part of those households. The nature of adoption as abandonment discussed in the literature necessitated this criterion. The abandonment described particularly in clinical studies generates unique psychological struggles that would likely differ from those adoptees who were adopted by other biological relatives. To that end, cases of offenders adopted by step-parents were excluded as the offenders knew them through their biological parents. Lastly, information related to judicial proceedings such as the criminal charges, pleas, convictions, and sentencings were essential for inclusion to characterize the criminal justice system's reaction to this phenomenon.

Initially, 43 cases met the above inclusion criteria. Four cases were subsequently removed from the sample. Two adoptees were acquitted of all charges, which suggests the homicides may have not been parricides. Another two cases were dropped as appellate courts ruled the offenders' confessions were coerced. Hence, 39 subjects comprised the final sample.

Although the gathering of cases was appropriately carried out, the sample may not completely represent parricides committed by adoptees in the US for a variety of reasons. Primarily, cases had to be reported by the media and digitized to be located using the online databases. Adoption practices have also changed throughout the sample's timespan, especially with adoptions increasingly becoming open adoptions with contact with birth parents and relatives, possibly impacting the nature of the parricides. Given the dearth of information available on parricides by adopted children, this research constitutes a necessary first step using available data to learn more about the nature of these killings. Moreover, the articles are indeed worthy of scientific examination as the public utilizes media sources more often than scientific sources to construct opinions, especially when scientific studies are in demand for a topic.

8.3.2 Variables

Analogous to the study by Boots and Heide (2006), data obtained from the articles were used to code 136 variables across seven domains. These domains included suggested motive, variables of clinical concern, incident level characteristics, individual level characteristics, criminal justice system processing, post-disposition outcomes, and traits aligned with Heide's parricide offender typology (Heide, 2013b).[1]

Suggested motives included romance, freedom, business disputes, money/insurance policies, fights/conflicts/disturbances, substance-induced homicides, psychosis/mental illnesses, mercy killings, abuse, and the favoring of biological children over the adoptee. Variables of clinical concern encompassed whether the offender was in a dissociative state, whether the killing was intentional, and whether the victims were dismembered or decapitated. Incident-level data consisted of the number of victims and offenders in the incident, the location, the date, what weapons were employed, and whether the victims included an adoptive mother and/or adoptive father.

The individual-level data gathered were the names, genders, ages, and races of offenders, accomplices, and victims. The age at which the offender was adopted was noted when reported. Victim-offender relationships and accomplice-offender relationships were also coded. Variables related to criminal justice system processing included the initial charge for the homicide, indicators of other crimes related to the homicide incident, whether juvenile offenders were processed as adults, whether prosecutors pursued the death penalty, charge date, trial date, conviction status, conviction date, sentence, mandatory treatment, and minimum years of confinement. Post-disposition data included amended sentences from appeals and any post-release recidivism.

[1]The authors of this study decided not to classify offenders by the typology due to insufficient evidence from news accounts. To successfully place offenders into the typology, in-depth evaluations and review of official records are needed.

Lastly, variables pertinent to Heide's parricide offender typology were individually coded in terms of the presence or absence of the item in the news accounts. For the *severely abused parricide offender* type, items entailed whether the murder was committed due to terror or desperation and was intended to end the abuse, if it was done in self-defense, if there was a history of abuse in the household, and if the homicide victim was alleged to be a substance abuser. Variables coded for the *severely mentally ill parricide offender* included signs of severe mental illness in the offender, evidence of hallucinations or delusions or other bizarre conduct, and if the killing appeared to result from mental illness. *Dangerously antisocial parricide offender* traits included if the homicide was the means to a selfish or instrumental end, if the offender presented past antisocial behavior, if serious efforts were made to avoid detection by authorities, and if the offender went on a buying spree after the homicide incident. Lastly, *enraged parricide offender* characteristics encompassed evidence of enragement during the incident, if the offender was intoxicated at the time of the homicide, and if the intoxication was due to drugs and/or alcohol.

8.3.3 Data Analysis Plan

Per the exploratory nature of the study, analyses are limited to descriptive data. Two of the authors of this study independently coded each case. Ten cases were used to determine inter-rater reliability, which was 93.8% agreement across 1360 ratings of 136 variables for each case. Coding by both raters then proceeded as planned for the remaining cases. Any discrepancies between the raters were debated and ultimately resolved by them.

8.4 Results

All 39 incidents occurred in the US between 1975 and 2018. One case took place in the 1970s while five were in the 1980s, nine were in the 1990s, nine were in the early 2000s, and 15 were from 2010 to 2018. Therefore, almost 62% of cases occurred after 2000. Additionally, only one case took place in a US territory with the remaining cases transpiring in the Western (37%), Southern (32%), Northeastern (18%) and Midwestern (13%) regions per the FBI's classification of states.

8.4.1 Incident Characteristics

As depicted in Table 8.1, 34 adoptees targeted their adoptive mothers and 33 adoptees targeted their adoptive fathers. In over three-fourths of the incidents (77%), adopted children killed or attempted to kill both adoptive parents. This includes one case

Table 8.1 Incident characteristics

Variable	N (%)
Victim type (n = 39)	
Adopted mother	34 (87.2)
Adopted father	33 (84.6)
Both parents	30 (76.9)
Other	8 (20.5)
Homicide situation type (n = 39)	
Single victim × single offender	7 (17.9)
Single victim × multiple offender	1 (2.6)
Multiple victim × single offender	24 (61.5)
Multiple victim × multiple offender	7 (17.9)
Adopted child type and accomplice presence (n = 39)	
Adopted son alone	30 (76.9)
Adopted son with non-family members	5 (12.8)
Adopted daughter with non-family members	2 (5.1)
Adopted daughter alone	1 (2.6)
Adopted siblings (both daughters) together	1 (2.6)
Other victim-offender relationships (n = 14)	
Sibling	10 (71.4)
Other relative	4 (28.6)
Weapon type (n = 39)	
Multiple weapons	12 (30.8)
Firearm	11 (28.2)
Sharp object	7 (18.0)
Blunt object	5 (12.8)
Fire	2 (5.1)
Strangulation	2 (5.1)

of an offender adopted by a same-sex male couple. In these parricidal incidents, 14 other victims were assaulted or killed. All of these other victims were relatives; approximately 71% were siblings. The majority of cases were single-offender and multiple-victim situations (62%) followed equally by incidents with a single victim and multiple offenders, and those with multiple victims and multiple offenders; these two categories represented 36% of cases in total. Only one case was a single-victim and multiple-offender incident.

All cases of single-offender and multiple-victim parricides were committed by adopted sons alone. Interestingly, only one out of four adopted daughters acted alone compared to 86% of 35 adopted sons. Five male and three female offenders had accomplices, one of whom acted with her adopted sister. One male offender killed with his biological mother. Friends constituted 64% of all accomplices. All friends who assisted were male. Accomplices ranged in age from 15 to 35 years and averaged 21 years.

Regarding weapons used in the incidents, offenders frequently chose firearms (44%), as their sole weapon (28%) or with other weapons (16%). Half of all offenders who employed multiple weapons (31%) used firearms. Nearly one-third of adoptees wielded sharp objects such as knives (18%) or blunt objects such as hammers (13%) only in the incidents. In the remaining 10% of incidents, the offenders strangled their victims or killed them by setting a fire. The weapon choice of adopted parricide offenders notably differs from US homicides overall as approximately two-thirds of US homicides committed between the early 1980s and 2016 involved firearms (Rosenfeld & Fox, 2019).

8.4.2 Offender Characteristics

As shown in Table 8.2, adopted parricide offenders were typically juveniles (56%) or in their late teens or early twenties (33%). On average, offenders were 19 years old at the time of the offense with a median age of 17 years. They were also predominately White (74%) and male (90%). Black offenders comprised 15% of cases collected

Table 8.2 Adopted parricide offenders characteristics

Variable	
Age at homicide incident	
N	39
Mean (median)	19.1 (17.0)
Range	14–37
	N (%)
Age category	
14–15	9 (23.1)
16–17	13 (33.3)
18–19	5 (12.8)
20–24	8 (20.5)
25 and older	4 (10.2)
Total	39 (100.0)
Age at adoption	
1 or younger	15 (42.9)
Older than 1	20 (57.1)
Total	35 (100.0)[a]

(continued)

Table 8.2 (continued)

Variable	
Race	
White	25 (73.5)
Black	5 (14.7)
Other	4 (11.8)
Total	34 (100.0)[b]
Gender	
Male	35 (89.7)
Female	4 (10.3)
Total	39 (100.0)

[a]Age at adoption was unknown for four offenders
[b]Race was unknown for five offenders

where race data were available while 12% were of other races. Only four adopted offenders were female. At the time of adoption, 57% of offenders for whom adoption age was known were over the age of 1, while 43% were one-year-olds or younger. The mean age at adoption was 4 years, 11 months, with a median age of five years.

8.4.3 Victim Characteristics

Thirty-four adoptive mothers and 34 adoptive fathers were victims in these cases, as shown in Table 8.3. Mothers and fathers were close in age with averages of 53.2 years and 53.5 years and median ages of 51 years and 52 years, respectively. They similarly ranged in age from 37 to 76 years for mothers and 36 to 77 years for fathers. Race information was available for 23 mothers and 24 fathers. Over 91% of mothers were White as were over 87% of fathers. The remainder of mothers and fathers were Black.

8.4.4 Judicial System Processing of Adopted Parricide Offenders

As revealed in Table 8.4, roughly three-fourths of offenders were initially charged with first degree murder; over 78% were charged with more than one homicide charge. Of the 22 offenders who were juveniles at the time of the homicide, all but three were charged as adults. Additionally, prosecutors sought the death penalty in half of all eligible cases. This high percentage of capital cases at first glance seems unusual because typically, prosecutors are unlikely to seek the death penalty in most homicides (see Baldus et al., 2002; Marceau et al., 2013). However, the prosecutorial

Table 8.3 Adoptive parent characteristics

Variable	Adoptive mother	Adoptive father
Age at homicide incident		
N	34	34[a]
Mean (median)	53.2 (51.0)	53.5 (52.0)
Range	37–76	36–77
	N (%)	N (%)
Race		
White	21 (91.3)	21 (87.5)
Black	2 (8.7)	3 (12.5)
Total	23 (100.0)[b]	24 (100.0)[c]

[a]Only 33 adoptees targeted their adoptive fathers, however one was adopted by a same-sex male couple
[b]Race information was unknown in 11 cases; mothers were not victims in five cases
[c]Race information was unknown in 11 cases; fathers were not victims in five cases. In one case, however, two victims were fathers

Table 8.4 System processing information for adopted parricide offender

Variable	N (%)
Initial charge ($n = 39$)	
1st degree murder	29 (74.4)
2nd degree murder	2 (5.1)
Unspecified homicide charge	5 (12.8)
Attempted 1st degree murder	1 (2.6)
Violation of juvenile code	2 (5.1)
Number of homicide charges ($n = 36$)[a]	
1	8 (22.2)
2	21 (58.3)
3–5	7 (19.4)
Involvement in non-homicide offenses ($n = 39$)[b]	
Larceny	11 (28.2)
Burglary	9 (23.1)
Auto theft	6 (15.4)
Arson	6 (15.4)
Robbery	5 (12.8)
Narcotics-related homicide	3 (7.7)
Rape	2 (5.1)
Other sex offenses	2 (5.1)
Other violent felonies	2 (5.1)

(continued)

Table 8.4 (continued)

Variable	N (%)
Charged as adult if juvenile? (n = 22)	
Yes	19 (86.4)
No	3 (13.6)
Prosecutor sought death penalty? (n = 26)[c]	
Yes	12 (46.2)
No	12 (46.2)
Non-death penalty state	2 (7.7)
Convicted of homicide related charge? (n = 36)	
Yes	34 (94.4)
No	2 (5.6)
Most serious sentence (n = 35)	
Death sentence	2 (5.7)
Life without parole	6 (17.1)
Life with parole/unspecified life	13 (37.1)
Other prison sentence	10 (28.6)
Others[d]	4 (11.4)

[a]No homicide charge in two cases; one additional case was in progress and charges were unknown
[b]Some cases included more than one non-homicide offense
[c]13 cases were juveniles and not eligible due to a Supreme Court decision
[d]Included offenders sentenced to juvenile facilities and mental hospitals

decision to seek the death penalty might have been due to multiple victim deaths in nearly 80% of all cases in the current sample. A murder involving multiple victims is considered an aggravating factor in death penalty statutes (see e.g., Florida Statutes 921 (7), 2019).

Thirty-four (94%) of the 36 adoptive parricide offenders charged with homicide were convicted. With respect to sentencing, only two of 12 offenders who faced a possible death sentence received one. Over half (54%) received life sentences with 17% receiving life without parole and 37% receiving life sentences with parole. Approximately 29% received other prison sentences and 11% were sentenced to juvenile facilities or mental hospitals.

Newspaper articles discussed crimes other than murder committed during the incidents. Specifically, the crimes in which some offenders engaged included property crimes such as larceny, burglary, automobile theft, and arson at rates of 28%, 23%, 15%, and 15%, respectively. The articles also indicated that at least 13% of offenders committed robberies as part of the incidents, and two (5%) perpetrated other violent felonies. Rape and other sexual offenses, namely desecration of a corpse, rarely occurred with only 5% of cases containing evidence of each.

8.4.5 Suggested Motives as Described by the Media

As shown in Table 8.5, details provided in newspaper articles conveyed that one-third of adoptees killed for financial gain. Other selfish motives included freedom from parents and romance, occurring in 21% and 10% of incidents, respectively. Fights or conflicts between offenders and their adoptive parents precipitated 28% of parricides. Psychosis or mental illnesses were suggested in over one-fourth (26%) of cases. Only 21% of cases mentioned abuse as a possible motive. Noteworthily, only two cases appeared to be substance-induced.

8.4.6 Characteristics of Heide's Parricide Offender Typology

Unique attributes of Heide's parricide offender typology (Heide, 2013a, 2013b) are summarized in Table 8.6. Notably, less than one-fourth of cases (23%) alluded to any abuse, which is an essential requirement for the severely abused offender type. Newspaper articles portrayed only one offender to have killed in self-defense. In terms of the severely mentally ill offender type, news accounts suggested 18% of adoptees suffered from severe mental illnesses. Five of the killings appeared to be due to the offenders' mental illnesses; four of the 39 offenders reportedly had been diagnosed with schizophrenia.

Adoptees most commonly demonstrated traits relevant to dangerously antisocial parricide offenders. Two-thirds of the sample killed for selfish motivations, and 59% exhibited earlier histories of antisocial behavior. One-third of homicides contained efforts to avoid detection, which were typically arsons of the murder scenes.

News reports also presented evidence in relation to the enraged offender type. Over 60% of adoptees had histories of poor impulse control usually identified through problems in school. News accounts intimated that approximately 39% were enraged during the homicidal incidents. Pertinent to Kirschner's Adopted Child Syndrome,

Table 8.5 Suggested motivation for the killing

Motivation	N (%)
Money/insurance policy	13 (33.3)
Fight/conflict	11 (28.2)
Psychosis/mental illness	10 (25.6)
Freedom from parents	8 (20.5)
Abuse	8 (20.5)
Romance	4 (10.3)
Substance-induced	2 (5.1)

Note More than one motive per case is possible

Table 8.6 Factors related to Heide's four types of parricide offenders

Variable	N (%)
Severely abused offender	
Killed out of terror or desperation	0
Killed to protect self or others	1 (2.6)
Long-standing history of abuse alleged	9 (23.1)
Homicide victim was a drinker	3 (7.7)
Abuse types	
Physical only	2 (5.1)
Verbal only	1 (2.6)
Multiple types including sexual	1 (2.6)
Multiple types without sexual	5 (12.8)
Abuse present but type unknown	1 (2.6)
No abuse	29 (74.4)
Total	39 (100.0)
Severely mentally ill offenders	
Suggestion of severe mental illness	7 (17.9)
Delusion, hallucinations, and bizarre behavior	5 (12.8)
Killing mostly due to mental illness	5 (12.8)
Dangerously antisocial offenders	
Killed for selfish motivation	26 (66.7)
History of antisocial behavior	23 (59.0)
Serious effort to avoid detection	13 (33.3)
Evidence of a buying spree	5 (12.8)
Enraged offenders	
Offender was enraged during killing	15 (38.5)
History of poor impulse control	24 (61.5)
Evidence that biological sibling was favored	3 (7.7)

reports in three (8%) of the cases claimed the adoptive parents' biological children were favored over the adopted children.

8.5 Discussion

This is the first study to have examined in depth the characteristics of parricides committed by a non-clinical sample of adopted offenders. Newspaper accounts on 39 adoptive parricide cases from the US were used to provide a more complete portrait of the dynamics involved in these types of parricides, as well as the response by the criminal justice system. At first glance, the sample size may seem small; however, it is relatively large given the fact that only about 250 offenders on average are arrested each year in the United States for killing biological parents and stepparents. As previously mentioned, large homicide data sets compiled by the FBI do not include a code for adoption status, which makes it impossible to determine how many of these parricide cases may have actually involved adoptive parents.

Based on his clinical evaluations and prior research, Kirschner (1992) has estimated that adopted children are more likely to kill their adoptive parents, and especially their mothers, than biological children due to severe dissociated rage caused by adoptees feeling that they were abandoned by their biological parents or stolen by their adoptive parents. The lack of data on this type of homicide is especially troubling in light of the fact that more than 110,000 children are adopted in the US each year (Child Welfare Information Gateway, 2016).

8.5.1 Differences Between Biological and Adopted Parricide Offenders

It would be reasonable to assume that reporting of incident characteristics as well as offender and victim demographic data in newspaper articles on adoptive parricide cases was fairly accurate (Taylor & Sorenson, 2002). These types of data are within the realm of "basic facts," and journalists are trained to pay attention to these details. When comparing findings from these 39 US adoptive parricide cases to analyses based on biological parricide cases, four noteworthy differences emerge.

First, adopted parricide offenders targeted both adoptive parents in nearly 77% of cases in this study, compared to less than 8% of biological parricide offenders. Second, adoptive parricide cases are more likely to involve juvenile offenders than parricides committed by biological offspring (56% versus less than 18%). Third, adopted parricide offenders are more likely to be under the age 25 than their biological counterparts (90% versus 43%). Lastly, 28% of adopted parricide offenders used firearms as the sole means of killing, compared to 55% of offenders who target their biological parents (Heide, 2013b; Heide & Petee, 2007).

These differences suggest that the dynamics involved in cases of adoptive parricide differ from those found in parricides against biological parents. The much greater proportion of offenders under 25 in general, and those under the age 18 in particular, among adopted parricide offenders points to the role of attachment issues in these killings. Lack of attachment may also be relevant to the fact that adopted offenders were more likely to choose methods of killing other than firearms, which would require them to be in closer proximity to their victims at the time of the homicide. As discussed further below, the parricides cases in this sample may be tied to rage emanating from underlying feelings of abandonment.

8.5.2 Important Observations from the Findings

Evidence provided by newspaper accounts suggests that adopted parricide offenders tend to be criminally oriented (almost 60% had a history of antisocial behavior) prior to the homicide incident and driven by selfish motivation, possibly fueled by underlying anger related to rejection and abandonment. Two-thirds of the offenders in the sample killed an adoptive parent for a selfish or antisocial motive, such as gaining freedom from chores/parental nagging, freedom to romantically date whomever the adoptee wanted, or monetary reasons (e.g., life insurance, money to buy drugs). The calculated nature of the majority of killings also explains why offenders were charged with murder in the first degree in almost 75% of the cases.

At the same time, close to 40% of offenders in the sample displayed evidence of rage at the time of the homicide. Supplemental descriptive analyses indicated that 44% of cases showed evidence of overkill, which means that offenders used more force than would be necessary to kill the victim (Safarik & Jarvis, 2005). Additionally, only three of the 17 cases that contained overkill involved a fight/conflict that escalated to a lethal event. This observation suggests that excessive force used by adopted parricide offenders may not be typically a product of rage due to some immediate event; instead, this rage may be the result of the accumulation of anger over years, possibly resulting from poor attachment during infancy (Magid & McKelvey, 1987).

The majority of parricides in this sample were committed by juvenile offenders, as opposed to samples of biological parricides. This finding can be attributed to possible lack of contact between adoptees and their parents as they grow older. Analyses by Heide (2013b) showed that offenders under the age of 18 were more likely to kill stepparents than biological parents, which may be a function of distance between adults and their stepparents and thus a lower likelihood of conflict and murder in later life. This dynamic may also apply to the relationship between adopted children and their adoptive caretakers after adoptees reach adulthood and leave the house.

The findings discussed above also highlight the difference between clinical samples and more general samples. For example, in a small sample of adoptees who killed their parents, Kirschner (1992) found that the majority of offenders experienced a dissociative state at the time of the parricide incident. Conversely, in this non-clinical sample, very little evidence of dissociation was found, despite the fact that many offenders were enraged during the killing. This difference may be due to the fact that Kirschner personally evaluated these adoptive parricide offenders, compared to the data available to a reporter.

8.5.3 Limitations and Directions for Future Research

The study has several limitations associated with reliance on newspaper accounts (e.g., Shon & Roberts, 2010). First, the sample only includes cases that were covered by media sources and available online at the time the study took place in 2018. Accordingly, the extent to which the sample is representative of the overall population of adoptive parricides is unknown. A large nationwide sample of adoptive parricides will help determine whether these cases are genuinely distinct from those perpetrated by biological children; it is possible that parricides committed by juvenile offenders for instrumental motives and using excessive violence are simply more interesting to reporters, but are not reflective of the overall trends related to this type of homicide.

Second, the amount of media coverage varied per case, and information sought by the authors was sometimes unavailable. For example, information on victims' race was missing in 11 cases. Third, media coverage of a homicide event is not always objective; sometimes information is deliberately withheld by law enforcement or the victims' relatives or omitted by journalists in order to protect the privacy of the family, among other reasons. For instance, information on abuse within the family or mental illness suffered by the offenders or the victims may have been hidden from reporters or excluded by them, out of respect for the deceased. Therefore, the absence of information does not necessarily mean that a certain variable is absent from the family's history. There may have been known family pathologies not reported in newspaper accounts of the homicide incident, which would have influenced the findings substantially, with respect to motivation and other offense dynamics. This limitation was addressed to the extent possible by collecting data from at least two media sources for each case.

Future research on adoptive parricide would benefit from using police reports of the incidents, presentencing reports, interviews with convicted adopted parricide offenders and survivors of their crimes, and with the offender's permission, discussions with defense attorneys and perusal of psychological evaluations. In cases of juvenile adopted parricide offenders who were sentenced to life in prison without the possibility of parole before 2012, transcripts of resentencing proceedings that took place as a result of the *Miller v. Alabama* (2012) Supreme Court ruling may also provide valuable insights regarding offender motivation and possible precipitating events prior to the homicide.

Knowledge regarding psychological precursors of adoptive parricide events, using a larger sample, could alter the portrait of the typical adopted parricide offender that emerged from this study. More importantly, awareness of risk factors preceding adoptive parricide is needed to develop more effective interventions for families that struggle with adopted children. Otherwise, many adoptive parents will remain oblivious to the fact that their child may erupt in rage at any moment and cause significant harm to them.

Previous research suggests that future studies using larger samples should include cases that occurred outside the US, in order to assess whether US cases are representative of adoptive parricides across the globe. Boots and Heide (2006) investigated differences between the US and non-US countries in 226 cases of parricide. Victims in this study were identified as biological parents in more than 95% of the cases; stepmothers and stepfathers were identified as killed in only 1% and 5% of the incidents, respectively. Twelve significant differences emerged between the US and other countries in terms of the characteristics of parricide incidents, system processing of offenders in reported parricide incidents, and motives and other areas of clinical interest (Boots & Heide, 2006). A larger sample of parricides would also allow researchers to examine whether juvenile and adult offenders who kill their adoptive parents differ in terms of use of accomplices, choice of weapon, motivation, clinical variables, and other factors related to the homicide. Clearly, further research is needed.

References

Allen, B. (2011). The use and abuse of attachment theory in clinical practice with maltreated children, part I: Diagnosis and assessment. *Trauma, Violence, & Abuse, 12*(1), 3–12.

American Psychiatric Association. (2013). *Diagnostic and statistical manual of mental disorders* (5th ed.). American Psychiatric Publishing.

Baldus, D. C., Woodworth, G., Gross, C. M., & Christ, A. M. (2002). Arbitrariness and discrimination in the administration of the death penalty: Legal and empirical analysis of the Nebraska experience (1973–1999). *Nebraska Law Review, 81*(2), 486–756.

Barone, L., & Lionetti, F. (2011). Attachment and emotional understanding: A study on late-adopted pre-schoolers and their parents. *Child: Care, Health and Development, 38*(5), 690–696. https://doi.org/10.1111/j.1365-2214.2011.01296.x

Block, R. L. (1977). *Violent crime: Environment, interaction, and death.* Lexington Books.

Boots, D. P., & Heide, K. M. (2006). Parricides in the media: A content analysis of available reports across cultures. *International Journal of Offender Therapy and Comparative Criminology, 50*(4), 418–445. https://doi.org/10.1177/0306624X05285103

Carangelo, L. (2018). *How an adoption ignited a fire.* Access Press.

Carangelo, L. (2019). *Adopted killers: 430 adoptees who killed—How and why they did it.* Access Press.

Child Welfare Information Gateway. (2016). *Trends in US adoptions: 2008–2012.* U.S. Department of Health and Human Services, Children's Bureau.

Fegadel, A. R., & Heide, K. M. (2015). Double parricide: An in-depth look at two victim homicides involving parents as victims. *Behavioral Sciences & the Law, 33*(6), 723–739. https://doi.org/10.1002/bsl.2189

Florida Statutes. (2019). Retrieved May 2, 2020 from http://www.leg.state.fl.us/statutes/index.cfm?App_mode=Display_Statute&URL=0900-0999/0921/Sections/0921.142.html

Grotevant, H. D., Dulmen, M. H., Dunbar, N., Nelson-Christinedaughter, J., Christensen, M., Fan, X., & Miller, B. C. (2006). Antisocial behavior of adoptees and nonadoptees: Prediction from early history and adolescent relationships. *Journal of Research on Adolescence, 16*(1), 105–131. https://doi.org/10.1111/j.1532-7795.2006.00124.x

Hall, S. E., & Geher, G. (2003). Behavioral and personality characteristics of children with reactive attachment disorder. *The Journal of Psychology, 137*(2), 145–162. https://doi.org/10.1080/00223980309600605

Heide, K. M. (1993). Parents who get killed and the children who kill them. *Journal of Interpersonal Violence, 8*(4), 531–544. https://doi.org/10.1177/088626093008004008

Heide, K. M. (2013a). Matricide and stepmatricide victims and offenders: An empirical analysis of US arrest data. *Behavioral Sciences & the Law, 31*(2), 203–214. https://doi.org/10.1002/bsl.2056

Heide, K. M. (2013b). *Understanding parricide: When sons and daughters kill parents.* Oxford University Press.

Heide, K. M. (2014). Patricide and steppatricide victims and offenders. *International Journal of Offender Therapy and Comparative Criminology, 58*(11), 1261–1278. https://doi.org/10.1177/0306624X13495168

Heide, K. M., & Petee, T. A. (2007). Weapons used by juveniles and adult offenders in US parricide cases. *Journal of Interpersonal Violence, 22*(11), 1400–1414. https://doi.org/10.1177/0886260507305528

Heide, K. M., Spencer, E., Thompson, A., & Solomon, E. P. (2001). Who's in, who's out, and who's back: Follow-up data on 59 juveniles incarcerated for murder or attempted murder in the early 1980s. *Behavioral Sciences & the Law, 19,* 97–108. https://doi.org/10.1002/bsl.423

Hopkins, B., & Abram, S. (2006, August 8). Motive in killings remains mystery. *The Daily News of Los Angeles*, p. N1.

Hubbell, J. T., Heide, K. M., & Khachatryan, N. (2019). Adoptees who kill their adoptive parents. *Behavioral Sciences & the Law, 37*(5), 473–492.

Hubbell, J. T., Heide, K. M., Wagers, S. M. (in press). Adopted children who kill their adoptive parents: An examination through the lens of attachment theory. *Behavioral Sciences & the Law.*

Jaffé, P. D. (1997). Adoption and murder. In *Advances in psychology and law: International contributions* (pp. 274–280).

Keeney, B. T., & Heide, K. M. (1994). Gender differences in serial murderers. *Journal of Interpersonal Violence, 9*(3), 383–398. https://doi.org/10.1177/088626094009003007

Kerr, D., Leve, L., Harold, G., Natsuaki, M., Neiderhiser, J., Shaw, D., & Reiss, D. (2013). Influences of biological and adoptive mothers' depression and antisocial behavior on adoptees' early behavior trajectories. *Journal of Abnormal Child Psychology, 41*(5), 723–734. https://doi.org/10.1007/s10802-013-9711-6

Kety, S. S., Rosenthal, D., Wender, P. H., & Schulsinger, F. (1968). The types and prevalence of mental illness in the biological and adoptive families of adopted schizophrenics. In D. Rosenthal & S. S. Kety (Eds.), *The transmission of schizophrenia* (pp. 345–362). Pergamon Press.

Kirschner, D. (1992). Understanding adoptees who kill: Dissociation, patricide, and the psychodynamics of adoption. *International Journal of Offender Therapy and Comparative Criminology, 36*(4), 323–333. https://doi.org/10.1177/0306624X9203600406

Kirschner, D., & Nagel, L. S. (1996). Catathymic violence, dissociation, and adoption pathology: Implications for the mental status defense. *International Journal of Offender Therapy and Comparative Criminology, 40*(3), 204–211. https://doi.org/10.1177/0306624X9604000304

Langevin, R., Paitich, D., Orchard, B., & Russon, A. (1983). Childhood and family background of killers seen for psychiatric assessment: A controlled study. *Journal of the American Academy of Psychiatry and the Law, 11*(4), 331–341.

Lewis, D. O., Yeager, C. A., Gidlow, B., & Lewis, M. (2001). Six adoptees who murdered: Neuropsychiatric vulnerabilities and characteristics of biological and adoptive parents. *Journal of the American Academy of Psychiatry and the Law, 29*(4), 390–397.

Magid, K., & McKelvey, C. A. (1987). *High risk: Children without a conscience.* Bantam Books.

Main, M., & Solomon, J. (1990). Procedures for identifying infants as disorganized/disoriented during the Ainsworth Strange Situation. In M. T. Greenberg, D. Cicchetti, & E. M. Cummings (Eds.), *Attachment in the preschool years: Theory, research, and intervention* (pp. 121–160). University of Chicago Press.

Marceau, J., Kamin, S., & Foglia, W. (2013). Death eligibility in Colorado: Many are called, few are chosen. *University of Colorado Law Review, 84*(4), 1069–1116.

Mednick, S. A., Gabrielli, W. F., Jr., & Hutchings, B. (1984). Genetic influences in criminal convictions: Evidence from an adoption cohort. *Science, 224*(4651), 891–894. https://doi.org/10.1126/science.6719119

Menlove, F. L. (1965). Aggressive symptoms in emotionally disturbed adopted children. *Child Development, 36*(2), 519–532. https://doi.org/10.2307/1126474

Miller v. Alabama, 132 S. Ct. 2455. (2012).

Moffitt, T. E. (1987). Parental mental disorder and offspring criminal behavior: An adoption study. *Psychiatry, 50,* 346–360. https://doi.org/10.1080/00332747.1987.11024366.

Northridge man gets life in prison for murdering adoptive family. (2011, June 3). *The Daily News of Los Angeles*, p. A3.

Pedhazur, E. J., & Schmelkin, L. P. (1991). *Measurement, design, and analysis: An integrated approach.* Lawrence Erlbaum.

Robson, C. (2002). *Real world research.* Blackwell.

Rosenfeld, R., & Fox, J. A. (2019). Anatomy of the homicide rise. *Homicide Studies, 23*(3), 202–224. https://doi.org/10.1177/1088767919848821

Safarik, M. E., & Jarvis, J. P. (2005). Examining attributes of homicides: Toward quantifying qualitative values of injury severity. *Homicide Studies, 9*(3), 183–203. https://doi.org/10.1177/1088767905277144

Shon, P. C. H., & Roberts, M. A. (2010). An archival exploration of homicide-suicide and mass murder in the context of 19th century American parricides. *International Journal of Offender Therapy and Comparative Criminology, 54*(1), 43–60. https://doi.org/10.1177/0306624X08324472

Sodders, L. M. (2006, August 5). Son, 20, jailed in slayings of family; Dad, mom, sister stabbed to death. *The Daily News of Los Angeles*, p. N1.

Taylor, C. A., & Sorenson, S. B. (2002). The nature of newspaper coverage of homicide. *Injury Prevention, 8*(2), 121–127. https://doi.org/10.1136/ip.8.2.121

van IJzendoorn, M. H., Schuengel, C., & Bakermans-Kranenburg, M. J. (1999). Disorganized attachment in early childhood: Meta-analysis of precursors, concomitants, and sequelae. *Development and Psychopathology, 11*(2), 225–249. https://doi.org/10.1017/S0954579499002035

Walsh, J. A., Krienert, J. L., & Crowder, D. (2008). Innocence lost: A gender-based study of parricide offender, victim, and incident characteristics in a national sample, 1976–2003. *Journal of Aggression, Maltreatment & Trauma, 16*(2), 202–227. https://doi.org/10.1080/10926770801921584

Wierzbicki, M. (1993). Psychological adjustment of adoptees: A meta-analysis. *Journal of Clinical Child Psychology, 22*(4), 447–454. https://doi.org/10.1207/s15374424jccp2204_5

James T. Hubbell M.A. is a doctoral student at the School of Criminal Justice, University at Albany, SUNY. He has a master's degree in criminology in addition to bachelor's degrees in criminology as well as cell and molecular biology from the University of South Florida. He has previously had an article published on adoptive parricide in *Behavioral Sciences & the Law.* He is currently working with Dr. Kathleen M. Heide on a project examining the effects of age at adoption on incident characteristics in adoptive parricide. His research interests also include queer criminology and violence.

Kathleen M. Heide Ph.D., Distinguished University Professor, University of South Florida, Department of Criminology, is an internationally recognized researcher, consultant, and lecturer on homicide. Dr. Heide was elected as a Fellow in the AAAS for distinguished contributions in Criminology, particularly with respect to juvenile homicide and parricide. She is the author or co-author of four books and approximately 120 other scholarly publications. Professor Heide is a licensed mental health professional and court-appointed expert. She earned her B.A. from Vassar College, where she was elected to Phi Beta Kappa, and both her M.A. and Ph.D. from the University at Albany, where she was recognized as a distinguished alumna.

Norair Khachatryan M.A. is a doctoral candidate in the Department of Criminology at the University of South Florida in Tampa, where he has taught courses on serial murder and criminological theories. He received his M.A. degree in criminology from the University of South Florida. He is a primarily a homicide researcher, and has several peer-reviewed publications in the areas of juvenile homicide, parricide, and cyber-initiated homicide. He has also been involved in research on auto theft perpetration and victimization, as well as hate crimes.

Lightning Source UK Ltd.
Milton Keynes UK
UKHW020642160522
403067UK00006B/510

9 789811 613333